SKILLS-BASED SOCIOLOGY

Series Editors: Tim Heaton and Tony Lawson

The *Skills-based Sociology* series is designed to cover the Core Skills for Sociology A level (and equivalent courses) and to bring students up to date with recent sociological thought in all the key areas. Students are given the opportunity to develop their skills through exercises which they can carry out themselves or in groups, as well as given practice in answering exam questions. The series also emphasises contemporary developments in sociological knowledge, with a focus on recent social theories such as postmodernism and the New Right.

Published

THEORY AND METHOD
Mel Churton

EDUCATION AND TRAINING
Tim Heaton and Tony Lawson

MASS MEDIA
Marsha Jones and Emma Jones

WEALTH, POVERTY AND WELFARE
Sharon Kane and Mark Kirby

CULTURE AND IDENTITY
Warren Kidd

STRATIFICATION AND DIFFERENTIATION
Mark Kirby

CRIME AND DEVIANCE
Tony Lawson and Tim Heaton

HEALTH AND ILLNESS
Michael Senior with Bruce Viveash

THE FAMILY
Liz Steel and Warren Kidd

Forthcoming

POLITICS
Warren Kidd and Karen Legge

RELIGION
Joan Garrod and Marsha Jones

Further titles are in preparation

Skills-based Sociology
Series Standing Order ISBN 0–333–69350–7
(*outside North America only*)

You can receive future titles in this series as they are published. To place a standing order please contact your bookseller or, in the case of difficulty, write to us at the address below with your name and address, the title of the series and the ISBN quoted above.

Customer Services Department, Macmillan Distribution Ltd
Houndmills, Basingstoke, Hampshire RG21 6XS, England

WEALTH, POVERTY AND WELFARE

Sharon Kane
and
Mark Kirby

palgrave
macmillan

First published 2003 by
PALGRAVE MACMILLAN
Houndmills, Basingstoke, Hampshire RG21 6XS and 175 Fifth Avenue, New York, N.Y. 10010
Companies and representatives throughout the world

PALGRAVE MACMILLAN is the global academic imprint of the Palgrave Macmillan division of St. Martin's Press, LLC and of Palgrave Macmillan Ltd. Macmillan® is a registered trademark in the United States, United Kingdom and other countries. Palgrave is a registered trademark in the European Union and other countries.

ISBN 0–333–71933–6

This book is printed on paper suitable for recycling and made from fully managed and sustained forest sources.

A catalogue record for this book is available from the British Library.

10   9   8   7   6   5   4   3   2   1
12   11   10   09   08   07   06   05   04   03

Printed and bound in Great Britain by
J.W. Arrowsmith Ltd, Bristol.

I dedicate this book to my mother and father, **Joyce** and **John Kane**, and to my daughter, **Lucy Verrill**, as I could not have done this without them.

Sharon Kane

I dedicate this book to my niece, **Megan Waters**, to my partner, **Frances Newman**, and to all my co-authors of the *Sociology in Perspective* books for their continued support.

Mark Kirby

Contents

Acknowledgements

Writing a book like this requires the help and support of lots of people, whom we would like to acknowledge here. First, thanks to Tim Heaton and Tony Lawson for asking us to contribute to their series and for the vast amount of editorial work and advice they provided.

Catherine Gray and Keith Povey both worked very hard to turn our scribblings into something that can be published and we would like to thank them for their expertise and advice.

Sharon Kane would like to thank students and colleagues at Middlesbrough College for their support and enthusiasm; Laura Taggart, Andy Leach, Hilary Jones, Francine Koubel and Maria Feeney for believing in her and spurring her on; and Nick for discussing Marxism with her.

Mark Kirby thanks the sociology students and teachers at Sir George Monoux College, and in particular Len Rawling, who put up with him while he was writing this book. He would also like to thank Dr Alison Kirton and Francine Koubel for their constant advice and support; and Neil Renton for shouldering some of his teaching burden during that year and for the memorable use of matches and fire to demonstrate Marxism, something that certainly livened up a dull afternoon. Finally thanks to Julian Dean, Rachel Hek and Nick Madry, for their friendship and support, and many thanks to Frances for her support, insight, humanity, wit and advice. It means a lot to me. Thanks.

The authors and publishers wish to thank the following for granting permission to reproduce copyright material in the form of extracts, figures and tables:

D. Brindle, 'Prejudiced firms warned over jobs for the blind' in *The Guardian*, 9 September 1996 (reproduced with permission of *The Guardian*); Crown copyright material is reproduced with the permission of the Controller of HMSO and the Queen's Printer for Scotland; extracts from L. Duckworth, 'Study Challenges Idea of the North–South Divide' in *The Independent*, 31 May 2001 (reproduced with permission of *The Independent*); R. Gilroy and R. Woods (1994) *Housing Women* (reproduced with permission of Routledge); R. Gilroy (1994) *Housing and Social Inequality* (reproduced with permission of Routledge); Alissa Goodman, Paul Johnson and Steven Webb (1997) *Inequality in the UK* © the authors, by permission of Oxford University Press; M. Haralambos and M. Holborn (2000)

Sociology, 5th edn (reproduced with permission of HarperCollins Publishers Ltd); D. Hencke, 'Thousands of disabled lost benefit' in *The Guardian*, 7 June 1996 (reproduced with permission of *The Guardian*); *Labour Research* (August 1995) p. 12 (reproduced with permission of Labour Research Department); J. Mack and S. Lansley, 'Chart of Poverty' in *Perspectives in Sociology* by Kirkby *et al.* (p. 574) (reprinted by permission of Heinemann Educational Publishers); G. Philo and D. Miller (2000) *Market Killing* (p. 208) (reprinted by permission of Pearson Education Limited); J. Scott (1994) *Poverty and Wealth* (p. 24) © Longman Group 1994 (reprinted by permission of Pearson Education Limited); S. Webb (1993) 'Women's incomes, past, present and prospects' in *Fiscal Studies*, vol. 14 (reproduced with permission of the Institute of Fiscal Studies); P. White, 'Where Income Support Falls Short' (March 1995), taken from the magazine *Young People Now*, published by the National Youth agency.

Every effort has been made to trace all the copyright-holders, but if any have been inadvertently overlooked the publishers will be pleased to make the necessary arrangement at the first opportunity.

1 Introduction

The philosophy behind the book

The philosophy that underpins this book is similar to that of the other books in the Skills-based Sociology series. The book focuses on the topics of inequality, poverty and the welfare state. Its aim is to provide you with an overview of sociological debates on wealth, poverty and the welfare state whilst involving you actively in your own learning and helping you to develop the skills needed for you to be successful in your A level or AS level examinations. As sociology lecturers in further education colleges, and having acted as A level examiners, we are aware of the demands placed upon students by the awarding bodies and of the criteria used by them when marking examinations. We have used this knowledge to provide information and exercises that reflect these requirements and therefore offer good practice for the examinations set by the awarding bodies.

Skills

The subject core for sociology A Level developed by the Qualifications and Curriculum Authority (QCA), as implemented in the Curriculum 2000 Awards, identifies the skills that students must demonstrate in all AS and A Level sociology examinations. The Dearing Review laid down a new sociology core and two assessment objectives that would apply from the year 2001. The skills are now referred to as Assessment Objective 1 (A01) and Assessment Objective 2 (AO2). AO1 consists of knowledge and understanding and AO2 consists of identification, analysis, interpretation and evaluation.

Knowledge and understanding tests what you know of sociology and the extent to which you understand it. Knowledge in this sense refers to facts you either know or do not know. For example, either you know that Seebohm Rowntree was the author of a number of famous studies of poverty in York or you do not (see page 49). Equally, it may be that you know this fact but you do not have real understanding of what Rowntree was saying. However if you do understand you could demonstrate it by providing an account of his work in your own words.

With regard to the skills tested by AO2, the skill of identification requires you to look at a variety of materials and convey your understanding of them in your answer, while the skill of interpretation requires you to look at material in one format, such as a table, graph or text, and to communicate your understanding of this material when answering the set question, often by putting it in a different format. Analysis requires you to select relevant material to answer the question and to look at all aspects of the question in a logical, ordered way, considering each part and linking them together to form a rounded answer. Evaluation requires you to assess sociological debates and points of view by considering all the available evidence and theories and considering which argument(s) present the strongest case.

All these skills are linked, since in order to evaluate something it is necessary for you not only to know and understand all the sociological facts, conclusions and debates but also to interpret and analyse them. In our experience the best way to develop these skills is to practise them on your own. For this reason, and with the skills-based philosophy in mind, a large number of exercises are presented throughout the book. The book also contains a substantial body of sociological information, both contemporary material and classical pieces to illustrate how current theories, ideologies and policies arose. For example the ideas of the New Right (which underpinned the policies of the Conservative governments between 1979 and 1997) arose from late-nineteenth-century and early-twentieth-century debates on the distinction between the deserving and undeserving poor.

Our aim is not only to help you to pass the examination, but also to enjoy your sociology course. It should be stressed that it is not enough just to read the text – if you are to derive full benefit from the book it is vital that you also do the exercises. You will be able to identify the skills needed to complete the exercises by the symbols presented next to the exercises: **k** for knowledge, **u** for understanding, **a** for analysis, **e** for evaluation and **i** for interpretation. There are also link exercises (which draw on material from more than one chapter) for you to complete to help you understand the interconnectedness of the various issues, theories and ideologies.

The exam

One of the major aims of this book is to help you achieve a good grade in your final examination. To this end the book includes examples of past examination questions, sometimes with answers and sometimes without. Completion of the examination sections at the end of some of the chapters will help you to develop your sociological skills and enhance your performance in the examination. As you will discover, you can complete these exercises with other students, on your own for revision purposes or as you progress through the course.

Subject content

The remainder of this book consists of nine chapters. Chapter 2 considers inequalities in the distribution of wealth and income within and between societies. The question of whether the rich are getting richer at the expense of the poor will be considered. Chapter 3 looks at how various sociological and non-sociological writers have addressed this issue, and at whether they consider equality to be a good or a bad thing. Chapter 4 considers the definitions and measurements of poverty that have been used from the late nineteenth century to the present day. It considers a variety of studies that underline the problematic and highly politicised nature of defining and measuring poverty. Chapter 5 addresses which groups of people are defined as poor and the reasons for their poverty. Chapter 6 looks at the various explanations of the existence and persistence of poverty. These competing perspectives try to explain why some groups of people find themselves living in poverty whilst others do not. The chapter considers classical and contemporary studies in order to compare and contrast the past with the present. Chapter 7 focuses on the impact of globalisation and the implications it is likely to have on spatial patterns of economic and social inequality.

Chapter 8 focuses on the origins of welfare and the welfare state. It explores how and why the welfare state developed in the way it did. The material encompasses the ideological nature of the original debates and how these ideologies helped to shape the nature of the welfare state in its early years. Chapter 9 considers the debates on the welfare state from its inception to the present day, and the predictions for its future. In 2020, will the welfare state be as we know it now, or will it have changed beyond all recognition? What factors will shape its future, and how will this affect future generations? Chapter 10 looks at social security spending, housing and social services provision, and the way in which these affect people's opportunities and life chances for better or worse.

2 Wealth, income and inequality

> By the end of this chapter you should be able to:
>
> - state what income and wealth are;
> - explain how wealth and income are distributed;
> - describe the impact that changes in the distribution of income and wealth have on inequality in contemporary UK society;
> - outline how taxation, privatisation and share ownership affect the distribution of income and wealth.

Introduction

This chapter focuses on the creation of economic inequality and the role that wealth and income play in this process. Although these are economic processes they are also social relationships. So when we talk about economic inequality, we are also talking about the social relationships in which these economic processes are embedded. For instance we can ask questions such as: are the rich benefiting at the expense of the poor, or do the rich help the poor? If we did not have the rich, would we still have the poor?

The chapter will first consider evidence on the distribution of income and wealth, and then look at the social significance of the economic processes mentioned above.

Before we start it is necessary to clarify the distinction between 'income' and 'wealth'. While both can be measured in monetary terms, they are different. Income is a flow of money that occurs on a regular basis. For instance people talk of how much income they earn in a week or a month. Wealth, on the other hand, is a stock of money and other objects that, with varying degrees of ease, can be turned into money, for instance stocks and shares, property and valuable items. While income flows in at regular (or sometimes irregular) intervals, wealth is a measure of the total amount of monetary value available to a person. There is a link between income and wealth in that income that is not immediately spent on daily or weekly consumption can accrue to become wealth.

Income

What do we mean by income?

Lawson and Garrod (1996, p. 42) define income as 'an inward flow of money over time. Many people's main income is wages from employment, but there other sources of income, including benefits, pensions, dividends from shares and rent from housing. There is a distinction between earned and unearned income: earned income derives from employment or self-employment and requires some form of labour, while unearned income does not require labour since it comes from investment or reinvestment.

ITEM A

Composition of household income, 1987–1998

	1987	1991	1996	1997	1998
Wages and salaries	60	58	54	55	56
Operating income	11	10	11	11	11
Net property income	7	8	9	9	8
Social benefits	19	19	21	21	21
Other current transfers	3	4	5	4	4
Total household income (£ billion at 1998 prices)	616	706	784	805	825
Taxes etc. as a percentage of total household income:					
Taxes on income	11	12	10	10	11
Social contributions	17	15	15	16	16
Other current taxes	2	2	2	2	2
Other current transfers	3	3	3	2	2
Total household disposable income (£ billion at 1998 prices)	416	481	546	566	566

(Sources: Social Trends dataset at www.statistics.gov.uk/statbase; ONS, 1998.)

ITEM A *Exercise 2.1*

Study Item A carefully and answer the following questions:

i 1. What happened to taxes on income as a percentage of household income between 1987 and 1998?

i 2. As sources of income, by how much did social benefits increase between 1987 and 1998?

k u 3. Briefly explain the difference between total household income and total household disposable income.

k u i 4. Using information in the rest of the chapter or any other source with which you are familiar, suggest two reasons why total household disposable income may have increased between 1987 and 1998.

Households or individuals – the problem of measuring income distribution

One important issue in relation to income statistics is exactly how the data are calculated and presented. For example they may be presented as *household* income or wealth or *individual* income or wealth.

Because most individuals live in households, most statistics relate to total household income (see Item A above), and it is assumed that all income or wealth is equally shared between the members of the household. The key problem with this assumption is that it hides the fact the income is often unequally distributed among the members of a household, and it prevents us from studying the extent of this inequality. However there is little to be done about this since, as Lazear and Michael (1988) point out, the assumption has to be made because the data that are available are generally limited. According to Goodman *et al.* (1997, p. 32), 'There tends to be some sharing within households. The trouble is that this fact tells us nothing about how much sharing there is. There is certainly no reason to suppose that the sharing is everywhere equal.' All we can do is to remain aware of this limitation when we look at the statistics and consider their significance.

A few relevant facts on income

Income received by households is subject to deductions such as income tax and National Insurance contributions (NICs). The amount that remains after these deductions is referred to as disposable income and is sometimes used as an indicator of the standard of living in society in general. As well as paying NICs and income tax, people in the UK also pay indirect taxes such as VAT (value added tax). This tax is called indirect because it is paid to retailers as part of the price of goods and the retailers then forward the money to the Treasury.

Exercise 2.2

k u 1. How much income do you have at the present time, and where does it come from? List the amounts and their sources in a table.

a 2. Do you think that this income is dependent on your age, gender or class? Give reasons for your answer.

k u 3. What are the sources of the income of the other members of your household? If they are different from yours, how and why are they different?

In 1995/6, on average a fifth of people's disposable income was absorbed by indirect taxes. In 1996 disposable income per capita (per head) was 14 times higher than it had been in 1971, but this figure has to be adjusted to take account of inflation over that period. Figures that take inflation into account are known as 'real' figures. Real disposable income did rise between 1971 and 1990, but it began to level out after that and has remained fairly consistent ever since.

The main source of income for most households is salaries and wages, which in 1996 accounted for 55 per cent of households' total income, but there was an increase in the proportion of income from private pensions and social security benefits in the period 1971–96.

The income of the nation comprises the income of individuals and the income of organisations (for example profits). The standard measure of economic performance is gross domestic product (GDP), which in the UK has been growing at an average annual rate of 2.5 per cent since 1951. GDP is also estimated at the regional level. Between 1990 and 1995 London had the highest per capita GDP of all the regions in the UK, and the per capita GDPs of the Eastern and South-East regions were above the national average.

Exercise 2.3

Go to your resource centre or library and ask for the most recent copy of *Regional Trends* and *Europe in Figures*. Look at the sections on GDP rates, note the year(s) in question and answer the following questions:

i
1. Which region of the UK had the lowest GDP for the year(s) in question? Which region had the highest GDP?

k *u*
2. What factors do you think explain the regional differences? (See Chapter 3 of this book to help you.)

i
3. Which country in Europe had the highest GDP? Which country had the lowest?

The distribution of income

Jan Pen and the income parade

The Dutch economist Jan Pen (1971) devised an original way to visualise the distribution of income. He suggested that we imagine a parade where everyone's height reflects their income. By noting down the height of all the people who pass by in an hour we can gain a picture of the national distribution of income.

This idea has been applied to income distribution in the UK by John Hills (1995), who provides the following scenario. Suppose that the average height in the UK parade is 5 feet 8 inches – this represents the height of people in households on average earnings. When the parade starts only very tiny people walk by. After three minutes a single unemployed mother with two small children goes by: she is 1 foot 10 inches tall. After nine minutes a single male pensioner claiming Income Support passes by: his height is 2 feet 6 inches. During the first twelve minutes all the people in the parade are smaller than 2 feet 10 inches (under half the average wage).

After 30 minutes all the people passing by are 4 feet 10 inches tall (83 per cent of the average wage). People with average incomes (5 feet 8 inches tall) do not arrive until 62 per cent of the parade has gone past. After 50 minutes the height of the people really begins to rise. A full-time personnel officer goes by: she is 8 feet 7 inches tall. A self-employed freelance journalist arrives: his height is 11 feet 11 inches. After 59 minutes a chief executive and his wife walk by: they are both 60 feet tall. In the very last seconds the height of the passers-by rises dramatically and the final arrivals – Britain's richest man and his partner – are both four miles high.

Exercise 2.4

Reread the description of the income parade, then answer the following questions:

[i] 1. What proportion of the population have below average incomes?

[i] 2. What proportion of the population have above average incomes? (l)

[i][a] 3. In the early 1990s the average wage in the UK was £17 000. Based on this and the heights and percentages listed above, calculate the income of the single unemployed mother and Britain's richest man. (Hint: If you know that a person earning £17 000 is 5 feet 8 inches tall you can calculate what is represented by 1 foot. The easiest way to do this is to convert the feet to inches. So 5 feet 8 inches is 68 inches, and dividing £17 000 by 68 gives an income of £250 per inch. Multiplying this by 12 gives an income of £3000 per foot. For Britain's richest man, the number of inches in 4 miles is the first thing to work out!)

The Centre for Analysis of Social Exclusion

It is important to look at the distribution of income between groups and determine the size of the gap between those at the bottom and those at the top of the income scale. A report by John Hills (1995) of the Centre for Analysis of Social Exclusion revealed that while the average income grew by 40 per cent between 1979 and 1995, the income of the richest tenth grew by 60–68 per cent and that of the poorest tenth fell by 8 per cent when housing costs were taken into consideration. The share of income going to the poorest 10 per cent of the population halved during the 1980s, falling from 4 per cent of the total to under 2 per cent. The share of the poorest half of the population fell from a third of the total to just under a quarter. In 1990 income inequality reached the highest recorded level since 1945, with the UK experiencing faster growth in inequality than any other industrialised country except New Zealand (Hills, 1995).

The Institute for Fiscal Studies

A study conducted for the Institute of Fiscal Studies in the 1990s (Goodman *et al.*, 1997) revealed that there had been an unprecedented rise in inequality in the preceding 20 years, reversing the trend of falling inequality since the 1950s. It was found that the combined income of the richest 10 per cent of the British population equalled the combined income of all the households in the bottom 50 per cent. Furthermore, while the average income rose by 36 per cent between 1979 and 1992, the income of the poorest tenth fell by 17 per cent. At the bottom of the income scale, because of the rise in unemployment more than 70 per cent of the income of the bottom 10 per cent of households was accounted for by means-tested benefits.

The report gave two reasons for the rise in inequality. First, the income of those with less than average earnings had risen more slowly than those with average or above average earnings. Second, changes to the tax system had largely benefited those with above average incomes. Treasury calculations showed that the proportion of income paid in taxes by the poorest 20 per cent of households had risen from 31 per cent to 39 per cent between 1979 and 1992, while that for the richest 20 per cent had fallen from 37 per cent to 34 per cent (Elliott *et al.*, 1994).

ITEM B

Income distribution by source of income: share of each income component received by each quintile

	Poorest 20%	Next 20%	Next 20%	Next 20%	Richest 20%	Total
Self-employment	2	8	12	18	58	100
Private pension	4	13	19	25	38	100
Investment income	3	7	11	17	61	100
Earnings	2	8	17	26	47	100
Social security	29	33	18	12	8	100

(Source: Goodman et al., 1997, p. 138.)

ITEM B   *Exercise 2.5*

Study Item B carefully and answer the following questions:

[i] 1. Which three sources of income are most common among the richest 20 per cent of the population?

[i] 2. Which source of income is most common among the poorest 40 per cent of the population?

[i] 3. What proportion of social security expenditure goes to the richest 20 per cent of households?

[k][u] 4. Refering to information in this chapter and elsewhere, suggest reasons for the differences in the distribution of the different types of income among the various sections of the population.

Distribution of income by social characteristics

Sociologists consider that these trends are best analysed using social criteria such as class, gender, ethnicity, age and locality. This section provides a picture of recent trends in the distribution of income according to these criteria. One key source of data on this is the *New Earnings Survey* (NES) (ONS, 1999).

Income distribution by gender The NES shows that among full-time workers, men earned 35 per cent more than women per week in April 1999 (£442 compared with £327), and that among part-time workers, men earned 21 per cent more than women (£155 compared with £128).

According to Byrne (1999), if we look at income in terms of individuals rather than households, then only one third of women have an income that is above the poverty level (less than 50 per cent of the average income). It is suggested by Kodias and Jones (1991, p. 161) that the slight improvement in women's average living standards is actually the result of gains by a minority of women, usually those in professional full-time employment, while living standards are 'static or deteriorating . . . for the majority of women who need work'.

In both the UK and the US, one group that is forced to survive on a low income is single-parent families, 90 per cent of which are headed by women. In the case of the US, Kodias and Jones suggest that the low income of these women is often due to their poor labour market prospects, and in particular to the low pay in the service sector jobs that are available to them.

Byrne (1997), following a study conducted in Leicester, shows how income inequality can operate on a spatial level and interact with gender. He found that in the affluent areas of the city 96 per cent of children were born to married parents, compared with less than 50 per cent of children in the poor areas. He argues that these divisions emerged as a result of deindustrialisation (the reduction of industrial production, see Chapter 7 pages 125–8) in the city. This is an example of how economic processes can create income inequalities that reinforce social divisions and perpetuate economic divisions.

Income distribution by ethnicity Ethnicity is another important factor in unequal income distribution in the UK.

Average hourly earnings of full-time employees, by ethnic group and sex, UK, 1994 (£s)

Ethnic group	All	Male	Female
All origins	7.42	7.97	6.39
White	7.44	8.00	6.40
Ethnic minority groups	6.82	7.15	6.31
Afro-Caribbean	6.92	7.03	6.77
Indian	6.70	7.29	5.77
Pakistani/Bangladeshi	5.39	5.47	5.15
Mixed/other origin	7.70	8.45	6.77

(Source: Adapted from Oppenheim and Harker, 1996, p. 118.)

ITEM C *Exercise 2.6*

[i] 1. Study Item C and identify the highest and lowest-paid ethnic groups in terms of (a) men and (b) women

[i] 2. For which of the two sexes does ethnic origin appear to have the greatest effect on income?

[k][u] 3. Suggest reasons for the patterns revealed by questions 1 and 2.

The principle causes of unequal household income by ethnicity are unemployment and/or low-paid jobs. For example, both Pakistani/Bangladeshi and Afro-Caribbean people suffer high levels of unemployment, but the average pay of Afro-Caribbeans is higher than that of Pakistani/Bangladeshis. When gender is taken into account we find that on average Afro-Caribbean women actually earn more than white women, but this is not true of Afro-Caribbean men and some Pakistani/Bangladeshi groups.

A report by Tariq Modood *et al.* (1997) points to increasing income diversity among ethnic minority groups in the UK. According to Modood *et al.*, four out of five Pakistani/Bangladeshi households exist on less than half the average income, but African Asians and Chinese people are more likely than white people to be earning more than £500 per week, and they also have a lower unemployment rate.

Income distribution by social class There are marked differences between the incomes of manual and non-manual workers. In April 1999 non-manual workers earned an average of £443 per week compared with £315 for manual workers – a difference of 40 per cent. Figures from the *New Earnings Survey* (ONS, 1999) also show that between April 1998 and April 1999 manual workers received an average pay rise of 2.6 per cent while non-manual workers received 3.8 per cent, indicating growing inequality between these groups.

According to Westergaard (1995), while the average real income rose by 30 per cent between 1979 and 1991, that of the poorest 50 per cent of households rose by just 10 per cent. He comments that 'Even people up to mid-point incomes, and a number some way above that level, have gained quite little either by comparison with the rich or by past standards of rising prosperity' (ibid., p. 133).

By way of comparison, Braun (1997), who has studied changes in income distribution in the US, argues that there has been a decline in the real wages of American people in the bottom two thirds of the income scale: 'since reaching its peak in 1972–1973 real average weekly earnings have fallen by nearly 19 per cent. . . . The average American worker is worse off today than at any time in the past third of a century' (ibid., p. 62).

To provide a contrast, Melissa Benn (2002) states: 'As Zgymunt Bauman recently pointed out, in the US just 10 years ago the income of company directors was 42 times higher than blue collar workers. It is now an astonishing 419 times higher.' (p. 19)

Income distribution by location   Paul Baldwin's (1999) study of the distribution of income by postcode enables us to consider location as a factor in the distribution of income (this issue will also be considered in Chapter 7). Baldwin found that nine of the 20 poorest postcode areas are in Liverpool, while high incomes are concentrated in central London areas such as Belgravia, Blackfriars and Barbican.

ITEM D

Counties with the highest average income		Counties with the lowest average income	
Surrey	£29700	Tyne and Wear	£17400
Berkshire	£28100	Cornwall and the Isles of Scilly	£17400
Buckinghamshire	£27900	South Yorkshire	£17500
Hertfordshire	£26900	Isle of Wight	£17700
Outer London	£25600	Mid Glamorgan	£17700

(Source: Baldwin, 1999.)

ITEM D   *Exercise 2.7*

i

1. Study Item D and then work out the average income of Surrey residents as a percentage of the average income of Tyne and Wear residents. (I)

2. Suggest reasons for the relative affluence or poverty of the ten counties listed in Item D.

Differences in income also occur at the regional level, and in general those living in the South-East have higher incomes than those in the

North-East (see Chapter 5, pages 91–4) due to occupational differences and the industrial structure of the latter.

Income levels are affected by economic factors such as the demand for different types of labour, inflation and the cost of living in certain areas. It is more expensive to live in the South-East than the North-East, so when housing costs are taken into consideration the income levels may be closer. Nonetheless people in the South-East still have higher incomes when other factors are taken into consideration.

So we can see that gender, social class, ethnicity and location all influence people's income and therefore their life-course.

ITEM E

The top twelve most highly paid directors in the UK

Director	Company (financial year)	Salary (£)	Percentage change
Bernie Ecclestone	Formula One Promo/International Sports World (1993)	30 750 109	+1647.0
Phil Collins	Philip Collins (1993)	22 281 412	+110.1
Crispin Odey	Odey Asset Management (1994)	19 256 000	+564.5
Elton John	Happenstance/J Bondi (1993)	17 938 053	+110.0
Peter Wood	Royal Bank of Scotland (1994)	17 402 251	−5.8
Kavah Alamouti	Tokai Bank/Capl Mkts (1993)	14 502 000	+97.0
Eric Clapton	Marshbrook (1993)	13 390 000	+83.8
Mark Levett	Winchester Commods (1994)	10 094 904	+762.2
Charles Vincent	Winchester Commods (1994)	9 722 906	+730.4
Cameron MacKintosh	Cameron MacKintosh (1994)	9 991 005	−2.7
Sir Andrew Lloyd Webber	Really Useful (1994)	7 058 000	+499.2
Jim Fifield	Thorn EMI (1995)	6 661 000	−6.9

In contrast, according to the *New Earnings Survey* (ONS, 1995) the average gross weekly pay of full-time workers on adult rates ranged from £175.30 per week (for female manual workers in East Anglia) to £506.30 per week (for male non-manual workers in the South-East) during the same period.

(Source: Table adapted from Labour Research, August 1995, p. 12.)

ITEM E **Exercise 2.8**

Study ITEM E, then answer the following questions:

[i] 1. What was the difference in salary between the most highly paid director and the twelfth most highly paid director?

[i] 2. How many of the companies were connected to the entertainment industry?

[i] 3. What is evident about the gender of the directors?

[i] 1. What percentage of the lowest average weekly wage was earned by the highest paid director?

[i] 2. What percentage of the highest average weekly wage was earned by the highest paid director?

[e] 3. To what extent do you feel such differences are justified?

According to the Labour Research Survey (1995), high earners can be divided into three categories:

- Directors of companies that are subsidiaries of another company.
- Private limited company directors who are the main shareholders and can sanction their own pay rises.
- Directors of public companies quoted on the stock exchange.

In July 1995 the Confederation of British Industry Committee, headed by Sir Richard Greenbury (chair of Marks and Spencer), published the findings of its enquiry into directors' pay and perks. The committee was set up at the request of Prime Minister John Major following a controversy over the 75 per cent pay rise received by Cedric Brown, chief executive of British Gas (raising his salary to £475 000). The 'Gas Greed' campaign was started after the rise was announced and the shareholders of British Gas, led by Professor Joseph Lamb, raised the issue at the annual meeting in May. Many were incensed by the rise as at the time British Gas was planning to cut the pay of thousands of showroom staff.

The committee was asked to examine four areas of top executives' pay:

- Remuneration packages such as share options, bonus schemes and contracts.
- The disclosure of directors' pay both as individuals and as part of a board.
- The constitution of remuneration committees.
- The ways in which shareholders were informed of pay policies and practices.

The committee consisted of 11 members, seven of whom had a combined employment income of £3.9 million. Sir Richard Greenbury had received a 5.9 per cent pay rise in 1994, which had taken his basic salary to £629 588 per year. Another member of the committee was Sir Iain Vallance (chair of British Telecom), whose total remuneration amounted to £652 853. He claimed that this reflected 'distributive justice', which in his mind appeared to justify the cutting of BT's workforce by 78 000.

Despite the changes recommended by this committee, publicity on executives' pay continued to feed public concern about 'fat cats'. Treanor (2001) reports that the salaries of executives of top companies rose by an average of 28 per cent in June 2001, compared with the average national pay rise of 4.8 per cent. As Finch (2001) points out, this suggests that British bosses considered their contribution to be worth 45 times that of ordinary workers. Furthermore Hurst (2001) notes that when these pay rises were awarded the total return on top companies' shares had fallen by 11.5%, putting into question the supposed link between executive pay and company performance. Sir Christopher Gent, chief executive of the mobile phone company Vodaphone, received a rise of 400 per cent. An important element of this was share options, which rose in value from £87 million in 1999 to £198 million in 2001. (ibid.)

ITEM F

Exercise 2.9

Study item F and answer the following questions:

i 1. On average, how much per week did a male manual worker receive?

a 2. What types of perk do you think a manual worker on a building site would receive?

a 3. What types of perk might a company director receive?

Wealth

Exercise 2.10

k u e Before reading this section list your ideas on what constitutes wealth (for example wealth includes ownership of land). At the end of the chapter review your list to see whether your ideas remain the same or have changed in light of what you have read.

What is wealth?

Webster's Third International Dictionary of the English Language (Gove Philip, 1993) defines wealth as an 'abundance of things that are objects of human desire, abundance of worldly estate, riches, material success', while *The Complete A–Z Sociology Handbook* (Lawson and Garrod, 1996, p. 10) defines it as 'The total value of the possessions held by an individual or a society'. The wealth of a nation generally consists of its economic capital – railways, houses, factories, roads, machines and stocks of capital goods available to use immediately or in the future. Economists view wealth as all the physical assets that make up our standard of living. One of the main concerns of economists is to increase the wealth of society so that it can flourish.

Personal wealth can be thought of in terms of money, material possessions and the ownership of land and property. A distinction should be made here between consumption property, which includes material possessions such as cars and owner-occupied housing, and productive property, which includes factories, land, and stocks and shares, all of which are used as capital in the process of producing things. As the UK has no general wealth tax, no overall wealth evaluations are made, although the Inland Revenue does produce estimates of wealth based on a sample of those who have died in a particular year. The only time that wealth is officially evaluated is when substantial amounts are transferred from one person to another, usually upon the death of one of the people as inherited wealth is taxable.

Summary facts on wealth

According to the United Nations Human Development Programme report (UNDP, 1996) the combined wealth of the world's seven richest men could wipe out poverty and provide basic social services for the quarter of the world's population who live in dire need. The Report (ibid. 1996) indicates an ever-growing divide between rich and poor, with the net wealth of ten billionaires amounting to 1.5 times the combined national income of the 48 least developed countries.

ITEM G

Richest individuals and families, US, 1999

	Net worth ($)	Source of wealth
Bill Gates	85 billion	Microsoft
Walton family	85 billion	Inheritance: Wal-Mart
Paul Allen	40 billion	Microsoft
Warren Buffett	31 billion	Berkshire Hathaway
Steven Ballmer	23 billion	Microsoft
Michael Dell	20 billion	Dell Computers
Gordon E. Moore	15 billion	Intel Corporation
DuPont family	13 billion	Inheritance: DuPont Corporation
Lawrence Ellison	13 billion	Oracle Corporation
John Werner Kluge	11 billion	Metromedia Corporation

(Source: Forbes 400 Web site: http://www.forbes.com/tool/toolbox/rich400/, quoted on www.inequality.org.)

ITEM D *Exercise 2.11*

Refer to Item G and:

i
k u i a

1. Calculate the total worth of the ten richest Americans.

2. Work out which of the companies' products you have used. (Hint: Wal-Mart now owns ASDA.)

Joe Lewis is thought to be the richest man in the UK, with an estimated personal fortune of £3 billion. He runs an international conglomerate called Tavistock, which has interests in financial services, property, food and transport. His biggest earnings come from the foreign exchange market, from which he is reported to have made a profit of £1 billion in 1997. He recently bought Glasgow Rangers football club for £40 million, which he regards as 'pocket money'. In 1994 Fergus McCann, the golfing holiday tycoon, invested £9 million in Glasgow Celtic football club. That £9 million is now estimated to be worth £70 million. Guy Hands of the Japanese company Nomura International earned a reputed £40 million in 1997, equal to £110 000 a day or £75 a minute. His pay packet is 2500 times the national average, or enough to pay the wages of the government cabinet for the next 17 years. A little further down the scale, 'Sugar' Myojin, a trader at Salomon Smith Barney in London, received about £31 million in 1996, and Joe Roby, a banker, earned £20 million in 1996.

The distribution of wealth in society

A report by the Institute of Fiscal Studies (IFS, 1997) shows that the UK is a far more unequal society than it was 20 or so years ago, and that it is divided into a handful of economic giants amid a sea of poverty-stricken dwarves. There are now over 200 billionaires in the world, and in the UK the 200 richest people are worth over £30 billion. The wealthiest 1 per cent of adults have consistently possessed about 20 per cent of the total marketable wealth of the nation over the past 20 years, while the least wealthy 50 per cent have held less than 10 per cent. According to *Social Trends* (ONS, 1998) the total amount of marketable wealth rose from £280 billion in 1976 to £1955 billion in 1994.

ITEM H

Marketable wealth minus value of dwellings

Percentage of wealth owned by	1976	1981	1986	1991	1994
Most wealthy 1%	29	26	25	29	28
Most wealthy 5%	47	45	46	51	52
Most wealthy 10%	57	56	58	64	65
Most wealthy 25%	73	74	75	80	82
Most wealthy 50%	88	87	89	93	94

(Source: ONS, 1998.)

Exercise 2.12

i   1. What happened to the marketable wealth of the wealthiest 1 per cent between 1976 and 1994?

i   2. Which group's marketable wealth increased most between 1976 and 1994?

i   3. Using the statistics in Item H, identify and summarise the trends in wealth distribution between 1976 and 1994.

k u i a   4. Using information in this section and other books, explain the trends you have identified.

The causes of income and wealth inequality

Statistics produced at regular intervals indicate that the rich are becoming richer at the expense of the poor. Economic factors such as taxation, share ownership and privatisation have to be examined to see why the divide between rich and poor is widening, and the implications of this.

Westergaard (1995) believes that wealth distribution changed in the 1980s and 1990s. Using data from *Social Trends* he identified a reversal of earlier trends and found that the share of marketable wealth of the richest 1 per cent of the population rose from 26 per cent to 29 per cent between 1980 and 1991.

In the following subsections we shall examine some of the reasons for this trend, focusing on changes in dividends, pensions and taxation, and the process of privatisation.

Dividends and pensions

In its quarterly bulletins the Bank of England reports on UK company profitability and dividend payments. In 1993–94, when the economy was in recession, total dividend payments rose by 18.3 per cent, so shareholders were doing well despite the recession. The top five increases in dividends were 29 per cent on average, with Associated British Foods' dividends rising by 73.3 per cent per share.

Besides their salaries and share dividends, many directors receive large pension payments. A Labour Research survey conducted in 1995 found that 41 directors in 38 companies had received more than £50 000 in pension contributions in that financial year. When this is calculated as a percentage of their salaries it is clear that they were receiving a much better deal than any of their employees. On the other hand the National Association of Pension Funds' annual survey of pension schemes revealed that on average employers contributed 7 per cent of their pay to occupational pension schemes but for company directors the contribution could be as high as 40 per cent.

Public money is also spent on pension funds and schemes. Twenty-five pence in every pound of the state funds given to the police and fire services is spent on bridging the gap between what current staff pay in contributions and the pension payments made to retired officers. In London, for example, there are more retired police officers than serving ones, so a large gap has to be filled by public money. Pension schemes can prove to be expensive for employers, so private schemes are being promoted in order to reduce the bill. The proportion of people in company pension schemes has decreased since 1983.

The social wage

The government spends a third of its budget on welfare services, and this kind of provision can be regarded as a 'social wage' for those at the bottom of the income hierarchy. Tom Sefton, working at the London School of Economics, has investigated who benefits most from this social wage. He charted the change in income distribution between 1979, when Margaret Thatcher's Conservative government came to power, and 1997, when Tony Blair's Labour government was elected. He found that the cash incomes of the poorest fifth rose by just 6 per cent during this period. When the social wage was included their incomes grew by 13 per cent, compared with over 60 per cent for the richest fifth. Therefore inequality increased despite welfare provision.

Taxation

At some point in our lives we all pay some form of tax, either directly or indirectly. The type of employment we have and the salary or wage we receive dictate the amount of income tax we pay, so taxation is an important factor in any consideration of wealth, income and inequality.

In modern market economies there are two main tools for correcting economic inequality: state benefits and progressive taxation (where the rich pay proportionately more tax than the poor). Income tax is a progressive tax since the tax rate is highest for those with the highest incomes. The theory behind progressive tax is that income is redistributed from the rich to the poor.

Between 1979 and 1997 people on high incomes benefited substantially from the Conservatives' policy of cutting taxes. In 1994 the Treasury calculated that the proportion of income paid in taxes by the poorest 20 per cent of households had risen from 31 per cent in 1979 to 39 per cent in 1992, while for the richest 20 per cent of households the proportion had fallen from 37 per cent to 34 per cent (Kirby, 1999). According to the Institute for Fiscal Studies, tax changes introduced after 1985 boosted the incomes of the richest 10 per cent by 6 per cent and cut the income of the poorest 10 per cent by 3 per cent (reported in Elliott *et al.*, 1994).

The Conservatives' key justification for tax cuts for the affluent was their expectation that the 'trickle down' effect would occur. This new right theory suggested that the additional wealth that would accrue to the rich by cutting the top tax rate would help the poor because some of it would trickle down to them. However, according to a report by the Joseph Rowntree Foundation (Hills, 1995), the trickle down effect failed to materialise. The poorest 20 per cent did not benefit from the economic growth of the mid to late 1980s – in fact the rich grew richer and the poor became even poorer. Income inequality has grown faster in the UK than in all other industrialised countries but New Zealand (Mann, 1995), and the gap is now wider than at any time since the Second World War.

In contrast to the Rowntree study, a report by the Social Market Foundation (Cooper *et al.*, 1995) found in favour of the trickle down theory. It estimated that the poorest 20 per cent had enjoyed a 28 per cent increase in benefits in kind (such as non-cash social transfers through public spending on health, education, housing, transport, school meals and so on) between 1987 and 1993, and to a lesser extent between 1979 and 1987. The report pointed out that the Rowntree study had ignored benefits in kind, and this was why the finding differed. Steve Webb and Alissa Goodman (1996) studied the spending patterns of different income groups, believing that how much people bought gave a better idea of their standard of living than how much they earned. Whilst Webb and Goodman agreed that the UK had become a less equal society, they found that inequality of spending had increased less than inequality of income.

Privatisation

It is important to address the issue of privatisation (the transfer of publicly owned enterprises to private ownership) because it affects us all, either directly or indirectly. Some people are employed by privatised companies and thus rely on them for their income. Most of us pay money to these companies to provide us with goods and services, hence some of our income keeps them running and contributes to their profits. Some of these profits are passed on to shareholders, the remainder are reinvested in the company to make even more profits. In the early days of privatisation its proponents argued that it would lead to improved economic efficiency and reduced reliance on public finances as privatised enterprises would be free to raise funds in the financial market.

During its first term of office (May 1979 to June 1983) the Thatcher government partially privatised British Aerospace, British Rail Hotels, Jaguar (car makers), Britoil and Enterprise Oil (oil production and exploration), Amersham International (manufacturer of radioactive materials), Cable and Wireless (telecommunications services), National Freight, British Rail and Sealink. In November 1984 the scale of privatisation was enlarged with the full sale of British Telecommunications (BT), followed by British Gas (in 1986), British Airways and the British Airports Authority (1987), British Steel (1989), the water authorities (1990), electricity supply (1991) and British Rail (1997).

When these corporations were privatised their property, rights and liabilities were first transferred to successor companies, then shares were created according to the Companies Act and each successor company was transferred to private ownership when its shares were sold to the public. Shareholders of privately owned companies have a right to receive dividends, paid out of the companies' profits. The companies are run by directors and managers whose aim is to maximise profits in the interests of shareholders. Shareholders may seek to persuade directors to act in their interests by voting at open meetings, or threatening to sell their shares to another set of directors so that they can take over the company.

Many of the large corporations earmarked for privatisation by the Conservative government were important to the national economy, and their sale would affect consumers of their products, employees, taxpayers and prospective shareholders. Naturally there were be people who would benefit from these privatisations and people who would lose, and they all tried to sway the rules to suit their own interests. For example there was bargaining between employees and management, and between the government and trade unions. We need to consider who lost and who gained from the process of privatisation, and its impact on the distribution of income and wealth.

One of the key arguments for privatisation was that rather than the public sector subsidising unprofitable industries, the private sector would be able to use private finance (via the stock market) to make the provision of the relevant goods and services more efficient. On the other hand it was argued that private sector provision would be more expensive in that there was always the risk that the privatised companies would go bankrupt, and since financiers would demand a premium to cover this risk, this would incur extra costs. Secondly, privatisation meant shareholders and shareholders meant dividend payments – yet another cost that did not apply with public ownership. Since one of the ways in which companies might seek to cut costs was through staff cuts or wage cuts, it was said that employees would be losers in the privatisation process, to the benefit of shareholders.

Pollack *et al.* (2001) consider the various claims and outcomes associated with privatisation. In particular they draw attention to employment changes and dividend payments. Their summary of this is presented in Item I.

Employment and dividends after privatisation

	Period	Fall in employment	Dividends (£m)
British Gas	1987–95	33 675 (38%)	4354
British Telecom	1988–95	89 000 (38%)	6745
10 water companies	1990–95	3 083 (8%)	6862
Electricity generation	1992–96	8 996 (43%)	1262
Railtrack	1996–99	520 (5%)	434

(Source: Pollack et al. 2001, p. 208.)

ITEM I

Exercise 2.13

[i] 1. Study Item I and identify the company with the largest fall in employment.

[i] 2. Calculate the total number of employees employed by each of the companies before and after privatisation.

According to Pollack *et al.*, 'The amount saved on labour costs was approximately equal to the amount paid out in dividends' (ibid., p. 208). This can be seen as a gain for shareholders and a loss for workers, not only for those who lost their income when they were laid off, but also for those who remained, as it was likely that they had to work longer hours for the same pay, which effectively meant a wage cut. Furthermore 'The railways present a similar story, albeit with more tragic results, as passengers lost their lives as maintenance and investment were cut back' (ibid.).

Another possible conflict envisaged before privatisation was between shareholders pressing for increased profits and customers affected by the price rises necessary to boost profits. Consequently the privatised industries were made subject to the authority of regulatory bodies, which were also required to keep the industries' monopoly powers in check. Whether these bodies have satisfactorily fulfilled their mandates is still a matter of debate, but it is clear that while there have been some falls in prices there have also been some very hefty price increases.

When the Labour Government took power in 1997, the large-scale privatisations ended and although there was no attempt to renationalise industries, Railtrack (one of the most notorious of the privatised companies, particularly after the Hatfield rail crash in 1999) was placed in administration by a government minister against the wishes of the directors and shareholders. Instead the government sought to create growth through such initiatives as the Private Finance Initiative (PFI) and public–private partnerships (PPPs). Some commentators consider that these initiatives are themselves a form of privatisation. For example PFI means that public buildings will be designed by private companies and leased back to the public sector for an annual fee. Furthermore Gaffney *et al.* (1999) estimate that not only will the cost of PFI hospitals be greater than public sector hospitals, but the PFI hospitals will also be smaller. In addition, since some of the money spent on heath provision will have to be used to pay the private companies, this will affect the level of health care provision.

After announcing its plans the government argued that PPPs would ensure that the financial risks inherent in large-scale projects would be shared with the private sector. However this argument was challenged when the newly elected mayor of London, Ken Livingstone, fought against the proposal to set up a PPP for the London Underground. It was argued that ultimately the risks would never be borne by private sector companies as they could avoid them through bankruptcy. This added risk would increase the cost of private sector involvement, a cost that would ultimately have to be passed on to consumers or paid for by cuts.

The Livingstone challenge failed in the courts, but this was not the end of the matter. Will Hutton (2001) claimed that the Underground PPP proposal was based on figures that were rigged to show that public sector provision would always be the more expensive option. For example the estimated cost of keeping the Underground in the public sector had been inflated by £700 million because it was assumed that a public sector organisation would fail to deliver good services and this would raise the cost to the public, and by a further £1.57 billion because it was considered that the public sector (unlike the private) would never learn from its mistakes. All in all the estimated cost of public sector provision had been inflated by a total of £2.5 billion on the basis of mere assumptions about the greater efficiency of the private sector. As Hutton said, the discovery of this placed severe question marks not only over the Underground proposal but also over all other PPP schemes:

What the accountants Deloitte and Touche have done in their confidential report on London's Public Private Partnership is to expose a mendacious gerrymander that sets out unfairly to rig the rules so that whatever LU [London Underground] does it can be depicted as less efficient that the private sector.

Despite their efforts to depict LU as an organisational no-hoper, the private contractors' bids are still higher than LU's artificially inflated costs – rigged by £2.5 billion. It is not just that the London Underground PPP is now in jeopardy as the full scale of the gerrymander is made public, it also undermines the whole philosophic and economic basis of public private partnerships (ibid., p. 6).

Shares

From the early 1980s the Conservative government set out to create a 'shareholding democracy' as part of its privatisation plan. People were encouraged to buy shares for the first time, but many of the first-time buyers sold their shares for a quick profit at the earliest opportunity. The shares they sold were snapped up by large institutional investors. For example the sale of 12 regional electricity companies in 1990 raised over £5 billion and created around nine million electricity shareholders. Just after the shares were floated on the stock market (offered for public sale) their price soared dramatically and the value of the companies rose to £7 billion. Within six months 60 per cent of shareholders had cashed in their shares.

This pattern was repeated with British Gas, the water and sewerage companies, Powergen and BT. Millions of small shareholders sold their shares, and some of those that remained became all too aware of the limitations of corporate democracy when they tried to do battle with the big shareholders. For example many of the small shareholders in British Gas were appalled by the huge pay rise the directors were to receive and tried to vote against it. Despite public outcry the insurance companies and pension funds that held the majority of shares voted in favour of the directors. A breakdown of shareholdings in privatised industries shows that because of their small numbers, the power of individual shareholders is very limited indeed. Bryan Hurl (1988, p. 56) presents the following statistics on the sale of public sector industries: 'Only 12 per cent of the shares were available directly to the British public, 6 per cent were reserved for employees, 20 per cent were placed abroad. The rest – nearly two-thirds – went under guarantee to the City's institutional investors. In the harsh reality of the marketplace capitalism triumphs over idealism.'

Hence the much-heralded growth of individual share ownership failed to materialise to any great extent. This issue was at the heart of a study conducted by Saunders and Harris (1994) before and after water privatisation. According to Saunders and Harris, 2.7 million people applied for shares in the various water companies, and the offer was oversubscribed by five times. Among the sample of small shareholders in their study, 20 per cent intended to sell their shares for quick gain, 25 per cent wished to retain them as a long-term investment and 20 per cent had invested because they thought they would pay good dividends. The remaining shareholders had bought shares for a variety of other motives. Saunders and Harris argue that only the third group reflected the enterprising skills that privatisation sought to encourage. However even among this group there was little interest in how the companies were doing, and only one in 240 shareholders attended the AGMs. Consequently Saunders and Harris conclude that

'Sociologically, the great privatisation crusade has turned out to be much ado about nothing' (ibid., p. 161).

Summary

While inequality in income and wealth lessened between 1945 and 1970, thereafter it began to increase. Indeed in global terms the UK has often been at the forefront of such inequality, particularly during the Thatcher period. However even under New Labour there has been scant attention to redistribution and there seems little immediate prospect of a return to redistributive policies. Instead New Labour seems more concerned with economic efficiency and perpetuating the business-friendly policies adopted by the Conservatives, so inequality and poverty are likely to be with us for a while yet.

3 Theories of equality and inequality

By the end of this chapter you should be able to:

- list theories that support greater inequality;
- list theories that support greater equality;
- describe the views associated with functionalism and the New Right;
- describe the views associated with social democracy, feminism, postmodernism and Marxism.

Introduction

One question implied in the previous chapter but never explicitly asked is whether the distribution of income and wealth matters. Unless we can show that it has some sociological significance, we might just as well provide you with data on the shoe sizes of the population. Fortunately sociologists do argue that the distribution of income and wealth matters. It matters for two key reasons:

- Money is an important if not the most important means of acquiring the goods and services that improve life. One simple example will suffice. If you have money you can, if you wish, purchase an education for your children at a private school. This will give them a much greater chance of getting into Oxbridge and thereby acquiring a well-paid job.
- Money is often seen as the main measure of the success or failure of individuals, and therefore the question of whether the distribution of money in society reflects talent or merit is important. A meritocracy (a society in which everyone has an equal chance of succeeding if they try hard enough, and where status is achieved through ability and effort and not through class or inherited advantage) may seem like an ideal vision, but it is important to consider whether such a society could or should be achieved.

A meritocracy could be considered an equal society since there are equal opportunities for all, but as talent and effort determine who becomes successful and therefore rich, there are bound to be inequalities in the distribution of income and wealth.

Exercise 3.1

A meritocracy is a society ruled by those with merit, in other words, a society where those with talent gain positions of influence.

 1. Think of as many different ways of measuring merit or talent that you can.

2. Create a rank order of the various forms of merit or talent that you think would be important.

3. Discuss your findings with other class members.

Whether society should be characterised by equality and exactly what is meant by equality have been central questions in sociology since its foundation. Sociology was born in the wake of the French Revolution, whose slogan 'Liberty, Equality and Fraternity' gave plenty of scope for debate on these questions and their implications for society. Hence the study of inequality has always been central to sociology and we have a large body of theory to draw upon to explain the empirical facts presented in Chapter 2.

This chapter considers a range of sociological theories on the subject and discusses their strengths and weaknesses. The first distinction we should make is between those who believe that inequality is important and those who argue for some degree of equality. As we shall see, there is no precise agreement about what is meant by equality and inequality.

Support for inequality in the distribution of income and wealth

Within sociology there is some support for a degree of inequality in income and wealth (and therefore opposition to the notion of equality) from two perspectives, namely functionalism and the New Right. We shall examine each in turn and consider the similarities and differences between them.

Functionalist views

Functionalism is based on the idea that everything that exists in society has arisen because it serves a purpose or has a function (hence the name functionalism). It should therefore not come as a surprise that sociologists writing from this perspective believe that economic inequality is functional for society.

Specifically, functionalist sociologists believe that those who have talent and realise their potential should be rewarded with high salaries.

This acts as an incentive for people to maximise their potential and benefit society with their expertise and talent. Inequality is seen in a positive light in that it acts as a spur to make people improve their position. Parsons (1977) argues that inequality is inevitable in society, and that this is recognised by most people. There is an unequal distribution of talent among the members of society, and this is a natural part of the ordered scheme of things. He argues that there are so many roles in contemporary society that we need to ensure that everyone is allocated to the job that best uses their talents. We must therefore encourage the most talented to train and develop themselves to take on the most difficult jobs. In order to do this we need to ensure that they will be amply rewarded for their sacrifices. In a situation of equal opportunity, those who grasp the opportunities presented to them and use their talents are rewarded. Those who do not must suffer the consequences. If the end result is inequality, then so be it. Society accepts this situation and therefore inequality is legitimated. Those who deserve monetary reward receive it, and this is seen as just and fair.

In perhaps the most famous overview of functionalist theories on inequality, Davis and Moore (1945) state that inequalities arise from the different values placed on various social roles, about which there is consensus in society. Hence jobs that are highly valued are well rewarded in terms of pay and those that are less well valued are rewarded less. Inequality is therefore seen as a legitimate and acceptable part of social life.

Exercise 3.2

In a copy of the table below, indicate whether or not the jobs listed are essential to and functional for society, and whether the people who do them are given high or low status by society.

Job	Functional?	Status given
Prime minister		
Sewerage worker		
Premier league footballer		
Pop singer (e.g. Robbie Williams)		
Beautician		
Electrician		
Farmer		

Functionalists therefore argue that society should be based on meritocratic principles, with people achieving success through their own efforts and their own merits. Everyone has the opportunity to succeed, but those who make the most effort will reap the most rewards and benefits.

One criticism of this view is that while some jobs are essential to and functional for society (waste disposal workers being a case in point) they are not highly rewarded economically, whereas less essential jobs (such as Premier League football players, who received an average annual salary of £400 000 in 2001) are. Both these jobs require people to use the skills and talents they have, but one is monetarily rewarded far more than the other.

Exactly how some jobs come to be seen as more essential than others is an important question for functionalists. Davis and Moore (1945) argue that jobs that are highly valued are highly rewarded, so if we ask 'how do we know that a job is highly valued?', the answer is 'because it is highly rewarded'. Since merit is effectively being measured by income level, this becomes a circular argument where income is supposedly measured by merit, but the key indicator of merit is income. This circularity (or tautology to give it its proper name) is a key weakness of functionalist theory.

Marxist theorist Claus Offe (1977 p. 67) considers that the so-called achievement principle model of society espoused by functionalists can be discredited. He too believes that the distribution of life chances is demonstrably at variance with performance criteria; that is, those who have the most talent or work the hardest are not necessarily those who receive the most reward.

Finally, John Scott (1994, p. 42) argues that a link must be made between the deprivation of the poor and the privilege of the wealthy:

> If deprivation is the condition of life of the poor, privilege is the condition of life of the wealthy. Deprivation and privilege can be seen as complementary terms, as two contrasting departures from the normal life style of the citizen. . . . [T]he causes of poverty can not be separated from the causes of wealth.

Here Scott is suggesting that poverty and wealth arise at the same time and under the same processes. They therefore have to be studied together, rather than as separate issues. To address only one issue is to limit research and leave avenues unexplored.

Exercise 3.3

1. What barriers might prevent people from utilising their talents?

2. Refer back Item E in Chapter 2 (the table of directors' pay). What kinds of talent have these people utilised?

3. In a two-column table, list the talents you think you have (good organiser, able to work co-operatively and so on), and how you utilise those talents in your everyday life (for example arranging matches for the school sports team).

4. In a table copied from the one below, list the strengths and weaknesses of the functionalist approach. The first ones have been done for you.

Weaknesses
1. It assumes that everyone sees inequality as fair and just.
2.
3.
Strengths
1. It has opened up a debate on whether inequality is a good thing rather than a bad thing.
2.
3.

New Right views

While functionalist theories were popular in sociology in the 1950s and 1960s they were later somewhat eclipsed by the emergence of New Right ideas. These were associated with the dominance of the political right in the 1980s and early 1990s, as characterised by the rise to power in the UK of Margaret Thatcher (Prime Minister from 1979–1990) and the Conservative Party (in government between 1979 and 1997); and in the US by Ronald Reagan (US president, 1980–88) and the Republican Party (in power from 1980–1992, and again from 2000). Like function-alists, new right thinkers believe that inequality exists and is justifiable, but they take the functionalist argument further by relating inequality to the free market.

The New Right see income inequality as necessary to expand resources and spur on economic growth. In this sense they agree with Davis and Moore (1945) that inequality is needed to motivate people to better themselves and utilise their talents to the full. In a free market economy the market provides information that enables producers to produce what is really wanted. If people do not produce what is wanted and the market collapses, there will be negative effects on society. It is therefore important to have a mechanism that rewards those who supply what people want and can afford, and discourages them from supplying things people do not want or cannot afford. The mechanism that can achieve this is inequality of monetary reward.

Peter Saunders (1995) argues that all societies are unequal in some way or other, and that such inequality is beneficial to society, not only because of the selection mechanism identified by Davis and Moore but also because inequality is a prime motivating force for capitalists who, in the process of pursuing personal riches, provide benefits to others: 'Successful entrepreneurs may well accumulate a fortune, but in so doing, they will have added to the productive power and wealth of the society as a whole' (Saunders, 1990, p. 53). Saunders also believes that talents are unequally distributed and that this may be genetically based, with the children of those who succeed going on to be successful themselves.

The New Right believe in the power of enterprise, and in the power of the market to allocate income in accordance with merit. One aspect of this is the 'trickle down' effect: if the rich are made even richer by granting them concessions such as tax cuts, some of their riches will, by stimulating the economy, trickle down to everyone else (see also Chapter 2). The New Right also believe in promoting market capitalism by spreading share ownership throughout the population, thus giving people a share in the means of production and putting them in charge of their own destiny.

Exercise 3.4

Reread pages 24–5

 Does the information on share ownership lead you to believe that the new right's ideas are correct? Give reasons for your answer.

The New Right are against the state intervening in people's lives. They believe that all individuals should be responsible for their own destiny and that government handouts are not the way forward. Nonetheless Saunders (1990) suggests that income and other assets need not be distributed through the market. He argues that there is an alternative, which he calls coercion. What he means by this is that the state could use its power to force people to take on certain roles or decide how much pay should be allocated to certain roles. However this would undermine individual liberty: 'The value of egalitarianism is not necessarily unattainable, but it could only be realised at the price of individual liberty. Equality and liberty are incompatible objectives. If we desire one, we must sacrifice the other' (ibid., p. 67). Since the New Right see individual liberty as the key to 'the good society', this statement implies that equality is undesirable. Indeed Saunders states that 'we should be wary of assuming that inequality is necessarily immoral or socially damaging' (ibid., p. 10). In a way it is the price that society has to pay for progress and economic expansion.

Criticisms of the New Right position

Critics of the New Right believe there is little evidence to support their claim that the free market offers the best way forward. Rather it seems to have contributed to the growth of inequality as far as living standards are concerned. The rich have benefited far more than the poor and the gap between the two has become wider, not narrower (see Chapter 2). The trickle down theory is undermined by this, as while the rich have grown richer under new right policies, it is not clear how the rest of the population have benefited.

A second criticism concerns the new right's stand against government intervention in the economy. According to writers such as Will Hutton (1996) economic growth tends to be higher in countries characterised by state intervention, such as Germany. Equally, although the spectacular economic growth of some East Asian economies in the early 1990s was presented as proof of the superiority of the market approach, in fact the state was heavily involved in the economic affairs of these countries.

Exercise 3.5

Form a small group of three or four people and assume the role of sociologists intending to research the way in which people in society view inequality in wealth and income.

How do you propose to carry out this research? Write a justification of your chosen methodology, along with a hypothesis for your study.

Support for equality in the distribution of income and wealth

In contrast to the theories discussed above, other schools of thought stress the need for total equality or at least greater equality. However there is disagreement between them over the exact meaning of the term 'equality', as well as how to measure and achieve it.

This section considers the following approaches: social democratic, feminist, Weberian, postmodernist and Marxist.

Social democratic views on equality

R. H. Tawney is probably most famous for his book *Equality* (1961), originally published during the Great Depression of the 1930s. In it Tawney provides strong theoretical arguments in favour of the creation of a society based on the principles of equality, and he outlines the unwelcome effects of inequality. This book was one of the first to discuss the problems of inequality at the societal level, and it became a cornerstone of Labour government policy after the Second World War. It can also be seen as providing the model for the sociological books of today that investigate the extent of inequality and debate its consequences (for example Glyn and Miliband, 1994; Goodman *et al.*, 1997).

What is particularly interesting is that Tawney (1961) carefully considers the different meanings of the term equality, thus heralding the way in which social democratic thinking was to be distinguished from more radical proposals for equality:

> the word 'Equality' possesses more than one meaning . . . it may either purport to state a fact, or convey the expression of an ethical judgement. On the one hand, it may affirm that men are, on the whole, very similar in their natural endowments of character and intelligence. On the other hand, it may assert that, while they differ profoundly as individuals in capacity or character, they are equally entitled as human beings to consideration and respect (ibid., p. 46).

Exercise 3.6

1. Rewrite the above quote in your own words, removing the sexism and clearly distinguishing between the two very different meanings of equality conveyed in the passage.

2. Suggest ways in which we could create an equal society in relation to each of these two meanings of the term.

Tawney draws a distinction between fundamental human equality on the one hand, and equal citizenship and human rights on the other. He clearly rejects the possibility of the first of these:

> the assertion of human equality is clearly untenable. It is a piece of mythology against which irresistible evidence has been accumulated by biologists and psychologists. In the light of the data presented – to mention only two recent examples – in such works as Dr Burt's admirable studies of the distribution of educational abilities among school-children, or the Report of the Mental Deficiency Committee, the fact that, quite apart from differences of environment and opportunity, individuals differ widely in their natural endowments, and in their capacity to develop them by education, is not open to question (ibid., p. 47).

Exercise 3.7

Refer to the education chapter in a sociology textbook (for example Kirby *et al.*, 2000, or Lawson and Heaton, 1996) to see whether it is in fact 'not open to question' that natural endowments differ widely. How has the debate on IQ and IQ testing led to a reassessment of Tawney's views.

The clear implication is that social democracy should pursue the notion of equality of opportunity. While this inevitably means that some inequality has to exist (reflecting the different talents identified by Tawney and therefore seen as legitimate, and much the same as functionalists argue), this should be kept within bounds as otherwise there will be negative social, political and moral consequences for society. This was the main concern of early Social Democrats and their solution was to provide public services so that societal surpluses would be redistributed to all. This provided the ideological basis for increased taxation and public expenditure and the emergence of the welfare state (see Chapter 8).

Since Tawney there have been arguments among social democrats over exactly what rights should be given to people and whether public provision is actually needed. For example T. H. Marshall (1963), writing about citizenship rights, argues that the concept of citizenship has developed over time to embrace civil, political and social issues:

- Civil citizenship means the right to individual freedom – essentially freedom of speech, freedom of thought and belief, the right to own property and the right to justice.
- Political citizenship means the right to vote and participate in political decision making.
- Social citizenship means the right to economic welfare and security, including the right to education, work and health care.

All liberal democracies support the first two sets of rights. However the third is more controversial as it effectively implies a social security budget financed by taxation, and therefore some redistribution of income and wealth. The extent to which this has actually occurred or is still an aspiration among social democratic thinkers is a matter of debate.

The early approach, as adopted by the Labour government elected in 1945, was based on state intervention in and control of key elements of the economy. As a result the state came to play a large part in the distribution of economic resources. Social expenditure also expanded in the postwar period. Between 1951 and 1979 social expenditure – mainly on the welfare state – rose by 250 per cent in real terms and increased its share of GNP from 16.1 per cent to 28.3 per cent (Judge, 1982).

Because of this increasing state involvement in economic affairs, Tony Crosland (1956) argued that capitalism had changed its spots and there was no longer a need for public ownership to ensure social justice. Intervention would be enough, he argued, to achieve both the efficiency gains of equality and a just society. This view reflected divisions within the Labour Party over whether economics (nationalisation) or morality (state intervention and moral exhortation to treat people fairly) was the best way to bring about equality.

If we look at the contemporary Labour Party under Tony Blair we can see that these arguments have again risen to the surface. One thing that is new about New Labour is its rejection of any notion of a greater public sector, believing instead (like Tony Crosland) that the private sector and the free market can be harnessed for progressive ends. This enthusiasm for the private sector flies in the face of the earlier Labour Party belief that nationalisation was needed to avoid the waste and inefficiency that characterised the free market. This change of attitude can be seen in the government's promotion of public–private partnerships (PPPs), which involve private funding for public sector projects (see Chapter 2, pp. 20–3, Chapter 9, pp. 171–3).

Another indication of New Labour's rejection of state intervention in the economy can be found in the figures on state expenditure. According to Toynbee and Walker (2001), government spending fell from 41.2 per cent of GDP during John Major's last year as Conservative prime minister (1996–97) to 37.7 per cent in 1999–2000. New Labour has shrunk the state even further than the Conservatives managed to do!

Added to this, all thoughts of a large-scale redistribution of income and wealth through tax measures seem to have disappeared. In essence, it appears that since the poor now only constitute a minority of the electorate and there is a need to keep the more numerous, relatively affluent middle classes voting for New Labour, this means not raising their taxes. When income supplements do need to be given to the poor, New Labour has targeted work rather than welfare as the main solution, seeing the private sector and the jobs it provides as more able than the welfare state to solve the problem of poverty. However it does have to be said that a small degree of redistribution has occurred through fiscal changes. Toynbee and Walker (ibid.), quoting Institite for Fiscal Studies statistics, show that fiscal reforms since July 1997 have made the poorest 10 per cent of people 8.8 per cent better off, while the richest 10 per cent of people have become 0.5 per cent worse off. It is also the case that legislative changes such as the minimum wage have had a positive impact, although many claim that it is too low, including groups such as TELCO (a coalition of religious and community groups in East London), which argues that a living wage would need to be set at £6.30 in 2001 figures, rather than the current minimum wage of £4.10. However it should be pointed out that the larger amount is based on there being only one main breadwinner in the family, and this might be seen as offensive by feminists.

Therefore while some redistribution has occurred, many view it as not enough. The need to keep business and the middle classes happy with New Labour's political project is seen as placing limits on the extent of any redistributive policy, and it has led many to argue that New Labour is based on very old ideas. For example Alan Ryan (1999, p. 77) argues that 'The third way first showed up in British policies ninety-five years ago. At that point it was, and in so far as it is coherent it remains, the ideology of the New Liberalism'. Equally Greg Philo and David Miller (2001, p. 18) argue that '"New Labour" is an odd term. With its commitment to free market liberalism, its moral tone, its exhortations to the lower orders to discover the merits of work and its designation of the deserving and undeserving poor, it is actually a version of old fashioned Christian Liberalism.'

Feminist views

Feminists in general and radical feminists in particular see women's inequality in all spheres of life as directly or indirectly related to patriarchy. Men generally oppress women, but this is most evident in the economic realm as women have less income and wealth than men. The assumption in society is that women are 'carers' who stay at home to look after their children. This usually excludes them from paid employment, and even if they do go out to work, it is often part-time to fit in with the needs of the children. In this way women are prevented from taking on certain types of employment (see Chapter 5, pp. 83–9). Furthermore, the fact that women may have to take maternity leave makes some employers reluctant to employ them, and although laws are in place to stop discrimination it still occurs, but this is difficult to prove.

Assumptions are made about the social roles of men and women, and social constructions are placed on sex differences. These differences are not just biological in nature, so women's position in society has to be seen as socially engineered, not simply biologically based. Human beings develop ideas about appropriate masculine and feminine behaviours, and from this emenates a sexual division of labour in the home and the workplace. The fact that women are very often economically dependent on men puts them in a weak position and reinforces their subordination in a male-dominated world. Women have far less access to financial resources than men. They are often in low-paid, part-time work, or are viewed as a 'reserve army' of labour, to be called upon in times of economic need and sent back to the kitchen when not needed. Wealthy women tend to be the daughters, wives or partners of wealthy men, rather than being wealthy in their own right. For example the ten richest people in the world are all men and between them they own more than the combined wealth of 560 million people. Of course some women are rich in their own right, for example Queen Elizabeth of Britain (whose wealth is inherited), Madonna (the American film star and singer) and Naomi Campbell (fashion model), but they are exceptions to the rule.

Marxist feminists have added to the debate on patriarchy and economic power by linking capitalism and patriarchy into a 'dual systems' theory. According to Michele Barrett (1988) and Sylvia Walby (1990), patriarchy and capitalism have to be seen as playing an interrelated part in maintaining economic inequality between men and women.

Exercise 3.8

k u a e

Drawing on the previous section, your sociology text(s) and the section on Feminism in Chapter 6, outline and assess two sociological explanations of the economic differences between men and women.

Weberian views

Weber argued that there are important social divisions in society other than social class. He developed a trilogy of 'class, status and party', reflecting his idea that as well as economic divisions (class), there are social divisions based on different degrees of status or prestige and different elements of political power.

Early in his career Weber studied the effect of changes in agricultural labour organisation in East Elbia (then part of Prussia, now a region of Germany). He was concerned that attempts to reduce production costs by employing Polish workers would lead to a decline in the political and cultural power of Prussia. The importance of factors other than the strictly economic can be seen in Weber's argument that the human legacy to be passed down should not be peace and happiness, 'but rather the eternal struggle to preserve and raise the quality of our national species' (quoted in Lassman and Speirs, 1994, p. 16).

Class, status and party are therefore seen as different aspects of power. Thus Weberians reject explanations based on a single overriding factor (most famously the pre-eminence placed on class relations by Marx) and attempt to explain inequality and poverty by considering a number of interacting and/or cross-cutting factors. One element of this is 'social closure', whereby groups and individuals seek to protect or enhance their economic position by preventing other individuals or groups from entering into competition with them. Examples of this are the way in which women are excluded by men from certain occupations, and Weber's own suggestion that the government should not allow Polish workers to take on agricultural jobs in the Elbian area.

The emphasis on the extent to which access to economic resources can be closed or open to different individuals and groups has given rise to studies of social mobility, which investigate whether people achieve their occupational positions on the basis of their social origin (positions that are closed to those with different origins) or regardless of their origin. Glass (1954), Goldthorpe (1980) and others suggest that access to some occupation is still not entirely open and thus social origin does have an effect on income distribution. Despite this, increased social mobility has led to fragmentation of the class structure so other aspects of people's identity have become more important explanations of the unequal distribution of income and wealth, for example gender, ethnicity, nationality and disability. The fragmentation of the social classes has also led to growing interest in the subject of individualisation, which is central to postmodernist views on the distribution of income and wealth.

Criticisms of the Weberian approaches

The key criticism of the Weberian approach is that while its emphasis on the multiplicity of social divisions provides a more accurate portrait of the complex society that exists today, it largely remains at the level of description and therefore no central mechanism of inequality and poverty is offered to give some dynamic to the account.

Secondly, it is argued that the Weberian model of inequality is little more than a hierarchical list of classes, without any logical limit to the number of classes or consideration of the relations that exist between them.

Postmodernist views

Postmodernist views on class can be linked to Weberian views in that they both place emphasis on the fragmentation of structures of inequality and on the Nietzschean argument that power is omnipresent. In effect, all aspects of life are a power struggle and we can never arrive at an agreed foundation for inequality, as suggested by functionalists, or at Marx's classless society.

Waters (1997) argues that we need to consider inequality in what he calls a postclass society. According to Waters, stratification in such a society is characterised by:

- Divisions other than class, such as gender and ethnicity.
- Stratification that is constantly in flux, shifting and unstable because of fragmented identities and associations, with an overlap between different aspects of social division.
- The classification of individuals according to political preference, educational level, general consumption and lifestyle, rather than class or occupation.
- Anxiety and uncertainty because of the continuously shifting stratification system.

This emphasis on cultural rather than economic divisions represents a move away from the Weberian and Marxist concern with the distribution of income and wealth and towards cultural factors such as lifestyle choice, which are seen by postmodernists as better predictors of how an individual will behave.

One aspect of social fragmentation relates to the sphere of employment. In the 1970s Bell (1973) suggested that technological changes were leading to increased demand for skilled and professional workers, and therefore income distribution would become bell-shaped when plotted as a graph, with most people grouped towards the middle. This can be contrasted with the Marxist immiseration thesis that people would become poorer as time went on, and with Andre Gorz's argument in *Farewell to the Working Class* (1982) that work was becoming a less important factor in people's lives, and therefore a less important source of income.

More recent postmodernist writers have placed greater emphasis on the process of individualisation, suggesting that social divisions such as class, gender and ethnicity are breaking down and that resources such as income and wealth are increasingly being distributed on the basis of individual attributes.

Criticisms of postmodernism

One criticism of postmodernism is that it tends to exaggerate the trends it identifies and therefore overemphasises the degree of change. For instance Madry and Kirby (1996) point out that post-Fordist and postindustrial arguments suggest that individuals have more choice in their lives than is actually the case, and Callinicos (1989) argues that the position of many workers in advanced industrial capitalist countries has worsened, leaving them with less rather than more choice. Furthermore Devine (1992) shows that people's everyday economic realities encroach upon and limit their choices, and as a result there is still some allegiance to collective identities such as social class, in opposition to the individualisation thesis advanced by postmodernists.

Marxist views

Marxists argue that inequalities of income and wealth are the result of differences in social class, rather the cause of those differences. At the basic level of Marxist theory there are two distinct classes, based on their relationship to the means of production: the owners of the means of production (the bourgeoisie) and the workers (the proletariat). The bourgeoisie have economic power and posses the wealth of society; the proletariat are paid less than their labour is worth and consequently they do not receive the wealth they deserve. In effect the bourgeoisie 'own' and control the proletariat and decide their economic fate. The proletariat are kept in a subordinate position from which they cannot escape. In order for capitalism to thrive inequalities have to exist, and the proletariat are not given the chance to better themselves because costs have to be kept low in the interest of profit.

Marx wrote a scathing critique of the operation and immorality of capitalism and its effects upon the working class. He devised two principles of equality that came to be known as the contribution principle and the needs principle. The contribution principle stressed that people should be rewarded in proportion to their contribution to the creation of wealth. Since Marx viewed owners not as entrepreneurs but as parasites who exploited the real creators of wealth, the contribution principle implied that they should receive no income. However this could also be applied to anyone outside paid employment, and hence the needs principle: 'From each according to their abilities, to each according to their needs' which did not require any contribution as a basis for entitlement, merely human need.

While this would provide the basis of a just distribution of material wealth, Marx believed that more fundamental change was needed, a point that has divided Marxists and other radical thinkers and social democrats to this day (see the discussion of social democratic views on page 32).

Exercise 3.9

i *a*

Reread the sections on feminism and Marxism, and in a table copied from the one below list the similarities and differences between feminism and Marxism. Examples have been provided to start you off.

Similarities	Differences
Oppression is evident	Gender is a major theme in feminism
Ownership is a central theme	

Case study on income distribution

The case study that follows looks at the way in which workers are after treated as expendable commodities that can be hired and fired at will. They lack power because they are hired on short-term contracts that offer no security, and they have little help from trade unions. Due to the impact of globalisation and the advent of flexible firms (see Chapter 7, pp. 125–38) work practices are changing dramatically and workers often have to choose between accepting these practices or suffering long-term unemployment and poverty.

On 14 February 1999 it was revealed by the *Observer* that Filipinos and Mauritians, working as painters and welders on British North Sea oil rigs were being paid just 81 pence an hour, ranking them amongst the worst paid in the UK. Some of the men had worked for 84 consecutive days, at the end of which they had been paid off, with commission being taken by the overseas agents who had obtained the jobs for them. Such working hours and conditions are illegal under European law, but oil rigs are exempt because they operate outside the twelve-mile limit.

On 21 February 1999 the newspaper disclosed that up to 20 of these workers had been sacked and told they would be sent back to their home countries. Despite being paid £90 a day less than British workers, these men were willing to go on working because the pay was still more than they could hope to receive in their own countries and the money they sent to their families went some way towards making their lives better. Anyone who loses a source of income in this way naturally becomes poorer.

Link Exercise 3.1

Using information in Chapter 7 and the case study, answer the following questions:

1. Why are employment laws able to be flouted by companies operating oil rigs?

2. Which sociological theory provides the best explanation of to why the workers were exploited? In 200 words, give reasons for your answer.

Exercise 3.10

Over the course of one week, make a note of any items on poverty and wealth in newspapers such as the *Guardian*, *The Times*, the *Telegraph* and *The Independent*, and magazines or journals such as *The Economist* and the *New Statesman*. If the print media were your only source of information, what would you understand about poverty and wealth?

4 Definitions and measurements of poverty

By the end of this chapter you should be able to:

- list the different definitions of poverty;
- outline the reasons why different definitions are used;
- outline how poverty is measured and why these measurements are used;
- discuss the strengths and weaknesses of different approaches to the definition and measurement of poverty;
- appreciate the extent of poverty;
- answer an exam question on this subject.

Introduction

> Poverty, like slavery, cannot be studied independently of its moral context and its effects on real human lives (Thomas, 1997).

This chapter examines the ways in which poverty is defined and measured. How poverty is defined shapes our perceptions of it in a variety of contexts and determines the way in which societies deal with it through social policies and actions. In this sense poverty is a political issue. The politicisation of poverty leads to new ideas, which in turn shape the way it is measured.

This chapter looks at the absolute and relative approaches to the definition and measurement of poverty, and considers the debate on whether defining and measuring poverty is an objective or a subjective (and thereby value laden) exercise. It then considers the more recent approach to poverty measurement developed by the Blair government, using social indicators in line with its policies on social inclusion.

This chapter should not be read in isolation but should be used in conjunction with the ideas raised in other chapters about how the poor are viewed.

Definitions of poverty

> Poverty is still the gravest insult to human dignity. Poverty is the scar on humanity's face (Brundtland, 1988).

If the above quotation is true, it is vital to be aware of what poverty is. Although the word poverty is used every day, do any of us really know what it means? We have to know this before we can begin to tackle the problems associated with it. However there is no universally agreed definition of poverty because it is an inherently political issue, in that all governments have to decide how to deal with it, produce some form of social policy on it and provide the economic funding necessary to support that policy (for example in the UK the welfare state is funded by National Insurance contributions and tax payments – see Chapter 9). Therefore any definition is problematic, subjective and particular to the individuals or groups who use it. Poverty is a highly contested issue and has been since the first studies were conducted in the late nineteenth century. There appears to be no objective definition of poverty and no real consensus on what constitutes poverty.

Exercise 4.1

Before reading this chapter write down your own definition of poverty. (After reading the chapter you will be asked to return to your answer to see whether your ideas have remained the same or changed.

According to Norwegian sociologist David Piachaud (1987, p. 62), 'If the term poverty carries with it the implication and moral imperative that something should be done about it, then the study of poverty is only ultimately justifiable if it influences individual and social attitudes and actions.'

Poverty is a problem that is unlikely to disappear in the foreseeable future in many countries due to their economic and/or political situation. For example if a country is experiencing civil war or unrest, if the government is unstable and there is raging inflation, then poverty is very likely to continue to exist. However in peaceful, affluent countries, as Piachaud points out, wherever and whenever it arises it is seen as a problem requiring a solution.

There are two main groups of definitions of poverty: absolute definitions and relative definitions. We shall examine each of these in turn.

Absolute definitions of poverty

- A definition of absolute poverty assumes that it is possible to define a minimum standard of living based on a person's biological needs for food, water, clothing and shelter (Oppenheim and Harker, 1996, p. 70).

The Concise Oxford School Dictionary defines poverty as:

- Poverty is 'Being poor, indigence, want, scarcity, deficiency' (Hawking *et al.*, 1997, p. 126).
- Absolute poverty is 'a condition characterised by severe deprivation of basic human needs, including food, safe drinking water, sanitation facilities, health, shelter, education and information. It depends not only on income but also on access to services' (UNDP, Human Development Report (1998) p. 167.)

Absolute or subsistence definitions of poverty were first proposed at the end of the nineteenth century, based on the prevailing thoughts of the time. As society evolved these ideas were challenged (for example by the advocates of more relative approaches) but absolute measures are still used today. For example in 1996 the United Nations stated that one in five people in the world lived in absolute poverty. In a British Social Attitudes survey conducted by Taylor-Gooby (1993) it was found that 60 per cent of the people surveyed thought of poverty in terms of subsistence.

Absolute definitions of poverty are based on the fact that all human beings require adequate food, clothing and shelter in order to sustain life, or in other words, to subsist. Seebohm Rowntree (1901) drew on this idea in his study of York. He concluded that poverty existed when 'total earnings are insufficient to obtain the minimum necessities for the maintenance of merely physical efficiency' (ibid., p. 136). What did Rowntree mean by 'physical efficiency'? Is it about being able to carry out the daily demands made of you, for example being able to do your job to your employer's satisfaction without becoming ill?

Exercise 4.2

1. Write a list of what you think makes a person physically efficient.

2. What criteria have you used to arrive at this opinion?

3. Compare your list with those of three other people. To what extent do you agree?

4. Are you physically efficient? How do you know?

5. Who would you consult to find out about physical efficiency?

6. Does physical efficiency mean the same now as it did, say, in 1899, 1936 and 1950?

People still view poverty as an absolute rather than a relative problem. In a speech in 1976 Keith Joseph (former Conservative secretary of state for social services) said: 'An absolute standard of means is defined by reference to the actual needs of the poor. A family is poor if it cannot afford to eat. By any absolute standards there is very little poverty in Britain today.' Likewise in a speech given on 9 June 1994 the Duke of Edinburgh said that absolute poverty no longer existed in the UK because the free health service and free universal education had alleviated two of the primary reasons for poverty – ill health and lack of education.

The strengths of absolute definitions of poverty

- Since they are ultimately based on biological notions of existence, absolute definitions provide a clearly understandable and universal notion of poverty that can be used to identify those living in poverty.
- These definitions closely fit our everyday, commonsense notion of what poverty means.
- Absolute definitions of poverty strongly influenced the Beveridge Report and consequently the nature of the new welfare state in the UK. As long as benefits continue to be based on the idea of subsistence (which in effect they are in the UK) studies of absolute poverty will continue to have an impact on social policy and the welfare state.

Criticisms of absolute definitions

The universal application of absolute definitions of poverty is problematic in that what counts as poverty differs from place to place and time to time. Human needs tend to be culturally defined, and what is defined as need in one place may not be in another. What were deemed as acceptable living standards when Rowntree began his studies are not acceptable now. Standards are not fixed; they can and do change. As Melanie Phillips (1992) says: 'Those who claim that only absolute standards are valid suffer from tunnel vision. Of course, poor people 50 years ago would not have had the material goods they enjoy today. So what? It's a bit like saying that anyone with an inside lavatory can't be poor because people used to use a shed in the back yard.'

Absolute definitions of poverty can also be criticised for assuming that needs can be measured in a scientific and objective manner. Needs tend to vary according to age, gender, race occupation and disability, so a single standard cannot be applied across the board, as absolute definitions infer. Postmodernists would echo this view and refute the idea that needs can be measured against a predetermined scale.

Exercise 4.3

a 1. List what you think are your basic needs.

e 2. To what extent do these needs depend on your age, locality, race and gender? Give reasons for your answer.

Criticism can be levelled at experts for using unrealistic assumptions when designing measures to alleviate the effects of poverty. Experts on nutrition and budgeting, such as those consulted by Rowntree, can draw up diet sheets aimed at ensuring adequate nutrition, but as Martin Rein (1970, p. 62) says, it is 'an unrealistic assumption of a no waste budget and extensive knowledge of marketing and cooking. An economical budget must be based on knowledge and skill which is least likely to be present in the low income groups.' How many people consult a nutritionist before buying and cooking food? Some people will be able to utilise the resources they have better than others, so what resources are available and to whom need to enter the equation.

Furthermore the absolute approach to poverty does not allow for personal taste and choice, which may be influenced by social class and geographical location. Thought should be given to how people prefer to spend their money rather than telling them how they should spend it.

Exercise 4.4

a 1. Keep a diary of everything you eat during the course of a week.

a 2. Estimate roughly how much it cost to feed you for the week.

e 3. Do you consider that what you ate was good nutritional food?

e 4. Was this week a typical one? Do you usually eat more or less?

Acccording to Joseph and Sumption (1979, p. 84): 'A family is poor if it can not afford to eat.' No consideration is taken here of the type or amount of food a family may be eating. To imply that if you can eat you are not poor is to ignore nutrition, health and children's physical development.

The Joseph Rowntree Foundation looked at how people would adapt to eating on a low income (Dobson, 1994). All the families studied managed to get enough to eat – but at a price, such as self-denial, family stress and unaccustomed shopping habits. The study found that:

- The cost of food took precedence over taste, cultural acceptability and healthy eating.
- Mothers had to ration supplies, find out where to shop economically and restrict their spending.

- Families had only a vague knowledge of food issues despite receiving information from a variety of sources.
- Advice on healthy eating was not considered feasible.
- Mothers deprived themselves to ensure that their children would not appear to be different from those who had sweets and 'treats'.

Postmodernists find absolute definitions of poverty too generalised and prescriptive, and as lacking relevance to the present. They argue that there is so much diversity and pluralism in society that to reduce poverty to a base level is to disregard important issues such as cultural and philosophical differences within and between societies. However, those on the New Right use absolute definitions to claim that poverty no longer exists in the UK because everyone has the basic necessities required to subsist. This contention, however, is debatable.

ITEM A

Dr Owen: . . . may I ask whether she [Prime Minister Margaret Thatcher] is aware that 15 million people in Britain – that is the official figure – will be living at or below the poverty line this Christmas?

The Prime Minister: I recognise the right hon. gentleman's very studied question. Before I answer him, may I ask him what definition of poverty he is using to reach that figure?

Dr Owen: It is the official Government statistics relating to the 3 million unemployed families, the 6 million families that are living on low wages and pensioners who face high costs for rented accommodation. If she checks that total, she will find that 15 million Britons are at or below the poverty line.

The Prime Minister: There is no Government definition of poverty. There are some 7 million people who live in families that are supported by supplementary benefit. There are many other different definitions of poverty, which is why I asked the right hon. gentleman to say which definition he was using. Many of the low-paid on supplementary benefit have incomes about 40 per cent above that level. They are wholly artificial definitions. The fact remains that people who are living in need are fully and properly provided for.

(Source: Hansard, 22 December 1983, quoted in Mack and Lansley, 1985, p. vii.)

ITEM A   **Exercise 4.5**

Read Item A and then conduct the following tasks:

i 1. List the types of family and individuals said to be living at or below the poverty line in 1983.

i u 2. Explain in your own words the prime minister's view that there were many different definitions of poverty and they were 'wholly artificial'.

i u a 3. What definition of poverty do you think Dr Owen was using in his statement, and what definition of poverty do you think would have been acceptable to Margaret Thatcher, if any?

Measuring absolute poverty

This section examines how poverty is measured according to absolute definitions. It should be stressed from the outset that absolute measures of poverty produce a lower figure for those living in poverty in advanced industrial societies compared with measures based on relative definitions. If poverty is based on absolute measures (based on minimal biological need) then few people in the UK could be said to be living in poverty, but relative measures compare the standard of living (rather than biological need) of one group (the poor) with that of more affluent groups, and therefore a greater number of people will be found to be in poverty.

Studies of poverty using absolute measures

Charles Booth   Charles Booth's 17-volume *The Life and Labour of the People in London* (1891–1903) was one of the pioneering sociological studies of poverty in the UK. Booth defined the poor as those with barely enough income to lead a decent independent life, and the very poor as those with insufficient income to lead a decent independent life. The key problem with this is, what is meant by a decent life?

Booth calculated that the income needed to avoid poverty at that time was £1.05 (21 shillings in the currency of the time) for a small family. Although this is often seen as establishing the concept of a poverty line, John Scott (1994, p. 24) points out that Booth himself did not use the term 'poverty line' and gave no justification for using the 21 shilling level as a divide between being poor and not being poor. Scott goes on to argue that since Booth talked about the ability to maintain the standard of living of the day, he implicitly acknowledged some element of relativity in determining the level of poverty. It is therefore possible to link Booth's study to the later (relative definition-based) work of Townsend (1979) and Mack and Lansley (1985). This undermines the clear distinction between the absolute and relative definitions of poverty that some sociologists try to maintain. Nonetheless Booth fits in with the absolute tradition because he did establish an effective poverty level (without using the word 'line') in his research.

Booth found that although over a third of people living in the East End of London were in poverty, the proportion was not much lower in the rest of London (Table 4.1).

According to Booth, the key causes of poverty were casual or irregular earnings and low pay. Poor employment practices, particularly in the case of sweatshops, had to be abolished if poverty was to be eliminated. He proposed that work be created for the poor by removing the privileges of some of the better off. With regard to the work-shy poor, Booth proposed a tightening of the Poor Law approach to instill-

Table 4.1 Poverty distribution in London, 1886–89 (per cent)

	Ordinary poor	Very poor	Total
East London	22.8	12.4	35.2
Central London	11.7	14.6	26.3
Battersea	27.8	5.6	33.4
All London	22.3	8.4	30.7

Source: Scott (1994), p. 24.

ing discipline in people by sending them to the workhouse. The Poor Law provided for those who were fit and healthy but lacked the means to support themselves (or the unemployed in today's terminology) to be sent to a workhouse, where the conditions were deliberately terrible in order to discourage people from applying for assistance and to encourage them to find a job. In effect Booth was suggesting a get-tough approach for those who avoided work.

Exercise 4.6

According to Trowler (1989, p. 42), early researchers' definition of absolute poverty was 'having inadequate income for proper food, clothing and shelter'.

i

1. In what way is this definition based on the biological notion of subsistence and need?

i u e

2. What potential problems might there be in the use of the term 'inadequate' to describe the absolute definition and distinguish it from a relative definition of poverty (see p. 51)?

Seebohm Rowntree   Another pioneering study of poverty in the UK was that conducted by Seebohm Rowntree (1901) in York. Rowntree adopted an absolute approach to poverty for ideological reasons, based on his belief that no one should have to live below a certain level. Rowntree calculated the cost of basic clothing and cheap but nutritional food (after taking expert advice from nutritionists). To this he added the cost of rent, fuel for heating and a small amount for other essentials. He then worked out a budget according to family, size, and any household whose income fell below this was defined as living in poverty. He also made a distinction between primary poverty and secondary poverty. Those in primary poverty spent their income carefully but still lacked basic essentials, for example meals had to be foregone because their income was too low to buy all the food needed. Those in secondary poverty had enough to buy the basic essentials but they did not spend their money wisely – for example they did not buy the cheapest food or they wasted their money on tobacco and alcohol – and consequently they remained in need.

Exercise 4.7

Mack and Lansley (1985, p. 28) argue that 'Rowntree's definition of primary poverty was in fact a rather narrow definition of "relative poverty" at the turn of the century'.

i **a** 1. From what you have so far read about Rowntree, do you agree or disagree with Mack and Lansley's statement?

i **a** 2. Reread the section on Charles Booth (particularly his notion of a 'decent life') and consider whether the statement can be applied to his views on poverty.

e 3. On the basis of your answers to questions 1 and 2, do you think it is possible for these to be a definition of poverty that contains no element of relativity.

Based on the above criteria, Rowntree concluded that 33 per cent of his survey population were living in poverty. In 1936 and 1950 he conducted further studies in York Rowntree, 1941 and Rowntree and Lavers 1951 using the same methodology but with a longer list of essentials. In 1936 the percentage of households in poverty had dropped to 18 per cent, and in 1950 these had been a further fall to 15 per cent. This, he explained, was because the causes of poverty had ameliorated over time – wages had risen in line with the growth of the economy and by 1950 the welfare state was in existence. Of course there were still pockets of poverty, but Rowntree believed the welfare state would eradicate these in time.

ITEM B

In 1899, 15.46 per cent of the working-class population of York (7230 persons) were living in primary poverty. In 1936, 6.8 per cent of the working-class population (3767 persons) were living in primary poverty. In other words there had been a reduction of more than one half in the number of working-class people living in abject poverty.

(Source: B. S. Rowntree (1941), Poverty and Progress: A Second Social Survey of York (London: Longmans Green.)

ITEM B ### Exercise 4.8

Read Item B and answer the following questions:

i 1. According to Item B, what percentage of the working-class population of York were living in primary poverty in 1899?

i 2. By how many percentage points did the extent of primary poverty decline between 1899 and 1936?

As Veit-Wilson (1994) points out, Rowntree's studies relied on his own subjective ideas about suitable lifestyles and on the judgements of the nutritionists who put together what they saw as a suitable diet. Despite these methodological problems, Rowntree's work served as a building block for further research. However, because he limited his study to the extent of poverty and methods of defining and measuring poverty, he set a precedent that resulted subsequent studies being restricted in scope.

Exercise 4.9

[a] 1. Why do you think Rowntree added to his original list of essentials in his second and third studies?

[e] 2. In an extended version of the table below, list what you consider to be the strengths and weaknesses of Rowntree's work. A couple of examples are provided to start you off.

Strengths	Weaknesses
He focused attention on a poverty line	His budget approach was too prescriptive

Relative definitions of poverty

The study by Rowntree (1901) is considered one of the classic studies of absolute poverty. However Rowntree himself hints at problems with his approach. For example his definition of primary poverty was receipt of an income that was 'insufficient to obtain the minimum necessities for the maintenance of merely physical efficiency' (1901, p. 167), thus making a clear distinction between merely existing and living. Rowntree also made reference to the need for people to ensure the 'maintenance of physical health'. While he thought that good health and physical fitness could be objectively and scientifically defined, they were defined by the standards of the day and would be considered differently now.

Mack and Lansley (1985, pp. 27–8) argue that Rowntree, rather than using an absolute definition, was in fact using a relative definition and the changes he made to his notion of subsistence in his later studies testify to this:

> Even Seebohm Rowntree, the man who had developed the idea of 'primary poverty', had, by the time of his second survey of York in 1936, incorporated into his definition of poverty some needs that were not related in any way to the maintenance of physical health. His 1936 definition allowed for items such as radio, books, newspapers, beer, tobacco, presents and holidays. . . . Rowntree's definition of primary poverty was in fact a rather narrow definition of 'relative poverty at the turn of the century.

What is considered 'adequate' changes over time. It is therefore a cultural and social definition rather than just based on biology and domestic science. This has led others to adopt an alternative approach known as the relative definition of poverty. Individuals and groups concerned with the problems of poverty and solutions to them have offered a variety of relative definitions of poverty, including the following: 'Relative poverty is defined in relation to a generally accepted standard of living in a specific society at a specific time and goes beyond basic biological needs' (Oppenheim and Harker, 1996, p. 6).

The measurement of a relative poverty involves comparing the standard of living of those who are considered to be poor with that of non-poor members of the same society. Relative approaches view poverty as a social construction, based on the belief that a certain standard of living is desirable for everyone in a given society at a given time. People in the 1990s expected more than people did in the 1970s – as standards improve, so do expectations. As the world is rapidly changing, definitions of poverty based on relative standards will also change rapidly because, as Rubinow (1969, p. 48) says, 'Luxuries become comforts, comforts become necessaries.'

Exercise 4.10

1. Write down what you consider to be luxuries. Why are they luxuries for you?

2. Compare your list with that of another student. Are your lists similar or different? Why do you think this is?

3. If possible ask a person of 65 or older to do the same exercise. Are his or her ideas the same as yours? If not, why do you think they are not?

The following quotes come from an organisation that tries to help the poor, an individual who has experienced poverty and a group of researchers into poverty. They give an indication of how multifaceted the issue of poverty is.

Poverty is not only about shortage of money. It is about rights and relationships; about how people are treated and how they regard themselves; about powerlessness, exclusion and loss of dignity. Yet the lack of an adequate income is at its heart (Oppenheim 1990).

Poverty means not having what you need. You have outer needs and inner needs, such as your body needs a house and food and your soul needs friendship and happiness. For us being poor means you have less and less (nine year-old Bijon, quoted in Oppenheim (1990), p. 15).

Poverty is an overall condition of inadequacy, lacking and scarcity. It is destitution and deficiency of economic, political and social resources. This broader perspective reflects the true dimensions of poverty (Kilty et al., 1997, p. 30).

Social poverty includes the lack of educational opportunity or provision, inadequate health care and substandard housing. Political poverty includes the absence of voting rights, civil rights and trade unions representation. Social poverty is as much of a problem as lack of money for those who experience it. Poverty is therefore a multifaceted problem and the diversity of opinion on what constitutes poverty makes it very difficult to define.

Peter Townsend opened his book *Poverty in the UK* (1979, p. 1) with the following words:

> Poverty can be defined objectively and applied consistently only in terms of the concept of relative deprivation. Individuals, families and groups in the population can be said to be in poverty when they lack the resources to obtain the types of diet, participate in the activities and have the living conditions and amenities that are customary in the societies to which they belong.

Non-Governmental Organisations (NGO) produced a Treaty on Poverty for the 1992 Earth Summit in Rio that defined poverty in the following way:

> Poverty is the state of deprivation of essential elements necessary for a human being to live and develop with dignity physically, mentally and spiritually, while accounting for specific needs relating to gender, ability/disability, cultural values, age and ethnicity." (NGO, 1992). This document can be examined at: *www.earthsummit2002. org/toolkits/Women/ngo-doku/ngo-conf/ngoearth22.htm*

Exercise 4.11

1. Reread the above definitions of relative poverty. What do they have in common?

2. What criteria did you use when you wrote your own definition of poverty for Exercise 4.1?

3. Is your definition similar to or different from the above definitions?

The strengths of relative definitions

- Relative definitions better reflect the way in which notions of poverty are socially constructed and relate to particular times and particular places.
- If measures of poverty are linked to debates about what is considered to be a decent standard of living at any one time, then they

are linked to wider debates in society, particularly those about citizenship.

- Since relative definitions of poverty do not rely on a fixed, unmoving poverty line they are better able to reflect the diversity of lifestyles that characterise contemporary societies. For example, Kirby *et al.* (1997, p. 579) argue that, 'in relation to Townsend's concept of deprivation, since it is not entirely reliant on the notion of income or the lack of it, it is possible to identify two different societies with essentially the same sort of distribution of income and therefore patterns of inequality, but with radically different levels of poverty, since the latter would be affected by the different societal norms operative in those two societies'.

Criticisms of relative definitions

- What most people consider to be poverty is more in line with absolute than with relative definitions. In an extension of this point, it can be said that relative poverty is actually a measure of inequality rather than poverty. There are those who believe that inequality is a good thing, such as functionalists and the New Right (see Chapter 3, pp. 27–32), and they argue that relative definitions of poverty attempt to use a moralistic term (poverty) to describe something they see as beneficial (inequality).
- It can be argued that relative measures are set at too high a level and consequently there is a danger of considerably overestimating the extent of poverty. This defeats the object of proving that poverty exists even in developed countries such as the UK.
- Relative definitions change as what are considered to be acceptable living standards and income change, so measures of poverty have to be adapted accordingly. But how frequently should this take place?

Studies of poverty based on relative definitions

Brian Abel-Smith and Peter Townsend

In the 1960s Abel-Smith and Townsend (1965) set out to construct a relative definition and measurement of poverty. They set a poverty line based on 140 per cent of a household's entitlement to National Assistance (now Income Support) plus rent and housing costs. They opted for the 140 per cent level because some of the resources of some claimants were disregarded when their benefits were calculated and additional allowances and grants were often made to claimants. They set a second line for those whose income fell below 120 per cent of the benefit level and found that 88 per cent of claimants had an income of less than 110 per cent of the basic benefit rate.

This line seems to have been an arbitrary one, and because it was based purely on income it would not have given a clear picture of relative deprivation, but its adoption marked a move towards a more relative approach to poverty.

Peter Townsend

Following his study of relative poverty in 1968–69, in the 1970s Peter Townsend (1979) carried out a survey of 1208 households and 3950 individuals in Belfast, Glasgow, Neath and Salford. Parallel research was conducted in another 51 parliamentary constituencies in the UK, bringing the total sample to 3260 households and 10 048 individuals. His 39-page questionnaire was divided into nine sections, covering housing and living facilities, employment, occupational facilities and fringe benefits, cash income, assets and savings, health and disability, social services, private income and style of living.

Townsend drew on three approaches to poverty measurement: the state's standard measure of poverty, based on low income; the relative income standard, whereby different income levels were compared and those beneath a certain income were deemed to be poor; and his own deprivation standard of poverty, whereby people who lacked certain goods and services were deemed to be deprived. Townsend found the deprivation standard to be the most useful measure. He drew up a list of 60 indicators of deprivation, from which he chose the 12 that he regarded as the most representative of deprivation. The resulting deprivation index (Table 4.2) Townsend enabled to identify those who were more disadvantaged than others in the UK because they lacked the items on the index.

Exercise 4.12

a 1. How many items on the index apply to you?

a 2. Why have you selected these? (For example it might be that you are a vegetarian by choice rather than necessity.)

a **e** 3. Draw up a deprivation index of your own. Have you used some of Townsend's indicators? Explain why you have or have not.

Townsend found that people on lower incomes tended to have a comparatively higher deprivation index, and that at income levels lower than 150 per cent of the Supplementary Benefit level (now Income Support) the degree of deprivation increased at a rapid rate. He classified 12.64 million people in the UK as being below this poverty line in 1968–69.

Table 4.2 Townsend's deprivation index

Characteristics	Percentage of population affected
1. Has not had a week's holiday away from home in last 12 months	53.6
2. Adults only. Has not had a relative or friend to the home for a meal or snack in the last four weeks	33.4
3. Adults only. Has not been out in the last four weeks to a relative or friend for a meal or snack	45.1
4. Children only (under 15). Has not had a friend to play or to tea in the last four weeks	36.3
5. Children only. Did not have a party on last birthday	56.6
6. Has not had an afternoon or evening out for entertainment in the last two weeks	47.0
7. Does not have fresh meat (including meals out) as many as four days a week	19.3
8. Has gone through one or more days in the past fortnight without a cooked meal	7.0
9. Has not had a cooked breakfast most days of the week	67.3
10. Household does not have a refrigerator	45.1
11. Household does not usually have a Sunday joint WC,	25.9
12. Household does not have sole use of indoor flush sink or washbasin, cold-water tap, fixed bath or shower, and gas/electric cooker	21.4

Source: Townsend (1979), p. 250.

One of the strengths of Townsend's work is that he took account of rising living standards and therefore his work can be seen as truly relative. Arguably his approach was also scientific in that he studied a large sample, and measured their resources and income to arrive at his 150 per cent cut-off point.

However Piachaud (1981) has criticised Townsend's deprivation index as poverty will be seen to exist if people choose not to eat meat or if children choose not to have a party, for example. It is vital to determine whether lack of an item is actually about poverty, free choice or deprivation, and Townsend's list makes choice seem like deprivation. This is more the case with some items than others, for example not having a fridge is far removed from not having meat because you are a vegetarian. It is this question of choice that lies at the heart of the debate on Townsend's work. Postmodernists argue that there is more personal choice than ever, but that it is limited for some groups in society because of their circumstances.

Exercise 4.13

Read the following statements, then in a three-column table list those which you think indicate (a) poverty, (b) personal choice and (c) deprivation.

1. I love meat but I can't afford to buy it.

2. I can't have a birthday party this year because it costs too much.

3. We've had our electricity cut off because we didn't pay the bill.

4. I hide when the milkman comes for his money. He'll stop delivering I know unless I pay.

5. We share a bathroom with four other families. It is dirty and horrible.

6. I'll finish paying for this Christmas by next Christmas and then it will start all over again.

7. I'd like to be able to give my children treats. They'd get fruit for a start.

8. We're not going on holiday this year because the house needs decorating.

9. I haven't eaten for three days. My benefit money ran out because I had to buy some shoes.

10. I hate sharing the bed with my two sisters, but I have to.

11. We're going to be evicted because we haven't paid the rent for three months. It's my fault – I'm a heroin addict and my money goes on feeding my habit.

12. I'm 80 years old and feel the cold but I daren't turn the heating on in winter because I'm scared I won't be able to pay the bill. I've only got the state pension to live on.

13. I owe six months' council tax but I need my 40 cigarettes a day. I'd go mad without them.

Joanna Mack and Stewart Lansley

In the 1980s and 1990s Mack and Lansley tried to establish a relative definition of poverty by asking the general public for their opinion. Their first study was undertaken in 1983, when they questioned a representative cross-section of the population on behalf of London Weekend Television. In their book *Poor Britain* (1985) they state that there was general agreement among the public about the necessities required to maintain a socially acceptable minimum standard of living. Of their list of 35 items, 22 were deemed essential by at least 50 per cent of the 1174 respondents. Based on this, Mack and Lansley decided that people who lacked three or more of these necessities because they could not afford them should be regarded as poor. According to this socially agreed definition of relative poverty, 7.5 million people were living in poverty in the UK.

Mack and Lansley conducted a follow-up study in 1990, again on behalf of London Weekend Television for its series *Breadline Britain*. The same methodological approach was used and the questionnaire, which included some new items, was completed by a sample of 1319 people. Items classified as necessities by over 50 per cent of the respondents were included in the list of essentials. In the 1990 survey the number of items considered essential rose from 22 to 32, reflecting the rise in living standards between the first and second surveys. Using the same definition of poverty as in the previous study, Mack and Lansley found that the number of people living in poverty had risen to 11 million.

ITEM C

A damp-free home	90	96	+2	Hobby or leisure activity	67	64	+3
An inside toilet (not shared with another household)	97	96	+1	New, not secondhand, clothers	65	84	+1
Heating to warm living areas of the home if it's cold	97	97	0	A roast joint or its vegetarian equivalent once a week[3]	64	67	−3
Beds for everyone in the household	95	94	+1	Leisure equipment for children, e.g. sports equipment or bicycle[3]	51	57	+1
Bath, not shared with another household	95	94	+1	A television	68	51	+7
A decent state of decoration in the home[3]	92	–	–	Telephone	56	43	+3
Fridge	92	77	+15	An annual week's holiday away, not with relatives	54	63	+9
Warm waterproof coat	81	87	+4	A best outing for special occasions	54	48	+5
Three meals a day for children[1]	90	82	+8	An outing for children once a week[1]	53	40	+1
Two meals a day (for adults)[4]	90	64	+26	Children's friends round for tea/snack fortnightly[1]	52	37	+1
Insurance[2]	88	–	–	A dressing gown	42	38	+1
Fresh fruit[2]	88	–	–	A night out fortnightly	42	36	+1
Toys for children, e.g. dolls or models[1]	84	71	+13	Fares to visit friends in other parts of the country four times a year[2]	39	–	–
Separate bedrooms for every child over 10 of different sexes[1]	82	77	+6	Special lessons such as music, dance or sport[1,2]	39	–	–
Carpets in living rooms and bedrooms in the home	78	70	+8	Friends/family for a meal monthly	37	32	–
Meat or fish or vegetarian equivalent every other day[3]	77	63	+14	A car	26	22	–
Celebrations on special occasions, such as Christmas	74	69	+5	Pack of cigarettes every other day	18	14	–
Two pairs of all-weather shoes	74	78	−4	Restaurant meal monthly[2]	17	–	–
Washing machine	73	67	+6	Holidays abroad annually[1]	17	–	–
Presents for friends or family once a year	69	63	+6	A video[2]	13	–	–
Out of school activities, e.g. sports orchestra, scouts[1,2]	69	–	–	A home computer[2]	5	–	–
Regular savings of £10 a month for 'rainy days' or retirement[2]	68	–	–	A dishwasher[2]	4	–	–

(Source: Mack and Lansley, 1985, p. 15.)

Exercise 4.14

Item C shows the results of Mack and Lansley's first survey of the public's perception of necessities. When you have studied the table, complete the following tasks.

a i

1. In a three-column table, list the items that you think are (a) most necessary, (b) necessary, (c) least necessary.

a e

2. Compare your answers with those of three other people. Do you agree or disagree? For those on which you disagree, explain how you reached your decision and discuss why you disagree.

Mack and Lansley's studies show that even over a relatively short period of time attitudes and expectations can change, which in turn changes people's perception of poverty. Their approach can be considered objective because the items on their lists of necessities were chosen by representative cross-sections of society. However, because Mack and Lansley drew up the original lists it can be argued that their results were biased.

Exercise 4.15

e

Using information in this section and other sources, draw up an evaluation table similar to the one below. You should identify at least three strengths and weaknesses of each work.

Study	Definition of poverty (relative or absolute)	How poverty is measured	Key findings (e.g. number in poverty)	Strengths	Weaknesses
Abel-Smith and Townsend (1965)					
Townsend (1979)					
Mack and Lansley (1985)					
Rowntree (1901)					

The latest consensus research

A study of poverty conducted in 1999 by Gordon *et al.* (2000) used the methodology developed by Mack and Lansley (1985), that is, they asked a sample of adults to state whether or not they considered certain items to be necessities and then drew up a list of the items selected by 50 per cent or more of the respondents. A comparison of Gordon *et al.*'s list with that of Mack and Lansley shows that what people considered as non-necessities changed somewhat between 1983 and 1999 (Table 4.3).

Table 4.3 Comparison of selected items in the 1983 and 1999 surveys (per cent)

	1983	1999
Items considered as non-necessities in 1983 but necessities in 1999:		
Telephone	48	71
Family round for a meal	32	64
An outfit for special occasions	48	51
Items considered as non-necessities in both 1983 and 1999:		
Car	22	38
Dressing gown	38	34
Access to the Internet	–	6
Satellite TV	–	5

Sources: Mack and Lansley (1985), p. 54; www.jrf.org.uk/knowledge/findings/socialpolicy/930.htm.

Exercise 4.16

Study Table 4.3 and answer the following questions:

i

1. Suggest reasons why the items seen as non-necessities in 1983 had become necessities by 1999.

i *a*

2. Suggest reasons why the items seen as non-necessities in 1983 remained so in 1999.

i *a*

3. Imagine that a further survey is conducted in 2020. What percentage of people do you think would view a car as a necessity by that date?

i *a*

4. Why were no figures available for the Internet and satellite TV in 1983? What implications does this have for the comparison of surveys over time?

Agencies that campaign on behalf of the poor (for example the Child Poverty Action Group) use relative definitions as they see them as more in keeping with the way in which most people view poverty these days. Because of this, their figures tend to be at variance with those of other agencies that use absolute definitions. For example, according to the Child Poverty Action Group the number of people living on incomes below 50 per cent of the national average rose from 13.9 million in 1991–92 to 14.1 million in 1992–93. However in June 1995 an all-party committee of MPs said that half (about 22.5 million) the adult population lived in a household in which someone was receiving a means-tested benefit.

In 1995 the Institute for Economic Affairs (Morgan, 1995) tated that a growing number of families were caught in a poverty trap of the government's making in that nearly 50 per cent of all families with four or more children were dependent on low state benefits. Furthermore 3.5 million children lived in homes where no one had a job. However government ministers insisted that these figures did not necessarily mean an increase in poverty, rather that the eligibility criteria for means-tested benefits had been relaxed. They also pointed out that the level of benefits had increased.

Exercise 4.17

Copy out the following passage and fill in the blanks with the words listed below (use each word just once).

'The approach to measuring ...... through absolute definitions, has, and will always have utility. Such a ...... offers a firm base on which to gauge trends, whereas a relativist approach in its simplest form (the *x* per cent with the ...... incomes) guarantees that the poor are always with us. But an ...... definition passes authority to some external judge – a physiologist or economist or medical expert – and ignores the ...... state of either the advantaged or ...... members of ...... The ...... approach strives for internal or participative judgement recognizing that we are 'members one of another'. Its notion of poverty is cultural. The ...... are poor in comparison with other members of society. They are ...... from sharing in the normal ...... of their country. So a relative ...... must be added for a full appraisal of poverty.' (Halsey, 1985, p. xxvii).

- absolute
- approach
- definition
- disadvantaged
- excluded
- life
- lowest
- poor
- poverty
- relative
- society
- subjective.

Now answer the following questions on the completed extract:

1. Identify one strength and one weakness of absolute definitions of poverty.

2. Identify one strength and one weakness of relative definitions of poverty.

Other measures of poverty

Capability poverty

Falkingham and Hills (1995) offers an alternative measure of poverty that they call 'capability poverty': the in ability to live a life characterised by qualities that cannot be measured in monetary terms, such as a healthy life, an informed and knowledgeable life, a feeling of personal security and the ability to participate actively in society. While it is clear that income-based and capability-based poverty overlap, the solutions to them differ.

The solution to income poverty is to increase the value of benefits or help people to find a job. This places the people concerned in a passive role – as objects of government action rather than active subjects. Conversely the solution to capability poverty is to offer encouragement and support to people so that they can take control of their own lives and become active in society. This approach fits in with citizenship-orientated ideas of poverty and it criticises income definitions of poverty as being overly economistic. The emphasis on the need to go beyond the income approach to poverty can also be seen in the social indicators approach.

The social indicators approach

In research based on the social indicators approach a number of indicators of poverty and social exclusion are identified for certain groups of people (for example children, young adults, adults over 25, older people or communities) and these are monitored at regular intervals. Examples of indicators include:

- Long-term receipt of benefits.
- Low birth weight.
- No GCSEs at grade C or above.
- Unemployment rates.
- Suicide statistics.
- Non-participation in civic organisations (voluntary organisations, political parties, pressure groups and so on).

As can be seen, this approach considers that social exclusion and poverty are more than a matter of lack of income, but it could be argued that lack of income is one of the key causes of some of the indicators listed above. This implies that something should be done about income distribution, which is at odds with the New Labour government's emphasis on success and enterprise and its reluctance to take steps to reduce income inequalities, other than establishing a minimum wage.

Two social indicator studies were published in the 1990s, the first broadly covering the period 1977–97 and the second covering the period 1997–99 (in essence, the situation that Labour inherited and what Labour had done since). First, Howarth *et al.* (1998) found that:

- The number living on low incomes was far higher than it had been 20 years previously. Households with less than half the average earnings rose from 4.0 million in 1982 to 10.5 million in 1997.
- More than 2.5 million children lived in jobless households, and children born in the bottom two social classes were 25 per cent more likely to be underweight as babies.
- Young men with no occupation were four times more likely to commit suicide than young employed men in social classes 1 and 2.
- Thirty per cent of pensioners were in the bottom fifth of the income distribution scale.

- Disadvantage was concentrated in certain communities. Eighty per cent of households in the social housing sector (council houses or accommodation rented from housing associations) had a weekly income of less than £200, and in 70 per cent of such households the head of household was not in paid work.

Second, Howarth *et al.* (1999) found that:

- Well over 10 million people lived in households with less than half the average income. When housing costs were taken into account the number rose to 13 million.
- Two thirds of those with incomes of less than half the national average lived in households where the head of household was not in paid work.
- Since 1995 the number on very low incomes (less than 40 per cent of the average income) had risen by over a million.
- Nearly a fifth of the population – around 10 million people – were on a low income for at least two years out of three.
- The proportion of the population in the North-East who were in receipt of government benefits was more than twice that in the South-East.
- In urban areas, 90 per cent of benefit claimants lived in wards where more than 10 per cent of the population were on benefits. In rural areas, 33 per cent of those on benefits lived in wards where more than 10 per cent of the population were on benefits.
- There were more children in the bottom fifth of the income distribution scale than in the top two fifths put together.
- The concentration of poor children in particular primary schools was increasing.
- Children in social classes IV and V were twice as likely to die in accidents as other children.
- Girls in social class V were 10 times more likely to become mothers in their teens than girls in social class I.
- More than 1.25 million young adults were paid less than half the male median hourly pay (£3.85 per hour in 1999). In all more than two million workers were paid less than this amount – 75 per cent of these were women.
- Young men without an occupation were four times more likely to commit suicide than young employed men in social classes I and II.
- Adults in social class V were four times more likely to suffer depression than those in social class I.
- In over two thirds of households in the social housing sector the head of household was not in paid work, compared with a third in households with other types of tenure.
- Households with no insurance were nearly twice as likely to be burgled as those with insurance.

- Nineteen per cent of Bangladeshi households and 8 per cent of Pakistani households were overcrowded, compared with less than 1 per cent of white households.

Subjective measures of poverty

All official poverty measures can be misleading because they are arbitrary constructs based on social judgements about needs and what the government considers acceptable at any given time. In the main, official research on poverty has been quantitative, using statistical evidence and a variety of criteria to count the number of people in poverty. According to Orshansky (1977, p. 3): 'Counting the poor is an exercise in the art of the possible. For deciding who is poor, prayers are more relevant than calculations because poverty, like beauty, lies in the eye of the beholder.' Identifying the true extent of poverty is impossible because so many methods are used and no agreement can be reached.

Exercise 4.18

a 1. What criteria would you use to measure the poor?

a 2. What made you decide on these criteria?

According to postmodernists, in the postmodern age there are no universal or objective truths. The world is too fragmented for anything to be universal, and therefore all truth has to be subjective. This assertion has implications for the definition of poverty, as definitions that worked in the age of modernity may not be appropriate now. In the view of postmodernists, because people are able to draw on a wide range of information and opinions via television, radio, films, books, magazines and tourism to different parts of the world, arriving at a definition that is universally acceptable is virtually impossible.

In 1989 Social Security Minister John Moore stated that relative poverty amounted to no more than simple inequality, so no matter how rich a society became the relatively less well off would be inaccurately perceived as poor. The poverty lobby would, on their definition, 'find poverty in paradise'.

In 1988 the term poverty was banished from government publications and replaced by 'people on low incomes'. Until 1979 the Department of Health and Social Security had published annual figures on low-income families, but thereafter it published them every two years. In 1988 it altered the basis on which the figures were calculated to huseholds with below average income and thereafter published them even less frequently.

The Institute for Fiscal Studies (an independent research organisation) produces statistics on low-income families based on figures from the *Family Expenditure Survey* (published by the DSS). These statistics relate to the number of people with an income of less than 140 per cent of Income Support. Individuals and organisations concerned with poverty have expressed concern about how these figures are arrived at and the fact that they are after published up to a year after their collection. Carey Oppenheim (1990) of the Child Poverty Action Group believes that the delay in publication is politically motivated, because 'If figures are out of date they are taken less seriously'. Furthermore Steven Webb (1991, p. 16), in a report for the Institute of Fiscal Studies, states that 'they give an incomplete picture of who is poor and who is not'.

According to Peter Townsend (1979) poverty statistics produced by the government are also misleading and based on false assumptions, and that the government tends to use an absolute definition to prove that poverty is declining. Tony Atkinson (*Guardian*, 6 November 1996) believes that the UK should adopt an official poverty line that is not coupled to benefit rate, that it is not enough to publish statistics on households with below average income because many people who are living in poverty do not appear on these figures (for example the homeless, those not registered for benefit, and convicts), and that there should be an explicit statement of intent and commitment to an antipoverty target that could be monitored. The main argument against this is that would be that there would be no agreement on the position of the poverty line, and even if there was the goal posts would probably be moved.

Exercise 4.19

In 1992 Mack and Lansley calculated that 11 million people were living in poverty. In 1968 (23 years earlier than Mack and Lansleys' study) Townsend (1979) concluded that 12.64 million were living in poverty, and in 1992–94 Oppenheim (1990) claimed that 14.1 million people were living in poverty.

1. What explanations can be given for the disparity between the above figures? (Hint: perhaps different methodologies were used.)

2. Which estimate do you find most convincing, and why?

As with other types of statistics poverty statistics do not reveal the full extent of the situation. The experience of poverty must be worse for some people than others, for example those who are 50 per cent below the poverty line will experience even more hardship than those who are 10 per cent below.

Exercise 4.20

1. At the beginning of the chapter you were asked to write down your definition of poverty. Have your views changed since then? If so, why and how?

2. As has been demonstrated in this chapter, official statistics can quickly become out of date. Update the statistics we have presented by consulting *Social Trends* and the most recent editions of *Sociology Update*. You might also explore the Internet.

Examination question

Using this chapter and your sociology text(s), answer the following question in 45 minutes. A mark scheme is presented below to help you to focus your answer.

Essay question

'Despite many sociological studies on poverty, it is still not possible to define a poverty line that will be supported by all' (AEB, Jone 1994). Critically examine the arguments for and against this view.

Mark scheme (knowledge and understanding, top mark band)

The following advice is adapted from the AEB (now AQA) mark scheme that examiners use when marking candidates' final examination papers.

6–9 marks   To reach this mark band you will have to show the examiner that you have a sound understanding of the theories behind the various definitions of poverty and the evidence and research methods used by sociologists in their studies. You will also have to demonstrate that you are aware of the links between theory and research methods. (Hint: you could refer to Rowntree, 1901, Abel-Smith and Townsend, 1965, Mack and Lansley, 1985, and Townsend, 1979, plus relative and absolute definitions of poverty and different types of measure, such as budget standards and the deprivation index.)

To obtain a top mark you will have to demonstrate that you have understood the set question (and not written a 'catch all', 'everything I know about poverty'). You will also have to demonstrate an understanding of the historical aspects of the debate (Rowntree's original work) along with the ideological debates (Marxist and New Right thought) that continue to the present day. You should support your argument with reference to specific issues such as the social policy implications of the official position adopted on the poverty line, and the question of individual responsibility. (Hint: your discussion of individual responsibility should include the new right theories of Marsland, 1996, and Murray, 1990, which are examined on pages 103–8 and 118–19, and welfare provision, which is discussed on pages 143–58.)

Besides knowledge and understanding you should also demonstrate your application, interpretation and evaluation skills. You should examine the strengths and weaknesses of the studies you quote, and arrive at a considered opinion after weighing up the evidence.

5 Who are the poor?

> By the end of this chapter you should be able to :
> - identify groups considered to be poor;
> - state the criteria used to assess poverty;
> - explain why certain groups are poor;
> - discuss different theories on the poor;
> - answer an exam question.

Introduction

> For everyone who has will be given more, and he will have an abundance. Whoever does not have, even what he has, will be taken from him. (Matthew, *The Parable of the Talents*, verse 25.)

This chapter looks at which social groups are more likely to live in poverty and the reasons why. It considers the various aspects of social stratification (for example class, age and regional differences) and the way in which these interact to determine life chances and cause some groups to have fewer opportunities than others and therefore a greater chance of finding themselves in poverty. By identifying which groups are more likely to live in poverty, these groups can be targeted by social policies and poverty can be tackled.

The chapter will also explore the key postmodernist idea of fragmented society, that is, society is not homogeneous because it is composed of unique individuals, and so to categorise people into groups is to ignore their fundamental differences, making research less valid and reliable.

Exercise 5.1

Write down which groups you think constitute the poor. Are the poor from (1) a particular social class, (2) a particular ethnic group, (3) a particular age group, (4) a particular locality? Does gender make any difference? Does disability play a part?

Poverty: some general trends

In July 1997 the Institute for Fiscal Studies (Goodman *et al.*, 1997) reported that inequality had grown among all age groups, regions and categories of people during the previous 20 years. This meant that traditionally poor groups may have experienced even greater poverty, although for others it was a short-term experience born of a change in circumstances, such as attendance at university. However for many, such as the disabled, poverty was long term and persistent.

Robert Walker (Walker and Leisering, 1998) has identified three types of poverty: transient, recurrent and permanent. Transient poverty is a temporary experience that lasts only a short period of time; recurrent poverty involves repeated episodes of poverty; and permanent poverty may last a lifetime. Walker believes that the poor tread a path between the various types of poverty throughout their lives, and that the way in which people move between the various phases is determined by their personal characteristics. This idea that people's experience of poverty changes during their lifetime was first proposed by Rowntree (1901), who identified five periods of poverty that alternated with relative plenty in a labourer's life: childhood, early working adulthood, parenthood, working life after the children have grown up, and old age.

Exercise 5.2

1. Why might a person live in permanent poverty? Write down your reasons.

2. What does Walker mean by transient poverty?

The structured experience of poverty

Although it is possible to identify personal characteristics of individuals that strengthen their likelihood of living in some form of poverty, a key assertion of sociology is that people's lives are strongly shaped by social structures beyond their control. Examination of these structures allows us to consider the unequal chances of escaping poverty in our society. In this section we shall look at structural inequalities that relate to social class, age, gender, ethnicity and locality.

Poverty and social class

Social class and poverty are closely linked, so social class is a vital factor to consider when discussing poverty. Nearly all discussions on social class derive from the work of Karl Marx (1818–83), who believed that all capitalist societies are characterised by class conflict (see Chapter 2 for an account of this). The conflict between the classes arises because the owners of the means of production do no work themselves but live off the surplus value generated by workers. This is known as exploitation. Workers have little choice but to sell their labour for low wages, and this is the main reason for working-class poverty.

An alternative view of social class is provided by Max Weber (1864–1920), whose work can be viewed as a debate with Marx. Weber argued that people's class depends on their position in the labour market, and the lack of marketable skills and qualifications among the working class and underclass places them at the bottom of the labour market and consequently at the bottom of the class structure. According to Weber this is the underlying cause of working-class poverty.

Exercise 5.3

From 1911 the registrar general used the following classification, which defined class according to six occupational groups. Since 1980 the classification has been based on occupational skill.

- Class 1: professional – for example lawyer, accountant, doctor.
- Class 2: intermediate – for example manager, teacher, nurse.
- Class 3N: skilled non-manual – for example clerk, secretary, shop assistant.
- Class 3M: skilled manual – for example bus driver, carpenter, coalminer.
- Class 4: semi-skilled manual – for example farm worker, bus conductor.
- Class 5: unskilled manual – for example labourer, cleaner.

1. What class do you belong to?

2. What criteria have you used to decide this? (For example the job your parents do, the area in which you live.)

3. The registrar general's scale of classification was been in use from 1911 to 1980. What problems might it present today?

In the last decade of the twentieth century attention was paid to the social characteristics of the poor and the emergence of an underclass. For the New Right, this underclass consisted of those whose main income derived from benefits, for example the unemployed, the sick, the disabled, pensioners and single parents. They were regarded as being below the working class as they were benefit-dependent and a drain on society's resources. (There is further discussion of the under-class in Chapter 7.)

In the mid 1990s there was reported to be a widening gap between deprived areas and more affluent ones (Central Statistical Office, 1994), giving support to the claim that the UK class structure was intensifying and its population polarising (see Chapter 2, pp. 5–25). Concern about the growing class and poverty divide was also raised by Hills (1995), who found that:

- The gap between rich and poor had widened considerably since 1980.
- Differences between pay levels had grown rapidly.
- Particular groups have faired disproportionately badly.
- Social security no longer had an impact on the growth of inequality.
- More people had become dependent on benefits as a result of higher unemployment and demographic factors.

Link Exercise 5.1

Refer back to Item B in Chapter 2 (p. 9). Use the information provided there and what you have have read so far in this chapter to answer the following questions:

1. Which socioeconomic group is likely to have the lowest income?

2. Does (a) ethnicity, (b) gender, (c) social class, (d) locality and (e) disability play a part in low income? Explain your answers.

Exercise 5.4

In 1845 Prime Minister Disraeli said that the rich and poor were like 'Two nations between who there is no intercourse and little sympathy, who are as ignorant of each other's habits, thoughts and feelings as if they were inhabitants of different planets'.

1. Do you think the above statement is relevant today? Why?

2. Hold a debate on the statement with two other students. One student should act as chairperson, one argue the points in favour and one the points against. The chairperson should allow both students equal time to put their case.

Poverty is not limited to the working class and the underclass. There is also 'genteel poverty' among middle-class people who have fallen on hard times. This group includes those who once had a profession that enabled them to purchase their own home in a suburban area and to live a comfortable life, but now they have little money to spare. Their pensions are not sufficient to maintain their previous lifestyle, but to admit to this would cause embarrassment. Outward appearances have to be kept up so that the outside world will not be aware of the shabbiness that lies below the surface gloss. Therefore the heating is turned down, or even off, less food is bought and clothes are made to last longer.

This section has explored how poverty is linked to social class. However postmodernists argue that class is an outmoded concept because it is derived from the metanarrative of Marxism (that is, it is a social theory that seeks to explain the way society is run on the basis of one central idea: that of class division). They argue that society is much more fragmented than this, and that factors such as gender, age and ethnicity have a crucial bearing on life chances. Nonetheless Marxists continue to argue that class is the main socioeconomic determinant of whether or not people experience poverty.

Poverty and age

Children and childhood poverty

For our purposes, children are defined as those aged 15 years and under, although the length of childhood varies from society to society (in the UK the official school leaving age and the age when marriage is legal with parental consent is 16). Childhood is a socially constructed concept and this has a bearing on when childhood is considered to end. Some societies allow marriage at the age of 13 and young people are regarded as adults from that age. Some societies have adulthood initiation ceremonies at which the community formally acknowledges an individual's attainment of adulthood. Many children in Third World countries work full-time from the age of 6 to help their families. Thus many children experience deprivation during their childhood and this differs from adult deprivation because children can usually do nothing about it.

James Speth, administrator of the United Nations Development Programme, said in a report 1996 that 'Poverty has become the greatest challenge facing our planet. It endangers the future of all our children and of coming generations.' Children living in poverty in the UK can usually be found in one or more of the following family types (Oppenheim and Harker, 1996):

- Families whose head is in full-time, low-paid work.
- Single parent families.
- Families whose head is unemployed.
- Families whose head is sick or disabled.

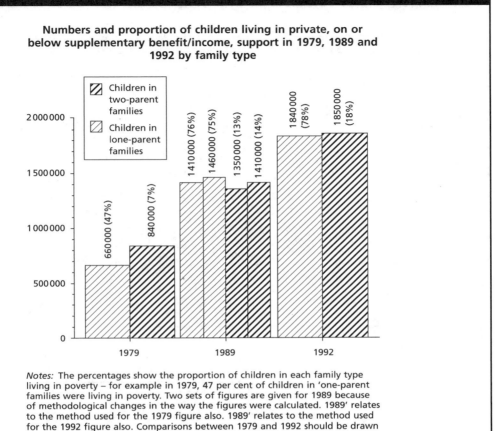

Numbers and proportion of children living in private, on or below supplementary benefit/income, support in 1979, 1989 and 1992 by family type

Legend:
- Children in two-parent families
- Children in lone-parent families

Data labels:
- 1979: 660 000 (47%); 840 000 (7%)
- 1989: 1 410 000 (76%); 1 460 000 (75%); 1 350 000 (13%); 1 410 000 (14%)
- 1992: 1 840 000 (78%); 1 850 000 (18%)

Notes: The percentages show the proportion of children in each family type living in poverty – for example in 1979, 47 per cent of children in 'one-parent families were living in poverty. Two sets of figures are given for 1989 because of methodological changes in the way the figures were calculated. 1989' relates to the method used for the 1979 figure also. 1989' relates to the method used for the 1992 figure also. Comparisons between 1979 and 1992 should be drawn with caution.

(Source: Oppenheim and Harker, 1996, p. 31.)

ITEM A   *Exercise 5.5*

Study Item A and answer the following questions:

i   1. What happened to the number of children living in poverty between 1979 and 1989?

e   2. Have any types of family group been omitted from the graph?

k *u*   3. Why have two sets of figures been given for 1989?

e   4. Why might sociologists not wish to rely exclusively on sources such as Item A when considering the number of children who live in poverty?

a   5. In 1979 the number of children living in a two-parent family was higher than those living in a lone-parent family but the percentage of lone-parent children was higher. How can this be explained?

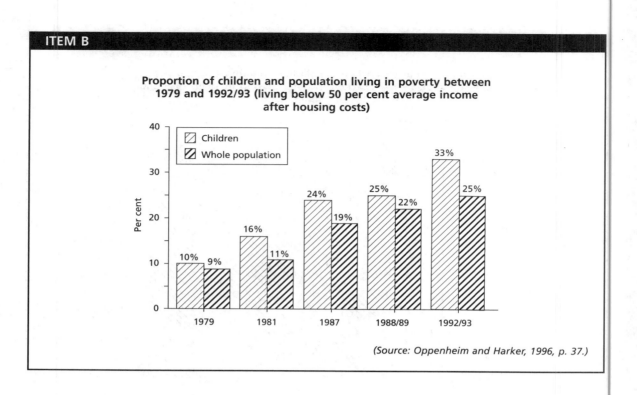

Proportion of children and population living in poverty between 1979 and 1992/93 (living below 50 per cent average income after housing costs)

(Source: Oppenheim and Harker, 1996, p. 37.)

ITEM B   *Exercise 5.6*

Study Item B and answer the following questions:

1. What percentage of children were in poverty in 1992/93?

2. Which group was most likely to be poor?

3. For what reasons might the proportion of children living in poverty have risen? (Hint: consider the rise of single parenthood.)

4. What was the percentage rise of children living in poverty between 1979 and 1992/93?

5. Summarise the trends in Item B.

In 1990 a study of child poverty and deprivation in the UK was commissioned by the UNICEF International Child Development Centre (Bradshaw *et al.*, 1990). It was found that there had been an increase in childhood poverty in the 1980s and this was attributed to three factors: demographic changes, economic trends and social policies.

● Demographically, there had been changes in family structure, with couples having fewer children and more children being raised in single parent households. It was estimated that over a third of all children would experience living in a single parent family. There is no doubt that the incidence of poverty would have been greater in single parent families than in two parent families.

- In the 1980s the Conservative government had been committed to reductions in taxation and public expenditure, which had detrimentally affected the poor more than any other group. Benefits and support had been cut back and the children of people on benefits had suffered further deprivation (see also Chapter 6, pp. 101–9). The state of the economy and whether parents had jobs with decent rates of pay had a strong bearing on children's likelihood of experiencing poverty.

When children suffer poverty it affects their education. For example Gary Foskett, a headteacher of a primary school in Southwark, London, said: 'I see children growing up in circumstances where there is barely enough money for food, clothes and shelter. There is no money for these kids to have books, toys or other things that well off families take for granted, they fall behind educationally and that makes them miserable and disadvantages them for life' (quoted in the *Guardian*, 14 March 1996). A self-fulfilling prophecy comes into operation, whereby poor children are labelled educational failures and behave as such.

Although parents know their children are disadvantaged at school and at home they feel helpless to do much about it. Parents interviewed in Bradford for a study on childhood nutrition and poverty said they were worried about not being able to provide their children with a healthy diet.

A study by The Food Commission (reported in *The Guardian*, 1 February 1994) found that DSS benefits did not include enough to pay for the diet for a child in a Victorian workhouse. The prescribed diet in a workhouse would have cost £5.46 a week at today's prices compared with the £4.15 allowed for in Income Support.

ITEM C   *Exercise 5.7*

Read Item C and answer the following questions:

i   1. According to Item C, how do children suffer when their families are dependent on state benefits?

k u a   2. Which aspect of poverty do you think affects children the most? Give reasons for your answer.

a i   3. Why might the CPAG regard mothers as the 'real experts' on a minimum budget for essential items?

Where income support falls short

How much money is needed to bring up a child? What is the true 'poverty line'? These are hotly debated questions, with many complications and little overall agreement.

Now a new measure has been defined, not by professionals but by the real experts – mothers. The campaigning Child Poverty Action Group (CPAG) has published a new report presenting a minimum budget standard of essential items which has been drawn up and agreed by around two hundred mothers from different parts of the country and different socioeconomic backgrounds.

They considered the things they regarded as the 'minimum essential' in the light of the United Nations Convention on the Rights of the Child: article 27 covers 'the right of every child to a standard of living adequate for the child's physical, mental, spiritual, moral and social development'.

All the mothers agreed that these amounts could not be reduced any further. Yet, for children under 11 they are on average £7.92 a week less than income support rates. For a boy aged form 2–5 the shortfall is as much as £11.75 a week.

The director of Child Poverty Action Group, Sally Witcher, said: 'The poverty line defined by mothers, who are surely the best placed to know, clearly reveals the inadequacy of income support.' Children are suffering, both in terms of their exclusion from childhood society and because their basic needs cannot be met from inadequate benefit.

Parents' minimum essential budget standard by age of child (£ per week)

	under 2	2–5	6–10	11–16
Food	6.85	9.36	9.72	10.11
Clothes: girl	5.57	7.13	6.94	5.83
boy	5.41	8.65	6.49	6.34
Possessions and equipment	4.75	3.13	2.20	4.13
Activities	1.75	7.53	7.45	7.36
Furniture and decorationg	0.17	0.54	0.54	0.62
Laundry	0.86	0.86	0.62	0.62
Toiletries: girl	6.54	2.18	0.65	2.45
boy	6.54	2.18	0.65	1.99
Total: girl	26.49	30.73	28.12	31.04
boy	26.33	32.25	27.67	31.09

(Source: White, 1995, p. 7.)

i 4. According to the table in Item C, how many pounds a week does it cost to feed 2–5 year olds?

i 5. What is the laundry cost for 11–16 year olds?

i 6. What is covered by Article 27 of the United Nations Convention on the Rights of the Child?

The economic factor that appears to have had the most impact on childhood poverty has been unemployment, especially long-term unemployment, which in the period 1981–89 increased from 26 per cent to 38 per cent. For children living in a household where the major wage earner had joined the ranks of the long-term unemployed, this meant a decline in living standards, and seven out of ten unemployed families lived in poverty.

Under UK law children cannot work full-time until they are 16 years of age, although they can work part-time for a restricted number of hours from the age of 13. When children are able to work and thus buy their own clothes and so on, this takes some of the financial pressure off their parents.

Exercise 5.8

[a] 1. Find out how many people in your class work part-time. How much per hour do they earn? Is it dependent on age?

[a] 2. The minimum wage was introduced in March 1999 (£3 per hour for 18–21 year olds, £3.60 per hour for over 21 year olds, no minimum wage at present for those under 18). In what ways, it any, has this affected people in your class?

[i][a] 3. What is the difference between the highest and lowest hourly rate of pay for part-time work among your classmates?

The elderly

The age profile of the UK population has changed considerably during the past century. As life expectancy has increased the number of elderly has increased (for example the number of people aged 65 and over increased from 1.7 million in 1901 to 10.6 million in 1993), and it is expected that this increase will continue. This has implications for everyone. How are the elderly to be provided for? Who will pay for state pensions? In fact should state pensions continue to be provided? In 1997 a quarter of all older citizens were dependent on Income Support. Worse still, many of those who were entitled to Income Support but for a variety of reasons did not receive it relied entirely on the state pension.

The state retirement pension has dropped as a proportion of average earnings since 1980 and now compares most unfavourably with occupational pensions. This is causing a divide between pensioners who had well-paid jobs with occupational pension schemes and those who were on low incomes and had no opportunity to join a pension scheme (see Chapter 10, pp. 175–88). Postmodernists argue that, like all groups in society, the elderly are not a uniform group, that their lifestyles and living standards vary according to their ethnicity, gender and social class. The way in which they spend their pension will differ, and their attitude towards receiving the state pension and the part it plays in their lives will vary.

One reason for keeping the state pension at a low level is that the government wants to minimise the cost to taxpayers and encourage the optake of private pensions. It hopes that in the future the majority of people will have private pensions, and it is possible that those who do need the state pension because they have not made adequate provision during their working life will be subject to a means test. The onus will be put on all individuals to provide for their retirement.

Exercise 5.9

k u 1. Go to the Post Office, a learning resource centre or library and find out how much the basic state pension is for a single person and a married couple.

a 2. Make a list of all the things needed to maintain an acceptable level of living (food, electrity and so on).

a 3. Do you think the pension will cover all these things? Why, or why not? (Bear in mind that due to the physiological condition and lifestyle of the very elderly they are likely to spend more on essential items such as fuel, but perhaps less on food.)

In October 1997 Pensions Minister John Denham said that growing inequality among pensioners was a major challenge to the government. By 2025 poor pensioners could be seven times worse off than well-off pensioners, compared with three times worse off in 1979. It is estimated that over the next 30 years the income of the poorest fifth of pensioners will to rise by 20 per cent whilst the income of the richest fifth will rise by 80 per cent.

Differences in pay, working conditions and opportunities during people's working lives will naturally affect them during retirement. Atkinson and Sutherland 1991 point out that those whose working lives were affected by the depression of the 1930s and the Second World War (1939–45) have very different expectations from younger generations who have enjoyed unbroken employment and higher rates of pay.

The age of the elderly person also needs to be taken into consideration because the older people are the more likely they are to need care and attention. A person of 65 who has just retired is in a different position from an 85 year old who has been retired for 20 years: the former is likely to be fitter, to have made provision for her or his retirement and to need less state help. Theoretically the elderly should be able to live on savings accrued during the course of their lives, with insurance policies and private pensions providing an additional income. However in actuality these savings can be reduced in value by inflation: £20 000 of savings does not have the same value in 2002 as it did in 1988. According to the National Association for Pensions Funds (Oppenheim 1990), individuals need to save at least 10 per cent of their income over their working lives to build up a pension that equals half their salary at retirement, and extra is needed to provide for care in old age. Very few people manage to achieve this, so face poverty rather than a comfortable, well provided for retirement.

ITEM D

Percentage of jobs where employer provides benefits, by gender, 1989

	Male full-timers	Female full-timers	Female part-timers
Pensions*	73	68	31
Sick pay*	66	58	27
Paid time off	64	48	30
Unpaid time off	54	54	57
Company car or	30	10	5
Free/subsidised transport	31	24	17
Goods at a discount	47	40	31
Free or subsidised meals	39	47	25
France/loans	21	20	12
Accommodation	14	17	5
Life assurance	39	19	5
Private health care	31	22	9
Recreation facilities	40	36	24
Maternity pay	n/a	31	16
Childcare	1	13	10

* Above basic government scheme.

(Source: Oppenheim and Harker, 1996, p. 105.)

ITEM D   *Exercise 5.10*

Study Item D carefully and answer the following questions:

i   1. What is the percentage difference between male and female full-timers with employer-provided pensions?

i   2. What is the percentage difference between male and female part-timers full-timers with employer-provided life insurance?

a   3. Could gender difference be the sole reason for these discrepancies?

4. In which category do male and female full-timers receive equal entitlement?

5. In which category do female full-timers benefit more than male full-timers?

Poverty and disability

When reading this section it is important to remember that disability is a sensitive issue because disabled people often feel that they are defined by their disability rather than who they are as people, and that some people react towards them in a different way than they do towards those with no obvious disability.

Exercise 5.11

1. Bearing in mind the sensitivity of the issue, jot down as many disabilities as you can think of.

2. Compare your list with that of another student. What are the similarities and what are the differences?

3. What criteria did you use to decide what constitutes a disability?

Disability is a catch-all term that encompasses physical conditions such as cerebral palsy and mental conditions such as schizophrenia. In a survey carried out by the OPCS (1995) a number of terms were used to distinguish between different groups:

- Impairment: loss of function.
- Disability: restriction of activity.
- Handicap: physical disadvantage.

Whatever the terminology used, many of those with a disability feel discriminated against and marginalised because they are stereotyped and treated as different and apart from others in society. If this were not the case and their abilities rather than their disabilities were concentrated on, perhaps progress could be made and fewer disabled people would find themselves living in poverty. Until there is less segregation and a willingness to give the disabled a fair chance the way they are treated is not likely to improve.

Different studies on the links between disability and poverty use different determinants of disability and different definitions of poverty, and it is important to bear this in mind when looking at the findings. The article in Item E addresses the issue of marginality.

Prejudiced firms warned over jobs for the blind

Employers have less than three months to re-think their attitudes towards taking on disabled people, the Royal National Institute for the Blind warns today.

The Disability Discrimination Act taking effect on December 2 will make it illegal to discriminate against disabled people in the labour market. Yet prejudice remains widespread, the RNIB says.

According to a survey by the independent Institute of Employment Studies, 51 per cent of employers would not take on anybody who had difficulty seeing.

The RNIB is this week launching initiatives designed to raise awareness of employment difficulties among the estimated 100 000 people of working age in Britain with sight difficulties. Of a sample of 60 such people interviewed by the charity, 63 per cent were not in work, 58 per cent had not worked in 10 years, and 53 per cent were on or below a poverty line.

Robert Latham, who is blind, represented Britain in the long and triple jumps in the Atlanta Paralympics. He received three job offers from four interviews, but had to apply for 136 jobs to get them.

Mr Latham, North Tyneside Council's information and advocacy officer for the visually impaired, said: 'No matter what I did, I was let down by the system.'

The RNIB is launching in partnership with the computer company ICL a job-matching service to bring blind and partially sighted people together with prospective employers.

(Source: Guardian, 9 September 1996.)

ITEM E **Exercise 5.12**

Read Item E and answer the following questions:

i 1. How many people are estimated to have sight difficulties in the UK?

k u a 2. Write down the reasons why you think a company might discriminate against job applicants who are visually impaired.

k u a 3. What kinds of job could visually impaired people do? (Contact your local branch of the Royal National Institute for the Blind to find out.)

i 4. According to Item E, how many employers would not take on anyone with sight difficulties?

i 5. How many jobs did Robert Latham apply for?

People with impairments or disabilities may not be able to take on a job for practical reasons, such as difficult access to the place of work, lack of suitable transport and inadequate facilities within the workplace. These problems must be addressed by institutions and companies in order to comply with antidiscrimination legislation.

Exercise 5.13

 1. Does the institution where you are studying have facilities for disabled students? If so, what are they?

 2. Is there information available for disabled students? If so, where is it located?

Many companies are reluctant to employ disabled people despite the existence of employment laws to prevent discrimination. Research shows that young disabled people, particularly school leavers wanting to enter the job market, are at greater risk of unemployment than the

---

ITEM F

Thousands of disabled lost benefit

The Government yesterday aditted 'very serious errors' which led to 24 000 severely disabled people losing up to £12 500 each in benefits.

Some died without ever knowing they were entitled to the cash becuase civil servants at the Department of Social Security failed to realise their entitlements.

A damning report by the Commons Public Accounts Committee highlights a failure by the ministry to help thousands of severely handicapped people living by themselves who needed state benefits to buy care over the last eight years.

A number, referred to as 'deceased customers' by the ministry, died before they could receive the money. But the ministry has not kept records of how many people died before they were told of their entitlements or how much they were owed.

Another 40 000 claims are being investigated, but 'there are no plans to take any specific steps in respect of customers now deceased', Ann Bowtell, permanent secretary at the Department of Social Security, says in a memorandum.

It has disclosed that about £90 million in benefit arrears was paid to claimants – varying between £30 and £12 500 each. Some 35 000 people were owed money.

The ministry supplied the information after Alan Williams, Labour MP for Swansea West, demanded an explanation of why 'some of the most disadvantaged people in our country could be deprived of money on that scale.

'We have had people die in poverty and in need when very large sums of money have been owed to them by the department. This amounts to grave robbing.'

Mrs Bowtell admitted: 'This was a very, very serious error on the part of our staff and I acknowledge that there have been large sums.'

The MPs were also severely critical of the ministry's ability to fight fraud and control public expenditure. They found it 'unacceptable' that £848 million had been paid or not paid in error. 'This extraordinarily high figure includes £546 million of cash overpayments, public money which should not have been spent, and £183 million of cash underpayments.'

(Source: Guardian, 7 June 1996.)

---

rest of the population. Because of their exclusion from paid employment the majority of disabled people have to rely on benefits as their primary income, and as disability lasts for life they are obviously on benefits for a longer time than others, which tends to exacerbate their problems. Even when the disabled do find work there is evidence that they receive lower pay and have poorer promotion prospects. Employers appear to view the disabled as unreliable on health grounds, and to see only their disability rather than the abilities they possess. Disabled people are also more likely to be in low-status, unskilled jobs. In 1994 the Royal Association for Disability and Rehabilitation found that 12 per cent of disabled workers were in managerial or professional jobs compared with 21 per cent of non-disabled workers, whilst 31 per cent of disabled workers were in low-paid manual jobs compared with 21 per cent of non-disabled workers (Oppenheim and Harker, 1996).

ITEM F   **Exercise 5.14**

Read Item F and answer the following questions:

i   1. How many severely disabled people had lost up to £12 500 in benefits?

i   2. How many more claims were being investigated?

a   3. What consequences might there have been for those who received less benefit than they were entitled to?

i   4. Who was to blame for the errors referred to in Item F?

A report by the Commons Public Accounts Committee (*Guardian*, 7 June 1996) highlighted the fact that severely disabled people living alone were not receiving the benefits to which they were entitled to pay for the care they needed. Many disabled people incur substantial costs as a result of their disability. They may need to have their homes specially adapted, heat their homes 24 hours a day, eat special diets or have someone there on a permanent basis to care for them. Having to spend money on such necessities can plunge the disabled into povety.

Poverty and gender

According to Glendenning and Millar (1987, p. 20), 'Self denial is still seen as women's special share of poverty.' Women who are poor have mainly been viewed as the partners of unemployed men or men in low-paid jobs, rather than as poor in their own right. In many instances men can and do control women's poverty by exercising control over how the family income is spent. They may 'dole out' a restricted amount for housekeeping and keep the rest for their personal use. Thus women are forced to buy wisely for the family whilst men can spend their money however they see fit.

Most studies of poverty use household or family income as indicators of poverty. This type of research obscures poverty differences between women and men because it assumes that the household income is shared equally. When share of income is taken into account, more women than men live in poverty. Women also tend to make sacrifices for their children and partners, going without themselves rather than have others go without new clothes, food or treats. As Land and Rose (1985, p. 129) say, 'Women bear the burden of managing poverty on a day to day basis. Whether they live alone or with a partner, on benefits or low earnings, it is usually women who are responsible for making ends meet and for managing the debts which result when they don't.'

Glendenning and Millar (1987) estimate that in 1985, 59 per cent of people living in poverty were women. Women make up 70 per cent of low earners and four out of five women employees work part-time. Social policy has been driven by the assumption that women are dependent on men and men must provide for women (see Chapter 8, pp. 153–4). Women's income is frequently viewed as less important than that of men in that it pays for a few extras but not basics such as rent or food. If a couple separate or divorce and the woman cannot find or is unable to continue in paid employment she cannot automatically rely on her ex-partner to provide for her and the children. The establishment of the Child Support Agency in 1993 to make ex-partners responsible for maintenance has hardly proved a success – many men are still not paying, and when they do pay the main beneficiary is the government (through reduced benefit payments), not women and children directly.

There has also been a 'feminisation' of poverty, particularly in the US, in that as poverty levels rise more women than men tend to experience it. Demographic changes have also a difference to the number of women who living in poverty, for example there are more single elderly women than ever before. The majority (59 per cent) of people receiving Income Support are women, and the majority of single-parent families are headed by women. In 1992 there were 1.4 million single mothers and they were more likely than any other group to be living in poverty. Well over half of single parents were on Income Support and 658 000 had been on Income Support for two years or more.

Comparisons between the way in which men and women experience poverty have been made by researchers such as Caroline Glendenning and Jane Millar (1994), who investigated:

- Access to income and other resources.
- The time spent on generating income and other resources.

- The transfer of these resources from certain members of the household to others.

They found that many mothers will go without particular things in order to improve their children's lives. Furthermore women are less able to earn an income than men because of the demands of caring for young children and the general lack of childcare resources. In a speech delivered on 22 January 1998 Joan Ruddock (minister for women) stated that 'Lack of affordable, quality childcare presents a barrier to work for many parents, especially lone parents. Lone mothers want to work, but they need and deserve high quality childcare to support them as well as to help them compete with others in the labour market' (Guardian, 23 January 1998). She pointed out that whilst three out of five women with children were working, many of them had poorly paid, part-time jobs. In response to these points the Labour government announced a £300 million package to provide out-of-school care throughout the UK. Childcare was to be made available before and after school hours and during school holidays (see Chapter 9).

ITEM G

Mean independent income of women by source and family type, 1991

Income source (£ per week)	Non-pensioners				Pensioners		
	Single with children	Married with children	Single no children	Married no children	Single	Married	All women
Earnings	37.00	54.70	92.40	90.60	4.20	6.10	53.40
Self-employment	4.70	5.10	2.70	7.10	0.20	0.40	3.80
Social security	61.50	16.40	12.20	3.50	57.40	30.40	23.40
Investments	2.80	5.00	6.70	13.10	18.90	18.20	11.00
Pensions/annuities	2.60	0.20	2.10	1.50	19.70	6.50	4.90
Other	15.20	3.80	4.10	3.40	0.80	0.60	3.40
Total	123.80	85.10	120.00	119.10	101.20	62.20	99.90

(Source: Webb, 1993.)

ITEM G | *Exercise 5.15*

Study Item G and answer the following questions:

k u a

1. Ask a local nursery and a childminder how much they charge to care for one child per week. How much would a person have to earn to make employment worthwhile?

Women are disproportionally represented in low-income jobs and the part-time, insecure employment offered by companies operating according to Post-Fordist work pratices. Entry into the job market is problematic for women who have stayed at home to bring up their children. Many lack the skills needed by employers and therefore can only obtain unskilled, low-paid jobs. Despite the Equal Pay Act, on average the gross weekly pay of women in 1994 was 72 per cent of that of men, and women made up two thirds of those earning less than the Council of Europe's 'decency threshold'. As much of their work is low paid and part-time, women also have less employment protection and fewer sickness benefits. They are also at greater risk of unemployment, and because they are unlikely to have paid full National Insurance contributions they are likely to be on a lower benefit scale.

ITEM H

Part-time employees, by gender, spring 1996 (per cent)*

	Males			Females		
	Manual	**Non-manual**	**All males**	**Manual**	**Non-manual**	**All females**
North-East	7.1	7.2	7.2	61.6	38.5	46.2
North-West and Merseyside	7.9	6.9	7.4	59.1	39.0	45.4
Yorkshire and the Humber	7.3	8.1	7.7	62.1	41.2	48.6
East Midlands	6.6	7.7	7.1	54.9	41.2	46.1
West Midlands	6.2	5.8	6.1	58.2	39.7	46.1
Eastern	9.3	6.4	7.6	61.0	40.2	46.2
London	11.6	7.9	9.2	52.7	28.0	33.0
South-East	10.0	7.0	8.1	61.8	38.9	45.2
South-West	11.7	7.8	9.3	61.8	45.5	50.2
United Kingdom	8.4	7.1	7.7	58.7	38.4	44.5
England	8.6	7.2	7.8	59.3	38.4	44.7
Wales	7.9	7.2	7.7	59.9	42.2	48.7
Scotland	7.2	7.0	7.1	54.2	36.9	42.2
Northern Ireland	6.5	4.1	5.3	52.7	36.0	40.5

* Part-time employees as a percentage of all employees.

(Source: Adapted from Labour Force Survey, Office for National Statistics; Department of Economic Development, Northern Ireland.)

ITEM H   *Exercise 5.16*

Study Item H and answer the following questions:

i a   1. In 1996 which area had the highest percentage of female part-time manual workers?

k u   2. What factors might have accounted for this?

i   3. Which area had the highest percentage of male part-time non-manual workers?

k u   4. What factors might have accounted for this?

Temporary employees, by type of work and gender, spring 1996*

	Seasonal work, agency temping, casual work and other temporary work		Contract for fixed period/fixed task		All temporary employees (thousands)	All temporary employees as a percentage of all employees
	Males (%)	Females (%)	Males (%)	Females (%)		
North-East	17.4	21.6	40.6	20.4	80	8.4
North-West and Merseyside	15.9	27.9	25.4	30.8	156	6.1
Yorkshire and the Humber	19.4	25.2	26.4	29.1	130	6.8
East Midlands	22.2	28.3	19.7	29.8	102	6.1
West Midlands	21.4	24.1	25.9	28.6	126	6.2
Eastern	24.0	27.1	20.7	28.1	144	6.8
London	21.0	30.3	20.9	27.8	228	8.8
South-East	21.0	30.3	23.0	25.6	217	6.9
South-West	23.4	32.3	17.1	27.2	133	7.4
United Kingdom	20.3	28.2	24.3	27.1	1586	7.1
England	20.7	28.1	23.5	27.7	1317	7.0
Wales	17.1	34.6	24.9	23.4	84	8.4
Scotland	18.9	25.3	31.3	24.5	156	7.9
Northern Ireland	n/a	n/a	n/a	n/a	29	5.7

* For some regions, sample sizes are too small to provide a reliable estimate. Includes those who did not state type of temporary work but percentages are based on totals excluding them.

(Source: Adapted from Labour Force Survey, Office for National Statistics; Department of Economic Development, Northern Ireland.)

ITEM H AND I   *Exercise 5.17*

Study Item I and answer the following questions:

i 1. In 1996 in England, what percentage of all employees were temporary employees?

i 2. Which area had the lowest percentage of females in temporary work (seasonal, agency and so on)?

i 3. What was the percentage difference between females and males contracted for a fixed period or task in the UK?

e 4. How reliable do you think these figures are? Give reasons for your answer.

i a 5. In no more than 100 words, summarise what the statistics in Items H and I tell you about gender and employment.

Women are often expected to care not only for their children but also for elderly relatives. While there is a state allowance for care work it remains largely unpaid, and if a woman is a single parent caring for a disabled child her chance of living in poverty is very high. In a survey of 978 adults Finch and Mason (1993) asked the respondents who should undertake the following:

- Caring for an elderly, confused male relative who lived alone and needed assistance several times a week. The response was as follows: son, 39 per cent; daughter, 30.6 per cent; all children, 9.2 per cent.
- Caring for an elderly female relative living on her own who needed help to get out of bed. The response was as follows: son 22.1 per cent; daughter, 67.8 per cent; all children, 10.4 per cent.

It can be seen from these responses that it is presumed natural for daughters to look after their elderly mothers and for sons to take care of their fathers, although the male–female gap was only 9 per cent in the latter case. On balance more burden is placed on women than men when it comes to caring.

At the global level, a significant effect of economic globalisation (see Chapter 7) has been increased poverty among women. Economic programmes and policies often fail to take gender into account and do not consider the effects they have on women. In the past decade or so the number of women living in poverty in developing countries has increased disproportionately in comparison with the number of men. There are also cultural factors to be considered as in some societies there are rigid, socially ascribed gender roles and women have extremely limited opportunities (see Chapter 7, pp. 125–8).

Exercise 5.18

1. Using information in this chapter, sociology text(s) and the Internet if available (for example www.un.org/womenwatch/daw/bejing/platform/poverty.htm), explain in 500 words why women are more likely than men to live in poverty.

2. As you have read, there are social consequences as well as economic consequences of poverty. How might women find themselves being sexually exploited due to poverty?

Following recognition that poverty is a major problem for many women, strategies have been put into place to alleviate the problem. For example the United Nations (1999) has set the following strategic objectives:

- To review, adopt and maintain macroeconomic policies and development strategies that address the needs of women in poverty.
- To revise laws and administrative processes to ensure that women have equal rights and access to economic resources.

- To provide women with access to savings and credit mechanisms and institutions.
- To develop gender-based methodologies and conduct research to address the feminisation of poverty.

Implementing these strategies is the task of governments and of women's groups working in isolation or in tandem. They are seen as long-term projects and not overnight solutions to a complex problem.

Poverty and ethnicity

Many ethnic minority groups in the UK (including refugees) experience discrimination and disadvantage because of their culture, religion and/or skin colour. This discrimination exists in the labour market, in housing and in other life chances. A postmodern approach would take into account the fragmented nature of ethnicity as different groups encounter different degrees of discrimination.

Link Exercise 5.2

This exercise is intended to heighten your awareness of the links between race, housing policies and poverty. Refer to Chapter 10, pp. 183–95.

$\boxed{i}$ 1. Which racial groups are most likely to find themselves poorly housed and living in poverty?

$\boxed{i}\boxed{a}$ 2. Does racism alone explain the differences between ethnic groups?

According to Oppenheim and Harker (1996) p. 42 in the late 1950s and early 1960s 'Immigrant workers were sucked into the economy where they were needed, whatever their qualifications – into those jobs that white people were becoming less inclined to do. The availability of jobs during labour shortages therefore laid the basis for the occupational inequalities that have persisted since.' These immigrant workers were exploited in that they worked longer hours for less pay and in worse working conditions than indigenous workers. They were seen as a source of cheap, expendable labour and were given little respect or opportunity to improve their prospects. Furthermore, as many of the jobs taken by immigrants were in the manual sector they suffered from the decline in manufacturing and the consequent rise in unemployment.

Many ethnic minorities work in poorly paid, insecure jobs such as catering and hotel work. Showed that between 1988–1990, 22 per cent of ethnic minority men worked in catering and related areas compared with 15 per cent of white men (Policy Studies Institute, Brown Lowter, 1993). While some ethnic minority groups fare better than others (for instance many Jewish people occupy high-levels jobs and do not live in poverty), Afro-Caribbeans, Pakistanis and Bangladeshis are heavily represented amongst those who live in poverty due to their lower educational qualifications. The latter are offer reliant on income support and consequently suffer severe deprivation. Even having qualifications does not necessarily help. Black graduates are even more likely to be unemployed than black non-graduates, and certainly more than white graduates.

Exercise 5.19

1. Go to your learning resource centre or library and look up the official unemployment figures by ethnic group in the latest issue of *Social Trends* or other publications (for example, if available, T. Jones *Britain's Ethnic Minorities*). Which group has the highest unemployment figure?

2. How you would account for this? Summarise your answer in 100 words.

In some circumstances ethnic minority people are discriminated against by social security policies. Immigrants can only enter this country if they can support and house themselves without the aid of the state. They have no right to housing benefit, income support or family credit, and this can lead to great hardship and poverty. The government's policy on welfare and housing provision serves to limit the number of migrants into the country, and it discriminates against those who already reside here and want their families to join them because they are required to prove that they have the means to support their families. Many immigrants do not claim the benefits to which they are entitled because they fear that their immigrant status will be brought into question and they will end up worse off than they were before.

During the 1960s a myth circulated that immigrants arriving in this country were immediately heading for the Department of Health and Social Security (as it was called at that time) to claim benefits that were denied to residents. Naturally this caused resentment and incited racism. According to Fiona Williams (1989, p. 33), 'The prevailing ideology was that black people had come on their own initiative and there was no need to make welfare provision for them. When black immigrants did use welfare services they were seen as scroungers.' However a survey in Batley, West Yorkshire (Gordon and Newnham, 1985), revealed that 39 per cent of immigrant households were not claiming the benefits to which they were entitled, compared with 23 per cent of indigenous households. Many of the migrants who arrived in the 1950s are now elderly and require care services, which for elderly black and Asian people are thinly spread and poorly focused. Many of the original immigrants did not plan to settle here permanently, but because of low incomes or poor health had no choice but to remain and live in poverty.

Poverty and locality

It is difficult to identify distinct geographical areas of poverty because wealth and poverty coexist every town, city and village. In some places, such as the London Borough of Hackney, extremes of wealth and poverty can be found within a quarter of a mile. It is often assumed there is a North–South divide, and that the South is inherently more wealthy than the North, but is this true?

Exercise 5.20

k u a

1. Write down which areas in your locality are rich and which are poor. Upon what criteria (for example, type of housing) have you based your decisions?

i

2. Go to a library, learning resource centre or geography department and find a map of your village, town or city. How close are the rich areas to the poor areas?

Because poverty statistics are not produced on a regional basis it is difficult to determine exactly where poverty is most severe, but indicators such as the number of free school meals taken in an area or the unemployment figures can be used to arrive at an estimate. As sociology students you will be aware of the limitations of statistics and that they can be misleading.

ITEM J

The North–South divide is irrelevant to the people of Manchester. The divide is on their own doorstep, between those who can afford to shop in the smart but ugly Arndale Centre and those who resort to the shabby shops in Oldham Street where almost everything is either second hand or second rate.

The second, poorer Manchester was spotlighted in a report published by the City Council, which found that a third of Manchester's 170 000 households were living in poverty. Instead of using the method of assessing poverty in terms of Income Support level, the researchers looked at people's ability to buy 16 goods and services which are generally accepted as basic necessities of life. Those who were unable to afford three or more of these items were considered poor.

(Source: Van Der Werff and Donellan 1996.)

ITEM J

Exercise 5.21

Read Item J and answer the following questions:

i

1. How many of Manchester's households lived in poverty at the time of the report?

i

2. What criterion did the researchers use to assess poverty?

3. In your opinion, why was the inability to buy three or more of the items used to decide that people were poor?

4. How accurate do you think the research findings were likely to have been?

ITEM K

Number and proportion of children on the school roll receiving free school meals in primary schools, 1994

	Number	%
North	69 965	24
Yorkshire and Humberside	89 220	19
North-West	148 296	23
East Midlands	54 456	15
West Midlands	71 399	14
East Anglia	24 031	14
South-East	301 813	20
South-West	56 249	15
England	815 436	19
Wales	72 246	25
Scotland	456 890	23
Northern Ireland	57 894	30

Note: 'Primary' includes nursery schools and middle schools.

(Source: Oppenheim and Harker, 1996, p. 138.)

ITEM K **Exercise 5.22**

Study Item K and answer the following questions:

i 1. In 1994, which region had the highest take-up of free meals? Which area had the lowest?

k u a 2. How might this be explained?

k u 3. Does the institution you attend provide free meals? What criteria are used to decide which students should be given free meals? (You could ask somebody at student services, if this exists at your institution, at the office or the catering manager for this information, but it may be sensitive and not freely available.)

Naturally some areas of the country have higher unemployment rates than others because the structure of employment has changed dramatically in the last 20 years or so, with the decline of traditional heavy industry in the North and the growth of service industries in the South. This trend does seem to indicate that the North–South divide idea is viable, but the recession of the early 1990s also hit the South-East and there is rising unemployment in that region, although it has maintained its dominant position in the national economy.

It is often assumed that poverty is found mainly in rundown inner-city areas, but there is also considerable poverty in rural areas. Eleven million people live and work in rural areas and one quarter of them live below or on the poverty threshold. This can be partly explained by the fact that traditional rural work is poorly paid, and that agriculture, forestry and fishing are in decline, with very little to replace them.

Exercise 5.23

 1. Why you think people in rural areas suffer from poverty?

2. Which types of rural people are likely to be poor?

Link Exercise 5.3

Use the information provided in Chapter 2 (pages 12–15) and Chapter 10 (pages 183–95) to answer the following questions:

 1. What type of rural people are likely to be wealthy?

2. What type of housing would they live in?

Rural poverty is usually less visible than urban poverty, and perhaps for this reason it attracts less attention and is viewed in a different light. The countryside is portrayed as idyllic, with cottages festooned with roses and apple-cheeked children enjoying the fresh air and a healthy lifestyle. It is difficult to imagine poverty in such a setting and even more difficult to persuade people that it exists. However poverty exists wherever unemployment is high and rural areas do have high rates of unemployment. Besides being poorly paid, many rural jobs are seasonal so unemployment rises and falls at certain times of the year. Two out of five rural businesses employ fewer than 10 people and Department of Trade financial assistance is only granted to businesses with 10 or more employees.

ITEM L

Labour market and economic statistics for Northumberland, 1995–7								
Northumberland	60.9	10.5	23.2	34.5	12	8.3	8.4	7581
Alnwick	56.0	1.0	23.9	36.8	13	7.3	8.8	1075
Berwick-upon-Tweed	61.7	0.9	24.9	20.0	12	6.9	8.1	1117
Blyth Valley	65.0	3.1	24.1	32.4	15	11.5	8.4	1026
Castle Morpeth	61.7	1.3	23.2	35.0	9	7.7	8.5	1339
Tynedale	61.4	1.3	26.6	31.4	9	7.1	7.4	2295
Wansbeck	57.2	2.8	19.8	42.7	14	12.0	4.8	728

(Source: Central Statistical Office, 1996.)

Exercise 5.24

Northumberland is a largely rural county where agriculture is the main source of employment.

Study Item L and answer the following questions:

a 1. In 1997, which group of people had the highest unemployment rate?

i 2. How many Income Support beneficiaries were there in Alnwick in 1995?

i 3. What was the percentage difference between the highest and lowest economically active areas in 1995–96?

i 4. How many businesses were registered for VAT in Wansbeck in 1995?

Exercise 5.25

i **e** 1. At the beginning of the chapter (Exercise 5.1) you were asked to write down the categories of people you thought might live in poverty. Have your ideas changed after reading this chapter or remained the same? Why?

a **e** 2. Put the following into what you consider to be their order of importance for research into socioeconomic inequalities: housing, disability, locality, social class, gender, ethnicity, age.

e 3. Write a paragraph to explain and justify your choice.

Examination question and student's answer

Question

'The claim that "the poor are themselves to blame for their poverty" is a feature of some explanations of poverty. Critically examine the sociological arguments for and against this view.' (AEB, June 1991).

Student's answer

The paragraphs in the following answer have been deliberately rearranged in an illogical way to show you how important it is to plan an essay that progresses logically and links relevant material. Read through the answer and rearrange the paragraphs so that the essay flows logically.

(a) Miliband argues that the poor are kept poor because they do not have the political power to get out of their situation. Miliband employs a Weberian perspective and argues that the bad market situation is the cause of their poverty. They have limited economic resources, which in turn maintains their situation as they cannot do anything about it. Also, due to false class consciousness and the stigma of poverty they are prevented from joining together to overthrow the ruling class.

(b) Some conflict theorists argue that the poor are poor because of the inadequacies of the welfare state. Le Grand argues that the welfare state does not redistribute wealth in society, therefore the poor cannot get out of their situation and in a way they are the cause of their problem. Marxists argue that the welfare state serves the interests of the ruling class and is not a neutral body. Wealth is not redistributed in favour of the lower classes so the wealth of the ruling class is not affected. However Le Grand argues that it is actually the middle classes who benefit most from the welfare state in the form of education and health care.

(c) However not all arguments are of this extreme nature. Others argue that their position in society and their subculture explain their situation, while Marxist and conflict theorists argue that they are kept in their situation and position in order to serve and benefit the ruling class.

(d) Some sociologists, such as Lewis, would agree with the statement to a certain extent and argue that the poor are poor because they are socialised into a culture of poverty; that is, they have different norms and values from the rest of society. Lewis argues that they are fatalistic and oriented towards the present, and that this attitude maintains them in poverty. Miller argues that the lower class in America have a different set of values and norms from those in mainstream American society. They are concerned with having a good time, being tough and suchlike, which prevents them from improving their situation. However this view is criticised by Liebow (1964), who argues that the poor he studied shared the same set of norms and values as the rest of society, but that their situational constraints prevented them from acting them out. Liebow argues the poor behave in the way they do to try to veil their real attitude, that their 'manly flows' and their failure to conform makes their behaviour appear to be present-orientated and fatalistic.

(e) It can therefore be seen that the poor may not have themselves to blame, and in Marxist terms it might be more realistic to say that the ruling class is to blame.

(f) Townsend argues that the poor are an underclass, consisting of individuals such as the ill, some women, ethnic minorities and other disadvantaged social groups. However Miliband argues that the poor should not be considered as a separate class, as in Marxist terms every social group, other than the owners of the means of production, are disadvantaged. The poor, however, suffer the greatest inequalities of all.

(g) Some sociologists argue the poor have only themselves to blame for their poverty. For example in the nineteen century argued that their laziness was the cause of the situation they were in. He argued that they should not be given help as they would become dependent on it, and instead should undergo self-help. Helping them would produce a culture of dependency, which would be a disadvantage for the state and society, as argued later by the new right sociologist Marsland.

(h) Kincaid, who adapts a Marxist view, argues that the poor are poor because the rich are rich. It can be argued that the poor serve the ruling class, who create the poor and maintain them in poverty in order to benefit themselves. An example of this is setting workers' wages low in order to keep high.

(Source: Student answer.)

The logical order is to be found on p. 206.

6 Explanations of poverty

By the end of this chapter you should be able to:

- explain and outline competing perspectives on poverty;
- evaluate the problems involved in establishing why poverty continues to exist;
- outline and evaluate the culture of poverty approach to studying poverty;
- outline and assess the new right perspective on poverty;
- outline and assess Marxist approaches to the study of poverty;
- outline and assess feminist perspectives on poverty;
- practice an examination question.

Introduction

This chapter examines the competing perspectives on why poverty exists and how to alleviate it. Some of these perspectives tend to, blame the poor for their plight, while others, such as the New Right, blame the government for perpetuating a too lenient and generous welfare system. In contrast Marxists argue that poverty is an inherent and inevitable part of the capitalist system. Therefore poverty, far from being the fault of the poor themselves, is a structural effect.

More recent approaches include those of postmodernists, who investigate the way in which globalisation and changing work practices such as Fordism and post-Fordism affect those who are experiencing poverty or are likely to experience it during the course of their lives, and feminist perspectives, which investigate the part played by gender relationships and the patriarchal system.

Exercise 6.1

a i e

Before you read this chapter, write down why you think poverty continues to exist. At the end of the chapter you will be asked to review your ideas to see whether they have remained the same or changed in light of what you have read.

The 'culture of poverty' explanation

The debate on whether a culture of poverty exists began in the 1960s and later influenced new right thinking on the persistence of poverty. The underlying assumption of the culture of poverty approach is that the poor are bound up in a poverty trap that is perpetuated from generation to generation. There is acceptance of a life of poverty from which there is no escape – the poor simply accept their lot and make no serious effort to improve it. Although some would argue that such ideas are outdated, they have served as the basis for research and therefore need to be considered in order to give a rounded view of the debate on the causes of poverty. According to Michael Harrington (1962, p. 12):

> The real explanation of why the poor are where they are is that they made the mistake of being born to the wrong parents in the wrong section of the country in the wrong industry or in the wrong racial or ethnic group. There are two important ways of saying this: the poor are caught in a vicious circle; or the poor live in a culture of poverty.

Harrington argues that those who live in poverty have had fewer life chances from the start, so there has been a continual struggle to survive. Harrington relates a conversation in which the American novelist F. Scott Fitzgerald remarked 'The rich are different', and the writer Ernest Hemingway replied 'Yes, they have money'. It seems that for many people the main difference between the rich and the poor is simply a matter of money, rather than a combination of factors that lead to some people having money in abundance and others having little or none.

Oscar Lewis (1965), an American anthropologist, based his research into poverty on the recorded life histories of families in Mexico and Puerto Rico in the 1950s and 1960s. He identified what he termed a culture or rather subculture of poverty, as exemplified by the Rios family, who had the opportunity to break away from their life of poverty but chose not to. Lewis identified a pattern of behaviour that persisted over time and had 62 characteristic traits. Twelve of these were universal, 13 were economic, 18 were social and psychological, seven were political and 12 were of various other types.

Some of the characteristics he identified were long-term unemployment, low life expectancy, a feeling of helplessness or inadequacy, violence in the household, early sexual experience, little ability to defer gratification poor work habits, short-term horizons rather than long-term goals, substance abuse and deviant family structures. These were self-perpetuating and transmitted from generation to generation. The poor reacted to their circumstances by developing their own norms and values, and in so doing became detached from mainstream society. These norms and values directed their behaviour and inhibited their attempts to break out of poverty. In this way poverty became self-perpetuating – a vicious circle that was difficult to break.

The implication behind the culture of poverty thesis is that if poverty is eradicated behaviour will change. Or is this, as the saying goes, putting the cart before the horse? Perhaps it is more a case of changing behaviour so that poverty will disappear.

Exercise 6.2

a 1. If you had a 'windfall' or a National Lottery win of £10 000, what you would do with it?

a 2. Would this depend on how much money you already had?

a 3. If your response to question 1 was spend, spend, spend, why was this so? If not, why not?

A later writer on the culture of poverty, Edward Banfield (1970), split the poor into two groups: those who lacked money but had middle-class values and would benefit from government support (mainly the disabled and unemployed single mothers who had been widowed or abandoned); and those he called the true lower class, who would live in squalor even if their incomes were doubled. These people had their own set of values and attached no importance to self-improvement, sacrifice or hard work. They lived in a culture of poverty and made no effort to escape from it. Benfield's work supported that of Lewis in that it pointed to the existence of a culture that involved resignation to poverty and the adoption of different norms and values from those of mainstream society.

In the 1970s the anthropologist Walter Miller (1962) argued that a distinct subculture existed among the bottom stratum of the American working class, who had their own set of what he called 'focal concerns'. These included the search for thrills, the desirability of masculinity and toughness, the need for immediate gratification and a willingness to leave everything to chance. There was a commitment to this subculture and even a preference for it. According to Miller these attitudes had been passed down the generations and therefore: 'Lower class culture [had become] a distinctive tradition with an integrity of its own' (ibid., p. 32). For Miller it was the values of these people that made them poor.

Exercise 6.3

a Write down what you think lower-class culture is. What social traditions does it include?

Criticisms of the culture of poverty explanation

A strength of the culture of poverty explanation is that it highlights the different lifestyles of the poor and tries to explain how these came about. It argues that the traditions of the poor have caused their separation from mainstream society. However, many of the culture of poverty ideas have been questioned. For example research by Ken Coates and Richard Silburn (1970) in the St Annes district of Nottingham revealed that while many of the people living there did indeed show signs of resignation and helplessness, this was a consequence of poverty rather than a cause of it. This ties in with the findings of Valentine (1968) and Liebow (1964) in the US. They concluded that poverty was the result of multiple deprivation: the poor had low-income jobs, if they were employed at all; and they lived in substandard housing, suffered from poor health and were poorly educated (see Chapter 4). It was not their attitudes, norms and values that made them poor but the lack of opportunities to better themselves.

Likewise Michael Rutter and Nicola Madge (1976, p. 107) state that 'There is little documentation of any communities in this country [the UK] which might correspond with the description of a culture of poverty given by Lewis.' However they have detected a chain of disadvantage in which the poverty of the parents is passed on to the children. This is evident in education, in that poor children miss schooling as a result of poor health brought about by poor housing conditions, poor diet and clothing that is unsuitable for the prevailing weather. Nonetheless, 'At least half the children born into a disadvantaged home do not repeat that disadvantage into the next generation' (ibid., p. 110). The poor do make an effort to improve their situation and parents do try to improve conditions for their children. However difficulties present themselves when money is at a premium and the children need new clothes and shoes.

Exercise 6.4

a 1. List the items of clothing that you consider necessary for an eight-year-old child over a period of three months.

a 2. List the clothes you are wearing at the moment and the cost of them. What is the total cost?

Research by the Institute of Fiscal Studies (Johnson and Reed, 1996) suggests that the economic standing of parents is an important determinant of where their children will eventually stand in the income distribution hierarchy. The main finding of the research is that today's income distribution reflects the inequalities suffered three or more generations ago. Poor people tend to come from disadvantaged backgrounds, and those who do escape from poverty tend to be the more able with better educational qualifications.

Other studies see situational constraints as the most important factor in poverty – poverty is not the fault of the poor themselves but the result of the situation in which they find themselves. For example Susan Mayer (1997) matched students' outcomes (progress) with parental income. Good outcomes were high examination scores, having a job by the age of 24 and earning a high income. Bad outcomes included dropping out of school or college, becoming an unmarried mother, and being unemployed and on benefit at the age of 24. According to Mayer, 'The parental characteristics that employers value and are willing to pay for, such as diligence, honesty, good health and reliability . . . improve children's chances independent of their effect on parents' incomes. Children of parents with these attributes do well even if their parents do not have much income' (ibid., p. 43).

Likewise research conducted in the US points away from the culture of poverty explanation and towards situational constraints as the main cause of poverty amongst certain groups of people who have to try harder than other groups to achieve the same levels of employment and income. For example David Gordon (1996) states that many young African American men have slim job prospects, are paid low wages when work is available and have little job security.

New Right perspectives

In 1935 President Roosevelt said the following in his State of the Union message: 'The lessons of history, confirmed by evidence immediately before me, show conclusively that continued dependence on relief induces a spiritual and moral disintegration fundamentally destructive to the national fibre. To dole out relief in this way is to administer a narcotic, a subtle destroyer of the human spirit.'

This view rose to prominence again in the 1980s and 1990s in both the US and UK with the emergence of the new right. In the UK the Conservative government, under the leadership of Margaret Thatcher (prime minister from 1979–90), believed that the poor were to blame for their poverty and it was up to them – not the state – to do something about it. One cabinet minister, Norman Tebbit, advised the unemployed to get on their bikes and look for work rather than expect the state to provide for them. The poor should not become part of a benefit culture or 'claiming class'.

At that point the media turned their attention to the behaviour of benefit claimants, with right-wing tabloid newspapers such as the *Sun* depicting benefit claimants as 'scroungers' who were enjoying a lavish lifestyle at the expense of hard-working taxpayers. This cudgel was taken up by Peter Lilley (social security minister until May 1997), who insisted that government policies had virtually eradicated poverty and that anyone who lived in poverty had chosen to do so. At the 1993 Conservative Party conference he proclaimed that the government was 'not in the business of subsidising scroungers'.

ITEM A

Jobless people who claim the dole but repeatedly refuse to look for work are to be targeted in a new Government crackdown. Ministers are drawing up fresh plans to weed out benefit 'malingerers' who say they are seeking jobs, but in reality are doing little or nothing to find work.

Social Security Secretary Peter Lilley wants tougher enforcement of the 'actively seeking work' rule, to make those suspected of dragging their heels provide greater proof of their quest. If they cannot supply adequate proof, or are discovered to have been giving false information, their benefit will be cut immediately.

Mr Lilley believes a hard core of claimants are flouting the rules introduced under the 1988 Social Security Act. Figures show [that] efforts to clamp down on the spongers have had little effect, with only a fraction of Britain's 2.9 million dole claimants – about 1200 annually – being refused benefit for failing to actively seek work.

New enforcement measures may include the issue of log books to suspected claimants, in which those thought to be slacking would be made to record details of jobs applied for. Benefit officers would then carry out spot checks with employers to discover whether a claimant's record of applications was genuine. Inspectors will also be given greater powers to demand copies of application letters from claimants, together with any replies they have received from job advertisers. The crackdown comes as Ministers try to find ways of curbing Britain's spiralling £70 million Social Security budget, targeting those who are deliberately milking the system and cheating the taxpayers. A senior social security source said: 'the whole method by which we check whether a claimant is actively seeking work is not working as it should. Most claimants do all they can to find work, but there are a hard core who know how to play the system and hoodwink benefit officials. We want those people to be forced to give greater proof.'

Dole and income support claimants are currently interviewed at three or six monthly intervals about their efforts to get a job. And they are sometimes asked to provide copies of application letters. But, social security chiefs admit the procedures for enforcing the 'actively seeking work' rule are too relaxed. They say it is relatively easy for those with long-term knowledge of the benefit system to flout it.

(Source: Sunday Express, 1 August 1993.)

ITEM A   *Exercise 6.5*

Read Item A and answer the following questions:

[i] 1. How many dole claimants a year were refused benefit for failing to seek work?

[i] 2. What powers were inspectors to be given to deal with benefit fraud?

[a] 3. What is your interpretation of 'actively seeking work'? Would this include going to the Job Centre every day?

The new right's theories strongly influenced the Conservative government and the proposals outlined in Item A reflected its views on how fraud should be dealt with and how benefit scroungers should be treated and viewed by society at large. The government focused public attention on the credibility of benefit claimants by saying, for example, that old people were not poor because many of them spent long holidays abroad during the winter months. Furthermore young single mothers should not have become pregnant in the first place and their families should take responsibility for them. As Peter Lilley said at the 1992 Conservative Party conference (adapting a song from a Gilbert and Sullivan operetta): 'I've got a little list of benefit offenders who I'll soon be rooting out. Young ladies who get pregnant just to jump the housing list.' In 1992 it was widely reported in pro-Conservative newspapers that young unmarried women were being put at the top of council housing waiting lists if they had young babies. The housing departments of many Labour-held councils were vilified in the media for adopting this policy rather than giving priority to married women with families. The debate centred on moral views of who deserved the most help in society.

Exercise 6.6

a 1. Who in your opinion really needs benefits?

a 2. How did you arrive at your choice?

a 3. Did you take account of factors such as race, gender, class and age?

(It should be noted that some of the policies mentioned in Item A still exist under the New Labour government, which has also shown signs of victim blaming – see Chapters 9 and 10, pages 158–74 and 175–98. Anyone who is claiming unemployment benefit must be able to produce written proof that they are actively seeking work – documents such as letters of application, a list of interviews attended, a dossier of jobs applied for and so on. If it is suspected that someone is not actively seeking work his or her benefits may be stopped. By shifting the blame for poverty to the poor themselves rather than focusing on policies to alleviate it, the government is effectively obscuring the situational constraints that cause poverty. It would seem that blaming the poor is a far easier option for the government than opening itself to criticism about the failure of its social policies.)

David Marsland (1996), a New Right British sociologist working in the 1980s and 1990s, developed the idea of 'dependency culture'. He was critical of universal benefits that were not means tested, for example Child Allowance and the state pension. All parents, no matter how rich or poor, were (and still are) entitled to Child Allowance if they wished to claim it. Marsland was of the opinion that the provision of was benefits creating a culture of dependency. For example he believed that handing out unemployment benefit encouraged people to remain unemployed – 'why work for a living if you can get money for doing nothing?' – and that the money would be put to better use if it was invested in industry and broadening the economic base of the country. He did not want to see all benefits abolished, but they should be restricted to people in genuine need who were unable to help themselves.

Exercise 6.7

In 1990 John Moore (then secretary of state for the DSS) declared, and quoted in the *Guardian*, that 'the poorest fifth of the population spend a tenth of their income on alcohol and cigarettes.'

a 1. Where do you think he obtained this information?

a 2. How could you check its accuracy?

a 3. If the statement was inaccurate, how could he have been challenged to prove his assertion?

Thus a moral dimension entered into the equation, with judgements being made about how the poor should live. The New Right marginalised the poor from the mainstream by implying that they should not drink alcohol or smoke tobacco because taxpayers were paying for them to enjoy that privilege. The poor must learn to help themselves, to take responsibility for their lives and make a determined effort to improve their lot.

Exercise 6.8

a 1. If you smoke tobacco and drink alcohol, on average how much per week do you spend on them? Is it a tenth of your income?

a 2. If you do not smoke or drink, find someone who does and is willing to tell you whether it costs more or less than a tenth of his or her income.

The poor are viewed by the New Right as different from mainstream society, having become detached from it due to their behaviour and lifestyle. They have become a separate, definable class below the working class, known as the underclass. Saunders (1990), a new right thinker, says that four features distinguish the underclass from the rest of society:

- They are socially marginalised.
- They are almost entirely dependent on state welfare.
- They have a culture of resigned fatalism (as discussed above in the section on the culture of poverty).
- They suffer multiple deprivations.

Saunders' ideas on the underclass of undeserving poor are also observable in the work of Charles Murray (1990), an American sociologist who, when visiting the UK in 1989, argued that a new underclass was emerging in the UK that was characterised by family instability, violent crime, lack of educational qualifications and dependency on the state. According to Murray, 'The underclass does not refer to a degree of poverty but a type of poverty' (ibid., p. 12). The term underclass, which was first used by the Swedish economist and sociologist Gunyar Myrdal (1962), implies that the people who comprise it are separate from mainstream society. According to Murray this underclass has always existed, there have always been deserving and undeserving poor, with the undeserving poor refusing to take responsibility for their lives, look for work, to obtain qualifications to better themselves or to contribute to society in a positive way. They are at the very bottom of society.

The deplorable behaviour of the underclass is the underlying theme of Murray's work. He blames the poor for the position they are in and the state for its overly generous welfare provision. He focuses on aspects of what he deems to be the socially unacceptable behaviour that lies at the heart of the way the poor live, as in the case of young women who deliberately have illegitimate children at an early age in the expectation that the state will support them. He claims that statistics show that the vast majority of illegitimate births are to women from lower social classes, where the lack of a husband is becoming the norm rather than the exception. Even when men are present they tend to be unemployed and uninterested in obtaining work. Murray argues that these men are happy to live off the state and to abdicate responsibility for their offspring. Having children is a way for them to prove their masculinity, but they are not family-oriented and often turn to crime. According to Murray, such men will only take responsibility for providing for their families if the state withdraws their benefits and forces them to work.

Lawrence Mead (1992) agrees with Murray. He too believes that the growth in welfare dependency is due to the poor refusing to take the jobs that are available or failing to keep the jobs they do take. They must be made to work in order to claim benefit; men must prove themselves as they did in the past by being providers and staying with their children: 'What matters for success is less whether your father was rich or poor, than whether you knew your father at all' (ibid., p. 23). Mead also considers that ethnic minority groups create problems, and he fuses together the underclass and ethnic minorities when he refers to 'ghetto culture'. The ghetto has a life of its own, characterised by what he refers to as a pathological culture. The poor, and especially poor blacks, live in a world of their own making. They have to make the effort to get out and if they will not do it of their own accord then measures must be taken to ensure they do.

In Murray's view, changes to the benefit system via Acts of Parliament lie at the heart of the rise in illegitimacy and poverty. For example in 1977 the Homeless Persons Act prioritised pregnant women and mothers in housing allocation and ensured the provision of single-parent benefit, Child Allowance, maternity payments and free school meals, as well as help with the acquisition of furniture and other essential items for the home. Murray argues that if mothers are able to obtain all these things, why should the fathers provide? He suggests that this produces a vicious circle in which everyone expects someone else (usually the state) to take responsibility, leading to the erosion of self-reliance and loss of the work ethic that once underpinned society.

Surprisingly, Murray does not propose that benefits should be cut drastically as this might produce additional problems, such as a rise in crime. What he does suggest is that local communities should become much more self-governing and take responsibility for such things as education, criminal justice and housing provision. People need to be given a 'stake' in society and a feeling of belonging, so that values and norms are established to the benefit of everyone. Murray also sees the underclass as the product of a decline in moral standards, and unless there is a return to high moral standards (coupled with a reduction in dependence on the state) there will always be an underclass and poverty.

Other writers have offered explanations of why some ethnic minority groups find themselves in the underclass, other than laziness and the possession of different values. For example, in their controversial book, *The Bell Curve*, Herrnstein and Murray (1994) state that that the lower position of some people, and especially ethnic minority groups in the US, is due to their inherently lower intelligence and cognitive ability (perception, intuition, reasoning and so on). According to Herrnstein and Murray, 60 per cent of intelligence depends on hereditary factors, so the lower intelligence that leads to inequality is mainly due to biological factors. The implication here is that is individuals who are unequal and not social groups as such, but (in the book) they do talk about differences between individuals and groups and the two groups that receive particular attention are race and class groups. The middle class and the underclass are compared, as are different racial groups. So their attempt to say they are not talking in terms of groups does not stand up to close investigation.

Some of the data used in *The Bell Curve* is derived from *Mankind*

Quarterly (see Rosen and Lane, 1995). This publication contains articles that reflect their authors' belief that racial differences are all-important, and there are identifiable links between this publication and various neo-Nazi and fascist groups. This kind of material is deliberately aimed at inciting racial prejudice and promoting white supremacy, to the detriment of all other ethnic groups.

Challenges have been made to the arguments presented in *The Bell Curve*. For example Gardner (1995) argues that at most only 20 per cent of socioeconomic inequality can be attributed to intelligence, which means, taking Herrnstein and Murray's argument further, that only 60 per cent of this 20 per cent can be explained in terms of heredity. The rest has to be due to structural and environmental factors that can and do change over time, which makes a mockery of the heredity explanation. Nisbett (1995) examined seven studies of the relationship between race and intelligence and found that only one of them (which coincidentally happens to be the one cited in *The Bell Curve*) gives tentative, but not wholehearted, backing to the heredity argument.

In summary, it seems that the new right believe that certain people are inferior in all ways and are incapable of finding their own way out of poverty. They must be forced to by means of policies instigated by those who are superior and hold the moral high ground.

Exercise 6.9

|a| 1. The term underclass often appears in inverted commas ('underclass'). Why do you think this is?

|a| 2. How useful is the term in adding to our understanding of why certain groups find themselves living in poverty?

Criticisms of the New Right perspectives

Critics of the new right consider that the arguments they put forward are not supported by empirical evidence. With regard to lone parenthood, Alan Walker (1997) states that official statistics on illegitimacy show that 60 per cent of births to women younger than 20 are registered by both parents, and Ermisch (1986) has found that on average lone parenthood for a never married woman in the 1980s only lasted about three years before marriage took place. Hence most children born to single mothers do not spend their entire childhood in a one-parent household.

Walker questions the New Right's arguments about the underclass. He argues that the underclass in fact have conventional attitudes about such things as employment, marriage and family life, but as so few employment opportunities are available to them they are unable to provide for a family. He sees the poor as victims of the system, as do Marxists and conflict theorists. In the words of Carol Walker (1993, p. 4), 'Despite sensational newspaper headlines, living on social assistance is not an option most people would choose, if they were offered a genuine alternative. Most find themselves in that position because of some traumatic event in their lives; the loss of a job, the loss of a partner or the onset of ill health.'

Hartley Dean and Peter Taylor-Gooby (1990) reject the new right's idea of a dependency culture as to a certain extent nearly everyone in society is dependent on someone. For example employees are dependent on their employers, consumers are dependent on manufacturers, and everybody is dependent on the state for physical security and the regulation of social structures. In 1990 Dean and Taylor-Gooby interviewed jobless social security claimants in South London and Kent. The vast majority of interviewees wanted to work and did not like living on benefit, although many referred to the fact that they would lose their means-tested benefits if they did take up employment, even if this was low-paid work. In general the attitudes and ambitions of the benefit claimants did not differ from those of other people, and they wanted to work and play a useful part in society. Dean and Taylor-Gooby conclude that 'The social security system does not foster a dependency culture, but it constructs, isolates and supervises a heterogeneous population of reluctant dependants' (ibid., p. 15). This conclusion is echoed by Bagguley and Mann (1992), who argue that the only thing that really distinguishes the underclass is their low income and the fact that they are the ones who are almost invariably blamed for social problems such as 'benefit scrounging' and juvenile delinquency.

Anthony Heath (1992) tested the New Right's claim that the attitudes of the underclass differ from those of the rest of society. He found that 86 per cent of those deemed to be a member of the underclass wanted a paid job just like everyone else in society. Using data from the British Election Survey of 1987 and the British Social Attitudes Survey of 1989 he identified those who were unemployed or not in paid employment and claiming income support and compared these people with families where one person at least was working. He found that their attitudes to wards marriage were similar, with marriage being seen as desirable, especially where children were involved. This finding was further researched by Elaine Kempson (1996) on behalf of the Joseph Rowntree Foundation. She drew up a report based on 31 research studies of life on a low income in the 1990s and concluded that 'People who live on low incomes are not an underclass with different attitudes and values to the rest of society. They aspire to a job, a decent home and an income that will cover their outgoings with a little to spare' (ibid., p. 112). Kempson believes that most people on a low income do try to make ends meet but often have to choose between cutting back on essentials or going into debt – a Catch 22 situation.

Exercise 6.10

1. Design a closed questionnaire to distribute to the rest of your sociology class to establish their perceptions of the underclass. There should be 10 questions with a choice of answers (for example: Which group is part of the underclass? The unemployed? The sick? The disabled?).

Postmodernist views on poverty

More recent ideas on poverty have come from postmodernist theorists, who argue that there is a wide range of fragmented groups in society, each with their own understanding of the situation in which they find themselves. Postmodernists maintain that not everyone who is unemployed is poor and part of the underclass, not all benefit claimants are 'scroungers', and if an underclass it will not and cannot be homogeneous. The poor are a very diverse group and do not have a collective identity, and there is little evidence to suggest that any section of the underclass has different values from the rest of society. As Ruth Lister (1991) points out, the term underclass is used to cover a wide range of people who have nothing in common but their reliance on some form of welfare benefit. The term provokes what she refers to as a 'pathological' view of the poor, who are seen as some sort of disease that is threatening the general well-being of society.

According to postmodernists, poverty is due to global factors and changed working practices. The flexible nature of contemporary work (see Chapter 3) means that many of the workforce are now employed as part-time or contract workers with low pay and poor working conditions.

Exercise 6.11

1. Do you think there is an underclass in the UK? Explain your response in 100 words.

2. If you have decided there is an underclass, who is part of it and why?

Structural explanations of poverty

Structural explanations of poverty differ from cultural explanations and new right ideas in that they are concerned with the part played by institutions such as the government in creating and maintaining poverty. The poor are not to blame for their plight – it is the way they are treated by institutions that leads them into a life of poverty.

Frank Field (a Labour MP who until June 1998 was in charge of welfare reform at the Department of Social Security) sees the underclass not as a dangerous group intent on subverting the norms of society but as victims of government policies. According to Field (1997) the underclass is composed of three main groups: the long-term unemployed, single-parent families with a continuing dependence on benefit, and pensioners dependent on state benefit. All these groups rely on benefits that are too low to allow an acceptable standard of living, and their situation is one from which there is no easy escape and to which there is no easy solution. Unlike New Right theorists, Field does not think that the situation in which the poor find themselves is of their own making.

Field believes that unemployment is much more likely to affect the working class than other groups, especially in the case of unskilled or semiskilled workers as changes to the structure of the economy mean that fewer jobs are available for them. Single parents have the problem of finding suitable but affordable childcare if they take up employment, and the cost of childcare can lead to their being worse off than they were on benefit. Finally, in real terms the value of the state pension has diminished in recent years, with the result that pensioners' living standards have fallen.

To alleviate the problems of the underclass Field proposed that certain jobs be moved to areas with high unemployment and that the unemployed be trained in skills that are essential to economic growth. Furthermore child benefit and pensions should be increased, the amount that single parents are allowed to earn before their benefits are cut should be raised, and inexpensive childcare should be made readily available. Naturally these measures would initially be expensive, but in the long term the gains would outweigh the losses and society as a whole would benefit.

In December 1997 the Labour government announced the establishment of a social exclusion unit, which is designed to tackle poverty by helping those who have fallen victim to poverty as a result of high unemployment, the high crime rate and poor housing. The twelve-member team's priorities include tackling truancy and exclusion from school, reducing the number of people sleeping rough, and developing new approaches to improving housing on the most rundown estates.

a

1. The following paragraph from Bradshaw and Holmes' (1989) study of poor families in the North-East of England echoes some of the themes considered above. Copy out the paragraph and fill in the blanks with appropriate words chosen from the list below.

'At a time when British poverty is again being discussed in terms of an ...... it is of crucial importance to recognise that these families, and probably millions more like them living on social security benefits, are in no sense a ...... and ...... group cut off from the rest of society. They are just the same people as the rest of our population, with the same ...... and ...... but with simply too little money to be able to share in the ...... and ...... of every day life with the rest of the population.'

- activities
- underclass
- detached
- culture
- possessions
- aspirations
- isolated

a **i**

2. Reread the section on structural explanations and then copy out and complete the table below.

Strengths	Weaknesses
It has added to the debate on poverty	It does not consider the role of the poor themselves

Marxist perspectives on poverty

Marxist theory is based on the idea that class conflict is a constant presence in society and that this conflict will bring about change. As discussed in Chapter 3, the owners of the means of production hold all the power and wealth in society. The workers are paid low wages to produce goods that the owners sell at large profits – profits that are not shared with the workers. According to Marxists, poverty is an inevitable outcome of this system. Inequalities of wealth, income, opportunities and power are deliberately created and perpetuated over-time so that one class is always dominant and the other subordinate. Capitalism – a system that puts price and commercial value ahead of all other values – is subject to erratic fluctuations, with periods of boom followed by periods of depression and unemployment, especially among the proletariat. It therefore polarises the rich and poor.

Marx saw capitalism as a particular stage of historical development that would eventually be replaced by communism (public rather than private ownership of the means of production and the equal distribution of profits). The classless society of the future would be based on abundance and the wealth created by industrial production would ensure that no one in society would live in poverty or be deprived. Society would be classless because private property owners would no longer be the organisers of industrial production. Rather production would be centrally planned according to human need, as opposed to the vagaries of the market. However this classless society would not be one in which everyone became the same, because the fair distribution of wealth would enable people to develop their individual talents, albeit within an organised framework.

John Westergaard and Henrietta Resler (1976), who take a structural approach to poverty, prefer the term inequality to poverty because preoccupation with the latter tends to obscure the reality. Drawing an arbitrary line to distinguish the poor from the rest of society diverts attention from the larger structures of inequality in which poverty is embedded. By viewing poverty as a cultural condition, the product of collective incompetence and lack of initiative among those who comprise the poor, structural causes are ignored and structural economic change is seen as infeasible.

According to Westergaard and Ressler, for capitalism to thrive there has to be a steady pool of labourers prepared to work for low wages, and everyone who is employed on a low wage or is unemployed can be viewed as a victim of the capitalist system. Rank and file wage earners live with the continual threat of poverty hanging over them due to their position in that system. Westergaard and Ressler consider that the only way to tackle inequality is to take collective action to replace the system with one in which resources are fairly allocated. Under capitalism, inequality breeds inequality and the public takes inequality for granted. Remedying this means transforming society.

Exercise 6.13

1. Write down three ways in which society could be changed to make it fairer. Explain in detail how these changes would bring about a transformation.

2. In 500 words write a commentary on the following statement:
   'Poverty cannot be eradicated under capitalism.'

Ralph Miliband (1969) has investigated why the poor are unable to compete for a fare share of society's resources. He is of the opinion that their lack of financial and political resources prevents them from forming powerful groups to represent their interests. Furthermore a vicious circle is in operation, whereby the poor are deliberately kept poor and powerless so that they can not threaten the established order by overturning the rich and becoming powerful in their own right.

Marxist criticisms of New Labour's approach

It appears that New Labour has no plans to redistribute income and wealth. This is made clear, for instance, by its promise not to raise income tax. Some in New Labour's orbit even reject the suggestion that redistribution is desirable. For example David Goodhart (1999, p. 27), writing in the Blairite publication *Prospect*, said:

> The old fixation with the 'gap' [between rich and poor] is the problem. A third way theory of fairness should state that the gap does not matter – or at least that it matters less than the life-chances of the people at the bottom. If these are rising steadily then it does not matter that the rich are getting even richer. . . . 'Gap' thinking is also based on a defunct zero-sum idea of wealth creation. In a 19th century mining village it was clear that the mine owner's wealth in a sense caused the poverty of the miners. Other than the odd sweat-shop, that is not the case today. The poverty of the poor does not create the richness of the rich and vice versa. Bill Gates has not amassed a fortune of $150 billion by exploiting the poor of Seattle.

Another potential area of debate arises from Howarth *et al.*'s (1999) comments on the monitoring of poverty and what is meant by living below the average income:

> In discussing poverty, the Government has tended to use the numbers below half-average (mean) income as its preferred measure. One alternative would be the numbers below half-average (median) income, where the median income is that of a person at the midpoint of the income distribution.
>
> One characteristics of the median measure, in comparison to the mean, is that is it less sensitive to changes in the incomes of groups in the population. For example, if everybody below half-average mean income were given enough money to bring them up to half mean, then assuming all else equal, the mean itself would rise. By contrast, if everybody below half of the median were given enough to bring them to that threshold, the median would remain the same. This gives the median a practical advantage in terms of setting targets and goals for the numbers below a certain threshold (ibid., p. 13).

Howarth *et al.* go on to point out that if what was understood as living on below half the average income was changed from mean average to median average, the estimated number of people living in poverty would fall from 14 million to nine million. It is unclear why use of this median would be better in terms of setting targets, but it is clear that it would reduce the official number of people living in poverty without the need to do anything about redistributing income.

Labour tax rises increase poverty gap

Higher taxes on cigarettes and alcohol have increased the gap in spending power between rich and poor households since Labour came to power, government figures revealed yesterday. Despite the chancellor's initiatives to boost the incomes of the poorest households, inequality in post-tax income has risen to its highest level for 10 years, according to the Office for National Statistics. The main reason appears to be changes to the indirect tax regime. The ONS figures show that inequality in disposable income – what people have to spend after direct taxes – has risen only slightly.

Indirect taxes such as excise duties and VAT hit the wallets of poorer households harder because they spend more of their income. While VAT rates have remained unchanged, excise duty on petrol, alcohol and cigarettes has risen sharply under Labour.

After falling for the first half of the 1990s, inequality in post-tax income started to rise in 1995, according to the ONS figures. It flattened out briefly then began rising again in 1997, reaching its highest level since 1990 last year.

The changes over the past three years are small by comparison with the rapid rise in inequality before and after tax which Britain experienced in the 1980s.

Wage inequality rose dramatically between 1979 and 1989. It fell slightly under John Major's government and has been largely stable since the mid 1990s.

Measures of income inequality after taxes are taken into account also rose steeply in the 1980s, particularly in the last half of the decade, when the then chancellor, Nigel Lawson, slashed the tax bills of top earners.

After-tax inequality fell under the Major government then resumed a rising trend under Labour.

(Source: Guardian, 18 April 2001.)

Exercise 6.14

[a][i]   1. With reference to the discussion in this section, explain the significance of using the median rather than mean as the basis of calculating the average wage.

[a][i]   2. With reference to Item B, list the evidence that the gap between the rich and the poor has increased under New Labour.

As we have seen, for Marxists poverty in its broadest sense includes all the inequalities that prevail in the social and economic spheres of society, and the unfair allocation of resources is at the heart of the problem. Those who live in poverty are not to blame for their plight – they lack power, are at the bottom of the social hierarchy, have only their labour to sell and are often unable to sell it.

Marxists paint a clear picture of the causes of poverty and why it exists and persists, but they fail to explain why particular groups in society become poor. They do not identify which sections of the working-class proletariat are poor, or why there is inequality even within the proletariat. Moreover capitalist society has not always existed, yet poverty has.

Exercise 6.15

a i In a copy of the table below, list the strengths and weaknesses of the Marxist perspective. Two examples are provided to start you off.

Strengths	Weaknesses
It focuses attention and debate on the capitalist system.	It does not take account of gender or ethnicity issues.

A feminist perspective

The Marxist feminist Margaret Benston argues that women are exploited by capitalism in that they are treated as a reserve army of cheap labour that enables profits to be kept up. In 1994, 6.41 million women were in low-paid jobs and on average women's full-time gross weekly pay was 72 per cent of that of men. The crux of the problem for women is their secondary position in the labour market, the continued use of them as a reserve army of labour and their role as secondary wage earners in the family.

Exercise 6.16

The following quote is from a woman interviewed by Walker *et al.* (1994) 'I was earning roughly £35 to £40 a week. It was piecework, 13p per skirt – you had to sew hundreds. I had to work, sometimes till midnight from nine in the morning just to pay the rent, electricity and gas.'

a 1. How many skirts per hour would she have to had sewn to make £5.88 (the hourly rate that the Council of Europe has set as the benchmark for low pay)?

e 2. What do you consider to be a decent living wage?

a 3. How many hours a week would she have to had worked to earn a decent living wage?

Social Democratic perspectives

According to Social Democrats the existence of poverty in capitalist societies is due to inequality in the labour market. Most of those living in poverty are members of groups that are excluded from the labour market or hold only a weak position in it. These groups include the unemployed, the sick, the disabled, the retired, ethnic minorities and women.

Peter Townsend (1979) argues that poverty and class are closely allied. Those in poverty generally tend to be unskilled or semiskilled manual workers from the working class. They have little opportunity to obtain well-paid employment and therefore are unable to escape from poverty. In the 1980s the charges made to the tax system by the Thatcher government and its promotion of a flexible economy resulted in even fewer opportunities being available to those who were already disadvantaged in society. To remedy this, Townsend suggests that the state should take measures to redistribute wealth and resources, and prioritise areas such as housing and job creation.

While exclusion from paid employment is a prime cause of poverty, those in low-paid employment also suffer because if their pay rises above a set threshold they lose their entitlement to certain benefits. Changes to the Jobseekers Allowance in 1996 have also meant that people who work on short, fixed-term contracts can no longer claim benefits during breaks between contracts (for example those employed in schools as ancillary staff- or meal providers). This obviously means a reduction of their annual income.

As stated above, poverty hits particular groups and these groups should be targeted by the state in a drive to reduce the number of those living in poverty. It is not envisaged that changes will take place overnight, or through revolution as the Marxists prescribe, rather the changes will be gradual and targeted. Such ideas formed the basis of the welfare state, which will be discussed in depth in Chapters 8 and 9.

Like Townsend, Rentoul (1987) advocates the redistribution of income and wealth. He estimates that £12 billion will be needed to eliminate poverty.

Julian Le Grand (1990) believes that the provision of social services has, in the main, benefited the better off more than the poor, particularly in the case of health care, education, housing and transport. For example he estimates that those in the top fifth of the income hierarchy have nearly three times as much spent on their children's education than those in the bottom fifth because their children are much more likely to stay on in education after the age of 16 and progress to university, which is the most expensive area of educational provision.

Frank Field (1997) has examined benefits received by employees that do not count as income, such as company cars, private health insurance, and assistance with housing and housing costs. Not surprisingly he found that those on higher incomes received far more of there resources than those on low incomes.

Another area of deprivation concerns citizenship. Citizenship should involve the extension of all rights to all people, but at present some rights seem to be granted only to those within the labour market.

Exercise 6.17

a i e

1. Return to your answer to Exercise 6.1. Have your ideas changed after reading this chapter or remained the same? Why?

2. In a copy of the table below, summarise the explanations of poverty provided in this chapter and other textbooks. Some ideas are provided to help you.

Name of explanation	How poverty is explained	Relevant empirical studies
Culture of poverty	The poor are caught in a vicious cycle where poverty is passed from generation to generation through the culture taught to children. Money alone will not therefore solve the problem of poverty	Lewis (1965) Banfield (1970) Miller (1962) **Critics** Coates and Silburn (1970) Liebow (1964) Johnson and Reed (1996)
Situational constraints		Mayer (1997)
New Right		Marsland (1996) Saunders (1990)
Marxist feminism		
Social democratic		

Examination question and student's answer

Question

'Assess the argument that different definitions and explanations of poverty reflect different ideologies' (AEB, June 1995).

Student's answer

The paragraphs in this essay have been deliberately jumbled up. Rearrange them in a logical order, as originally written.

(a) The British government has chosen not to produce an official definition of poverty, although unofficially it is those who earn less than 50 per cent of the average income. This allows the poverty figures to be manipulated to show a fall. The Conservative government promoted a New Right view and blamed the existence of poverty on the welfare state, claiming that it allowed a dependency culture to emerge and that the provision of universal benefits provided a disincentive to work and encouraged a sense of helplessness. Marsland (1996) agrees with this, and thinks that the welfare state is encouraging poverty to continue. Charles Murray (1990), in his study of the underclass, argues that the state allows (female headed) single parent families to depend on it, by taking over the male role as the breadwinner. Marxists refute this view, claiming that poverty is maintained by capitalism as it allows class divisions to increase and the rich to get richer whilst the poor become poorer and more exploited.

(b) Functionalists argue that the existence of poverty in fact provides an incentive to work though the transmission of values. This argument is opposed by Marxists, who claim that it is functional for the bourgeoisie to reinforce poverty among the proletariat, who are alienated through the use of capitalist tools and fall into the poverty trap and become dependant on the state.

(c) Poverty can be defined in absolute terms, where people are unable to afford the basic necessities to live a healthy life, or in relative terms, where poverty is relative to the average standard of living at a particular time. In the new right's explanation of poverty the poor themselves and the welfare state are blamed for its existence, while the far left blame capitalist society.

(d) According to liberal ideology a cycle of deprivation is caused by the poor having inadequate housing, which leads to their children having re-occurring illnesses that inevitably mean they spend less time on education. This puts them in a poor position for future life in that they lack the knowledge needed to get a good job and are forced to rely on the state. Oscar Lewis (1965) has also studied the issue of poverty and deprivation. In his study of urban life in Mexico and Puerto Rico he found that a culture of poverty existed and this was transmitted down the generations. The poor were fatalistic about their position, dependent on the state, did not defer gratification (did not save for future material rewards) and were marginalised from – they were society 'on the outside looking in'. It can be argued that Oscar Lewi's views reflect the new right idea that the blame for poverty lies with the poor, and that its existence is due to the culture of the poor, which is self-perpetrating. Herbert Spencer, a nineteenth-century writer, also blamed the poor for their position as they indulged in 'dissolute living'. Yet Liberals would argue that poverty exists because the state reinforces class divisions by setting state benefits too low and conducting means tests, and because the middle class 'soak up' the provisions of the state by staying longer in education and enjoying mortgage and tax relief, which inevitably increases the division between rich and poor.

(e) Marxists would agree with the Liberal view presented by Mack and Lansley in that the state reinforces divisions in wealth through its provisions, which the poor receive less of.

(f) However other definitions of poverty are provided by liberals such as Mack and Lansley (1985), who modified Townsend's relative deprivation index as it did not account for free choice and was rather subjective in its judgement of what was necessary. Mack and Lansley's questionnaire consisted of items considered by the public to be necessary, and it also took account of free choice. In the US the poor are defined as those who earn less than the amount needed for a healthy lifestyle.

(g) Poverty definitions such as the theoretical UK poverty line reflect a functionalist perspective in that it would manipulate statistics to show that poverty is not an increasing problem and that society is functioning harmoniously as poverty exists to provide incentives. The USA definition however is a little more radical as it allows for some 'luxury' good such as cars, however as liberals argue 'todays necessities were yesterdays luxuries'. Thus the US poverty line is quite liberal as it allows for this. Explanations of poverty. Those of the new right, for example Murray and Marsland would disagree with a functionalist view as it would argue that the state provides incentives to work whilst the New Right argues the opposite, with Oscar Lewis commenting that this is a result of its culture which transmits these attitudes. The most useful definition and explanation would remain to be that posed by the liberal perspective, that it is the state who reinforce poverty through establishing a vicious cycle of deprivation, indirectly benefiting the rich. This deprivation index also accounted for choice unlike Townsend – Marxist ideology is unlike Liberal in that poverty is reinforced through state provisions which keep the poor in their position reinforcing divisions in wealth. These different definitions and explanation reflect different ideology on whether poverty is essential for harmony (Functionalism) or whether it is for the promotion of a Capitalist society which marginalises the poor (Marxism).

The correct logical order is to be found on p. 206.

7 Globalisation, localities and poverty

> By the end of this chapter you should:
>
> - understand how globalisation and poverty are interlinked;
> - be aware of locality and poverty issues;
> - understand why certain countries and areas are poorer than others;
> - be aware of the effect that globalisation is having on economies.

Introduction

> The resources needed to eradicate poverty are a mere fraction of the resources available globally and in most countries (Richard Jolly, Special Advisor to the United Nations Development Programme, 1997).

This chapter focuses on the distribution of resources within and between societies. It investigates why certain areas within countries are richer or poorer than others and why certain countries are richer or poorer than others. It also looks at strategies for dealing with the problems inherent in this inequality.

Geographical inequalities in the UK: the North–South divide

One way of looking at regional inequalities in the UK is to divide the country into two by drawing a line from the Bristol Channel to the Wash. On either side of this line there are radically different styles and standards of living – or what is popularly known as the North–South divide. The North is seen as being dependent on once powerful but now declining manufacturing industries, and consequently as suffering from economic decline and social hardship, whereas the South is characterised by the rapid growth of lucrative service industries that provide the basis for social and economic affluence.

Balchin (1990, p. 46) has examined the myths and the realities of the North–South divide and argues that a range of indicators suggest that the North 'does worse on average than the South in most respects ... and throughout the 1980's there was a serious widening of the North–South divide'. Balchin identifies several key factors that have contributed to this situation, the most important of which is employment, or rather the lack of it. In the 1950s and 1960s government economic policy kept unemployment at around 1–4 per cent, but by 1981 there had been a substantial decrease in manufacturing employment (where people actually made things, such as in the car industry) and a significant increase in service employment (banking, warehousing, technology, fast food, education and so on). According to Balchin, in '1976–86 employment in manufacturing declined by, almost 2 million ... while employment in services expanded by 860 000' (ibid., p. 48). The distribution of these declines and expansions was geographically uneven, with three quarters of job losses happening in the North and two thirds of increases occurring in the South.

Future expansion also favoured the service sector and hence the South, so when the economic recovery of the 1990s took place the regional disparities in employment remained. Unlike the North, the South had the sites needed for expansion, easy access to airports and good road and rail links. For example a stretch of the M4 near Swindon became known as Silicon Valley because so many Silicon-Chip manufacturers had established factories there. These factories obviously offered employment opportunities for local inhabitants and encouraged local development.

Empolyment by region, 1997 (percentages and thousands)

| | In employment | | | | ILO unem-ployed | Total econom-ically active | Econom-ically inactive | All aged 16 or over[2] (= 100%) (thousands) | Economic activity rates (percentages) | |
| | Employees | | | | | | | | | |
	Full-time	Part-time	Self-employed	Total[1]					Males	Females
North-East	34.1	13.1	4.6	52.5	5.7	58.2	41.8	2040	66.8	50.1
North-West	36.5	12.2	6.2	55.8	4.1	59.9	40.1	5358	69.0	51.3
Yorkshire and the Humber	35.9	13.2	6.4	56.1	4.9	61.0	39.0	3943	70.0	52.4
East Midlands	39.0	14.2	6.5	60.3	4.1	64.4	35.6	3259	72.9	56.2
West Midlands	38.2	12.6	6.7	58.3	4.2	62.5	37.5	4135	72.7	52.8
Eastern	39.3	12.7	8.2	60.9	3.8	64.7	35.3	4164	74.1	55.6
London	39.7	10.6	7.9	58.7	5.9	64.6	35.4	5478	74.1	55.7
South-East (GOR)	38.8	13.7	9.1	62.1	3.4	65.6	34.4	6141	74.9	56.7
South-West	34.6	15.1	9.4	59.9	3.3	63.2	36.8	3841	71.8	55.0
England	37.6	12.9	7.5	58.7	4.3	63.0	37.0	38358	72.2	54.3
Wales	33.3	12.0	6.7	53.1	4.8	57.9	42.1	2292	66.4	50.0
Scotland	38.1	11.9	5.7	56.6	5.3	61.8	38.2	4026	70.6	53.8
Northern Ireland	35.8	9.7	7.2	55.1	4.5	59.5	40.5	1222	69.9	49.9

Notes:
1. Includes those on government-supported employment and training schemes, and unpaid family workers.
2. Population in private households, student halls of residence and NHS accommodation.

(Source: ONS 1998.)

ITEM A **Exercise 7.3**

Study Item A carefully and then answer the following questions:

i 1. In 1997, which region had the highest number of employees in full-time work?

i 2. Which region had the lowest number of employees in full-time work?

a 3. How do you think this difference can be explained?

i 4. Which region had the highest number of self-employed people?

i 5. Which region had the highest number of economically active females?

i *a* 6. Summarise any patterns you have identified and note the evident differences.

The end of manufacturing industry and the idea of a postindustrial economy

According to Daniel Bell (1973) the move towards a postindustrial economy will lead to greater prosperity and a better standard of living for those employed in the service sector. The implication of this is that we should not be worried about the decline of traditional manufacturing jobs but should welcome the growth of service sector jobs, which will solve the problem of unemployment and poverty in the North of the UK as much as they have in the the South.

However some jobs in the service sector are poorly paid and short term, and the conditions of work leave much to be desired.

Because traditional industries tended to be situated in the North, deindustrialisation (a decline in the share of manufacturing in economic production) has been far more extensive in the North than in the South, and almost all northern regions experienced a fall in manufacturing employment between 1979 and 1987. For example the North-East of England, which had been an important ship-building area for over a hundred years, went into decline, as did Sheffield with the closure of steel works and Birmingham with the collapse of engineering and small parts manufacturing. As a consequence these areas thus suffered a rise in both unemployment and social deprivation. Furthermore a considerable amount of manufacturing has been moved to countries where the production and labour costs are lower, such as Korea, Taiwan and Mexico, and it can be assumed that such industries have been lost to the UK for the foreseeable future.

Social inequalities

Balchin (1990) draws attention to other aspects of the North–South divide, including health and housing.

With regard to health, the inverse care law (Tudor-Hart, 1971) states that those most in need of health care often receive less, that is, certain groups of people in certain areas in the country receive less health care than their situation demands. Morbidity (disease) and mortality statistics reveal significant class, gender and race inequalities, and these inequalities are now at record levels. For instance Christopher Walker (*Independent on Sunday*, 11 February 2001) points out that the mortality difference between the top 10 per cent of geographical districts (those with the lowest mortality rates) and the bottom 10 per cent of geographical districts (those with the highest mortality rates) was higher in 2000 than in the 1950s. In the 1950s someone from the poorest 10 per cent of geographical areas was 1.6 times more likely to die than someone from the top 10 per cent of geographical areas, but by 2000 this likelihood had risen to 1.86 times. As can be seen, the relative chance of dying has indeed become more unequal.

There are also regional differences in housing provision and standards, and these will be discussed in detail in Chapter 10 of this book.

The North–South divide – fact or fiction?

Although much of the evidence examined thus far supports the notion of a North–South divide, Balchin (1990) suggests that:

- Disparities within regions (intraregional disparities) may be as marked as disparities between regions (interregional disparities).
- Inner-city decay exists in almost all regions but this is hidden by statistics based on averages.
- The South-East may be more prosperous in general, but Greater London has some of the highest levels of deprivation in Europe.

Hence Balchin suggests that, rather than a North–South divide, we should think more in terms of 'older industrial areas' and 'newer

ITEM B

Study challenges idea of North–South divide

Professor Richard Berthoud, of the Institute for Social and Economic Research, analysed the income of 50 000 households in 2600 neighbourhoods for his report, called *Rich Place Poor Place*. He shows that wealth and poverty are much more evenly spread across the UK than the common perception 'that rich and poor are segregated into different residential areas'. Every local neighbourhood has a wide cross-section of rich and poor families in the same way that incomes vary in a village, the professor says.

The distribution means that less than a third of households living below the poverty line, defined by [an] income of less than £150 a week, actually live in low-income areas. In fact, most poor people are spread across middle or higher-income areas.

In the most affluent areas, 40 per cent of households are likely to be in the top income bracket with a weekly income of more than £450. But 11 per cent of households are poor and 50 per cent have middle range incomes between £150 and £450 a week.

Across the country, Richmond upon Thames has the highest average income at £384 per week, while Kingston upon Hull has the lowest at £200 per week. Professor Berthoud says that regional differences in income are quite narrow when the much wider gap between the richest and poorest households [is] taken into account.

The least well-off regions are in the North of England, but they are not much worse off than elsewhere. About 25 per cent of the households in Tyneside, South Yorkshire and Merseyside are 'poor' on the measure used; but so are

15 per cent of households in the most prosperous region, the South East, and 17 per cent in London.

South Yorkshire emerges as the worst off region with an average income of £224 a week. That figure is £249 in Scotland, £242 in Greater Manchester, £251 in the East Midlands, £261 in East Anglia, £287 in London and £293 in the most affluent area, the South East.

Prof Berthoud, who based his study on detailed income figures collected by the Department of Social Security, says the income gap between rich and poor households has become wider in Britain than in most other European Union countries. But he adds that 'regional variations in the UK are substantially narrower than those observed in the other large countries'.

(Source: Lorna Duckworth, The Independent, 31 May 2001.)

centres of growth'. For example 'industrial Cornwall and the Medway towns of Kent are old while the "Silicon Glen" of Scotland is (comparatively) new' (ibid., p. 122).

It is also possible to consider this issue by analysing inequalities at the county or postcode level. In an article in the *Guardian*, Paul Baldwin (1999) states that the lowest incomes are to be found in the counties of Tyne and Wear, Cornwall and the Isles of Scilly (£17 400 per year on average). While Tyne and Wear is in the North, Cornwall and the Scillies are not, which tends to undermine the notion that poverty is restricted to the North. In case you think that this is an isolated example, the next three poorest counties were South Yorkshire (£17 500), the Isle of Wight (£17 700) and Mid-Glamorgan (£17 700), only one of which is situated in the North. However if we shift the analysis to postcode districts the poorest areas are found in the North, namely some parts of Bootle, Leicester, Middlesborough and Birkenhead.

Townsend and Lewis (1989) claim that the North–South divide is largely a media construct. However a number of media reports have presented a much more balanced picture of inequality and describe the North–South divide as something of an oversimplification, or at worst a nonsense.

Both North and South have rich and poor areas, and areas of high unemployment and low unemployment. Not all of the South is prosperous, and not all of the North is poor and deprived.

ITEM B | **Exercise 7.4**

[i] 1. According to Item B, what proportion of households in the most affluent areas are likely to be in the top income bracket?

[i] 2. What proportion of households in the most affluent areas are likely to be poor?

[i] 3. What proportion of households are poor in (a) Tyneside, (b) The South-East, (c) London?

[a][i][e] 4. Based on your answers to the questions above and other relevant material, do you think there is a North–South divide? Explain your answer.

Work practices

The term Fordism was first used by Antonio Gramsci (1891–1937), an Italian Marxist. The Fordist model of production (named after the Ford Motor Company, which introduced the system) was based on the application of technology and the strict and detailed division of labour, which effectively deskilled the labour force. The name Ford came to be synonymous with assembly-line mass production for a lucrative mass market. The products were standardised, for example in a run of mass produced cars identical headlights and all other components were fitted in exactly the same way to each unit.

While mass production was highly important, a new era has dawned in terms of job organisation, work practices and therefore income distribution. This era is often referred to as post-Fordism. We shall now examine some of the main arguments associated with this development, including the issue of globalisation.

Post-Fordism – the flexible firm

Post-Fordists believe that the future world of work will be based on flexible working patterns, in which individuality will be recognised and technology will be the basis for most production. People will work in isolation at home, but will be linked to others through the Internet, fax machines and mobile phones. For example Sabel (1982) claims that flexibility has become the buzz word as far as running businesses is concerned. Likewise Atkinson (1985, p. 38) argues that market stagnation (brought about by world recession in general and the UK's disproportionate share of that recession), job losses, uncertainty about future economic growth and technological change have forced firms to implement 'more flexible ways of manning which take account of these new market realities', and although there may be 'sectoral and company centred differences a new, more flexible model is emerging'.

According to Atkinson, this new model is based on two main types of worker: full-time, permanent core workers; and part-time, temporary or casual workers or those subcontracted for a particular job. This type of employment practice enables companies to achieve three types of flexibility:

- Numerical flexibility: fewer workers need to be employed on a permanent basis. Contracts can be short term and workers called upon when needed. Workers can be trained to be multiskilled, so that one person can do jobs previously done by two or more specialists.
- Functional flexibility: the firm concentrates on a single project at a time in order to obtain maxim efficiency for minimum cost. The firm makes use of new technologies and introduces new working methods. Multiskilled staff can be deployed to any area they are needed and conduct a variety of tasks.
- Economic flexibility: the bill for wages can be cut by employing fewer people, and concentrating on a particular area of expertise can reduce costs. Employing female part-time labour can also be financially beneficial as their wages are usually low. Furthermore women are seen as more expendable than men and are accustomed to being viewed and used as a reserve army of labour.

Exercise 7.5

Decide whether the following statements fit into the numerical, functional or economic flexibility categories:

 1. In my firm employees we trained to do a variety of jobs.

 2. My employees work in shifts.

 3. I've replaced some of my workers with agency staff or temporary or contract workers.

 4. I offer collective pay incentives to the workers.

 5. I have replaced full-time workers with part-time workers.

 6. I've reduced my wages bill by employing part-time women workers.

 7. I use the latest technology whereever and whenever I can.

One example of a flexible firm is McDonald's, where little skill is needed and all the tasks can be learnt in one day. Workers are called in when they are needed and none has a permanent contract. If sales go down in a particular branch the response is to cut the number of staff and make the remaining ones work harder.

Exercise 7.6

ku Visit your local McDonald's and assume the role of non-participant observer. Count how many tasks one worker completes in 15 minutes.

According to Piore and Sabel (1984), flexible production methods and the use of multiskilled workers to meet changing demands makes for the ideal firm.

The flexible firm is regarded as post-Fordist because the mass production assembly line has given way to multiskilled workers and teamwork structures that offer workers greater autonomy. However flexibility can also mean less job security and low pay, making the deficit between those with permanent, well-paid jobs and those with part-time or temporary contracts even greater.

Hence the flexible firm can create poverty for some and affluence for others. Whilst some people are always in danger of losing their jobs, others have to work long hours but their skills are transferable and this gives them the chance of transfer or promotion.

The global context

Postmodernists see globalisation as an important factor in everyone's lives. The countries and peoples of the world are becoming increasingly interconnected. Societies are becoming more multicultural and multifaceted, and this raises questions not only about culture and identity but also about the division of spoils between countries in the competition for limited resources. Societies are likely to become more fragmented, and poverty and wealth will be prominent amongst the issues that need to be addressed.

The term globalisation refers to the increasing interdependence and convergence of nations and national economies. No society lives in complete isolation from another. With globalisation, events and actions that take place in one part of the world affect people in many other parts of the world.

Globalisation involves the homogenisation of nation states and an increase in the number of international agencies and institutions (Robertson, 1992). In a globalised world, people and economies are interdependent. Capital and trade flow freely between countries. Transnational corporations (known as TNCs) wield vast economic power, and institutional investors can influence both currency and interest rates. In many cases this benefits First World countries to the detriment of Third World countries – TNCs use their power to make even bigger profits for themselves at the expense of poorer countries with cheaper workforces and weak infrastructure. Economic policy makers are constrained by global financial markets and international investors. As Ankie Hoogvelt (1982, p. 134) states: 'the global distribution of wealth and poverty is . . . a result of market forces reinforcing an accident of history which gave a headstart to European nations'.

Globalisation also has implications for the exploitation of child labour. From the child carpet weavers of Bangladesh, to children as young as eight working in the sex parlours of Thailand, to the child labourers in the charcoal mines of Brazil – child labour is exploited throughout the world to serve the interests of capitalists and capitalism. Companies are aware of the practice but turn a blind eye to it in the interest of profits.

Companies such as Nike and Gap have attracted bad publicity because child labour is used in the third world factories that produce their footwear and garments. The website www.nikesucks.org/ contains a list of claims about the activities of Nike. There are also websites that track the activities of other TNCs, for example www.mcspotlight.org/ tracks the activities of McDonald's.

While it is important to bear in mind that working for such companies may be preferable to the alternatives, this should not be seen as a defence of exploitative practices.

Exercise 7.7

Hold a debate on the motion 'This house believes that Third World workers are exploited.'

One student should act as chair person, one student should propose the motion and one student should oppose the motion. The chairperson should ensure that each student is given the same amount of time to speak and that questions are directed through the chair person to the speakers.

Global inequality

Inequality exists globally as well as locally in all areas of social and economic life. More than a quarter of the people in the developing world still live in poverty and about 1.3 million live on the equivalent of 50 pence a day.

ITEM C

We live in an age with an embarrassment of riches. At least for the lucky few. For them, the tech boom has created as many opportunities as previous industrial revolutions. The rail age had its Vanderbilts, with their gold-encrusted ballrooms; we have Bill Gates, whose personal wealth now equals the combined earnings of sub-Saharan Africa. One man enjoying the income of 137 million – now that's what I call inequality.

The growing global divide between rich and poor is well documented. If you broaden the 'rich' side of the equation from one man, Bill Gates, to the developed world's 200 wealthiest individuals, then you have the equivalent of the entire Third World's income.

(Source: Christopher Walker, Independent on Sunday, 11 February 2001.)

ITEM C **Exercise 7.8**

1. How many people's income does Bill Gates' wealth represent?

2. The riches of how many people do you have to add together to get the income of the entire Third World?

3. How do you feel about this degree of inequality?

Together the countries of South Asia, East Asia and South-East Asia have more than 950 million people who are income poor (do not earn enough to lift themselves out of poverty). Although a number of the economies in this part of the world boomed in the early 1990s, they experienced a very sharp decline and recession in the late 1990s. This was partly due to the irrational nature of the global market, with sudden changes in interest rates and investment decisions, and partly to poor economic policies.

Story of the blues

Fran Abrams in Tunisia and James Astill in Benin tell the tale behind a pair of jeans

Just off the Buttermarket in Ipswich, you will find it: Cromwell's Madhouse. A wide-open jumble of a shop on a corner site, piled high with jeans, sweatshirts, casual trousers and yet more jeans.

And somewhere in the middle, on a dais, there they are, under a huge sign saying: 'Famous Brands for £19.95.' 'Wash inside out separately', it says on the inside label. 100% cotton. But it doesn't say where they come from, which is perhaps just as well, for what would you put, if you really knew? 'Made in Tunisia, Italy, Germany, France, Northern Ireland, Pakistan, Turkey, Japan, Korea, Namibia, Benin, Australia, Hungary'?

For Cromwell's Madhouse is the last stop on a journey which, if it were put end to end, would go right around the earth and half way round again. At a very rough, very conservative estimate, a journey of about 40 000 miles on which components and raw materials criss-cross the globe in a sort of jerky, deranged dance.

These jeans, our jeans, arrived here a few days ago in a van that came up the A12 from Lee Cooper's warehouse at Staple's Corner, just at the bottom of the M1 in north London. There they had the Cromwell's label attached to them before being packaged up and posted off in plenty of time for the weekend rush. Before that, they came through the Channel tunnel on a lorry from a similar warehouse in Amiens, France and before that, by boat and train from Tunis in Tunisia. From Ras Jebel, to be more precise, a good hour's drive north of the city through flat Mediterranean farmland where the fields are fat with artichokes and the pencil cypresses sway in a surprisingly chilly spring breeze.

You can see the red Perspex Lee Cooper sign as you approach the outskirts of Ras Jebel. And it's fitting that you should, for Ras Jebel is Lee Cooperville. Here, 500 women work furiously, eyes down, every muscle clenched. Each has her own small part to play; zips, pockets, side-seams, hems. And each functions like an automaton, pulling a garment from a trolley by her side, throwing it on to her sewing machine, roaring down the seam at full throttle, ripping it off, throwing it back. Over and over. Bonuses depend on it. There are no safety guards on the machines and the women concentrate hard, keeping their fingers from the pounding needles. If they slip up, they can visit the factory nurse.

Trained machinists here take home 220 dinars a month – about £110, or 58p an hour. Comfortably above the legal minimum of 47p per hour before tax, but well below the Tunisian garment industry average of 92p per hour, according to a study published a few years ago. If they meet their targets they can make another 30 dinars, or £15, per month.

(Source: Guardian, 29 May 2001. You can read the full story on the Guardian website at www.guardian.co.uk/Archive/Article/0,4273,4193955,00.html)

For example South Korea, one of the so-called Tiger economies, built up its economy in a relatively short space of time. Property prices soared, foreign investment reached an all time high and manufacturing companies began to borrow very large sums with very little security other than the anticipated profits. Each month these companies had to borrow more in order to buy raw materials to continue production. However the goods they produced would only be paid for in the future, and then only if the demand remained for them. Erosion of the country's currency reserves and changes to the economy led to rapid currency sales and spiralling losses. The economy had few if any safety nets, so the hugely indebted businesses collapsed into bankruptcy.

Exercise 7.9

ITEM D   Read Item D and complete the following tasks:

1. List the advantages and disadvantages to UK consumers of this method of producing jeans.

2. List the advantages and disadvantages to UK workers of this method of producing jeans.

3. List the advantages and disadvantages to Tunisian workers of this method of producing jeans.

4. A pair of trainers is sold for £70 in the UK. The 45 people who made them share the equivalent of £1 between them. Can this be justified? Explain your answer.

Backlash against global forces

A Gallup poll held in 1997 found that two out of three Indians believed their standard of living had fallen since the reform. Many accused large corporations of twisting the economic system to their own ends, to the detriment of most of the population. In 1992 India launched an economic liberalisation policy aimed at development by means of globalisation. This policy resulted in wealth creation for an elite minority but increasing poverty for the vast majority. It also led to the rapid reduction of natural resources that many of the dispossessed relied upon for their very existence.

At the end of the twentieth century there was a backlash against global corporations and the economic policies of such institutions as the World Bank and the International Monetary Fund. Sweatshop workers, tribal groups, women's groups, subsistence farmers, villagers displaced by dams and fisher people opposed what they saw as the recolonisation of India by powerful interest groups and companies.

These coalitions of the dispossessed conducted embarrassing protests that made it difficult for TNCs to operate.

In January 1999 Medha Patkar (the 'Alternative Nobel Prize' winner) was arrested when demonstrating for peasants' rights. It was said that 450 peasant farmers had committed suicide because of the policies of the World Trade Organisation. According to Patkar, 'So-called modern technology has worked against the natural resource based community, undermining self-reliance and creating vulnerability through dependency on pesticides, fertilisers and on the market. They can't stand up against the corporate sector.' (www.worldtradeorg.) Likewise the environmentalist, Vandana Shiva, who led protests against the patenting of Indian seeds and plants by foreign corporations, stated that 'Patents on seeds would destroy 75% of Indian livelihoods linked to the land and the free availability and access to biodiversity (*Economic Review*, 1998)'.

Environmental issues and codes of conduct

In the face of unrest in many parts of the world, transnational corporations and government departments have adopted voluntary codes of environmental and corporate responsibility. In January 1999 the European Parliament proposed that legislation be passed to ensure that European transnational corporations operating in developing countries would comply with minimum standards on such matters as labour conditions, environmental protection, the rights of indigenous peoples and basic human rights in general.

Exercise 7.10

a 1. If you were setting up a code to curb exploitation, what standards would you apply?

a 2. Why have you chosen those particular standards?

e 3. How would you ensure the code was implemented?

a 4. If the code were broken, what sanctions would you bring to bear?

The European Parliament's legislative proposal met intense opposition from the transnationals, which believed that a voluntary code would be more than sufficient. One example of why legislation was considered necessary is that of Shell. This oil and petroleum company had had a code of conduct since the mid 1970s but this had not prevented it from exploiting the Nigerian delta nor did it intervene with the government to try to prevent the execution in November 1995 of Ken Saro-Wiwa, a supporter of the indigenous Ogoni people in their fight against dispossession and the environmental devastation being caused by the company. Ever since operations began, gas flares and oil spills had threatened the livelihood and health of the these people. In the words of one Ogoni song:

> The flames of Shell are flames of Hell,
> We bask below their light,
> Nought for us to serve the blight,
> Of cursed neglect and cursed Shell.

Shell, however, denied that a major problem existed: Naturally the definition of devastation is of paramount importance here. What the Ogoni people regarded as devastation Shell viewed as slight and unavoidable damage.

Almost 14 per cent of Shell's production outside the US takes place in Nigeria, and since operations began Ogoni has yielded about $30 billion in oil revenues. The Nigerian government has become very heavily dependent on oil sales and does all it can to ensure that Shell will continue its work.

Exercise 7.11

You will need to go to a learning resource centre, reference library or newspaper archive to complete this exercise.

$\boxed{i}$ 1. Using books, back issues of magazines (for example *The Economist*) and newspapers (for example November 1995 issues of the *Guardian* and *The Times*), plus the Internet (if available, www.gem.co.za/ELA ogoni.fact.html) find out as much as you can about Shell and the Ogoni situation.

$\boxed{i}\boxed{a}$ 2. Why was this situation allowed to develop?

The issue of debt

In the 1980s Mexico threatened to renege on its external debt repayments. This was seen as endangering Western financial markets and was eventually resolved by the Brady Initiative, which enabled Mexico to reduce the value of its debt.

When further debt crises occurred in the 1990s the International Monetary Fund and the World Bank announced an initiative to reduce external debt to a sustainable level. When a country is designated as a 'highly indebted poor country' its creditors are required to assess its indebtedness, based on the value of its export earnings, and share the burden of debt cancellation. A country's debt is considered unsustainable if it amounts to more than 2.5 times its annual export earnings, and 41 countries have been assessed to date.

Since the 1990s Africa, which is the world's most heavily indebted continent, has suffered a fall in investment, a drop in income levels and a rise in its infant and maternal mortality rates. Yet Africa is rich in mineral resources – it has 99 per cent of the world's chrome reserves,

85 per cent of its platinum, 68 per cent of its cobalt and 54 per cent of its gold. It is how these are exploited and who benefits from their exploitation that lies at the heart of the problem.

Many countries borrow extensively to overcome their balance of payments difficulties (when the value of imports amounts to more than the value of exports from the country). In the 1980s and 1990s rapid rises in interest rates meant that many countries were unable to service their debt repayments, and as a consequence some 700 million of the world's poorest people suffered a fall in their standard of living.

ITEM E

International debt, selected developing countries

	Total external debt 1994		Debt service as % of exports of goods and services	Total net official development assistance received (% of 1994 GNP)	Net foreign direct investment (% of GNP)	Terms of trade (1987 = 100)
	(US$ billion)	(% of GNP)				
Rep. of Korea	54.5	15	7	(.)	−0.2	92
Venezuela	36.8	66	21	0.1	−0.1	82
Malaysia	24.8	37	8	0.2	8.7	92
Brazil	151.1	28	36	0.1	−0.1	101
Sri Lanka	7.8	68	9	48.0	1.8	88
Indonesia	96.5	57	32	0.8	1.4	79
China	100.5	19	9	0.7	1.2	105
Ghana	5.4	102	25	12.1	1.8	64
India	99.0	34	27	0.6	0.2	100
Tanzania	7.4	230	20	–	0.8	82
Uganda	3.5	88	46	20.4	0.1	58
Mozambique	5.5	450	23	90.4	2.4	124
Ethiopia	5.1	110	12	18.7	–	74
Rwanda	0.5	165	15	122.8	0.2	75

(Source: Economic Review, Data Supplement, September 1998.)

ITEM E   *Exercise 7.12*

Study Item E and answer the following questions:

[i] 1. In which country had the highest debt?

[i] 2. Which country had the lowest debt?

[i] 3. What was the combined debt of these countries in 1994?

Debt repayments absorb money that could be used for purposes such as education, health care and housing, or to promote economic growth. So debt creates a vicious circle where the poor grow poorer instead of progressing.

The World Bank and IMF only grant aid or loans to countries that agree to run their economy in a prescribed manner. For example the stabilisation or structural adjustment programmes require governments to control their spending 'by limiting credit, cutting public social expenditure and sometimes public investment. For example the government of Morocco with the approval of the World Bank and the IMF has been carrying out a programme of cuts in domestic public expenditure which benefits the poor' (Hayter, 1989, p. 68).

Debt write-off

The devastation caused by Hurricane Mitch in November 1998 – the biggest natural disaster to strike Central America for 200 years – came after poor crop yields in 1997 had already severely affected the poverty-stricken people of the region. However the hurricane did draw press attention to the debt burden of developing countries, and the coalition Jubilee 2000 called on creditor nations to write off the debts of the poorest nations by the start of the new millennium. At the Brit Awards in February 1999 the Irish pop star Bono brought the campaign to the attention of the thousands of young people who watched the awards on TV, and the public was urged to place pressure on governments to write off the debts of countries devastated by disaster. To give some idea of the scale of the problem, Nicaragua – a victim of Hurricane Mitch – currently owes £800 per person, the world's highest per capita debt.

Exercise 7.13

kua Write a letter of appeal to the government on behalf of Jubilee 2000, clearly stating your case for wiping out Third World debt and justifying your arguments.

Gordon Brown (Chancellor of the Exchequer in the Labour government) has suggested that creditors should recognise a category of 'post-catastrophe' countries to be given what is termed fast track relief, but this would merely postpone their debts, rather than write them off. France, on the other hand, has already written off the debts owed to it by Honduras and Nicaragua.

Food issues

According to the United Nations Human Development Report (1996), between the 1960s and 1990s the poorest 20 per cent of the world's population experienced a decline in their share of global income from 2.3 per cent to 1.4 per cent. Economic decline has affected 100 countries and the income of 1.6 billion people has fallen. Populations have become even more economically polarised, both between and within countries.

In 1998 it was estimated that the number of hungry people in the world had risen to 828 million, following a decline in hunger over the previous 20 years. One in five people in the world is chronically hungry and it is thought that 30 million people die every year from lack of food. According to poor people in urban areas spend up to 80 per cent of their income on food.

In the late 1990s the head of the United Nations World Food Programme, Catherine Bertini, warned of the likelihood of a dramatic increase in hunger. In 1998 drought, poor harvests and high unemployment resulted in millions of new hungry poor in Indonesia alone. Children and the elderly in particular are expected to require hundreds of millions of dollars worth of food assistance if they are to survive.

The largest proportion of food-poor countries are in Africa, south of the Sahara Desert, and in Somalia famine killed 300 000 people in 1991 and 1992. In order for at least one of the family to be able to work and thus bring home food, that member has to be given food at the expense of the others, who may die in the interim.

Global wealth, global income

In Chapter 2, wealth and income were discussed in relation to gross domestic product and gross national product in the UK context. This section will apply these measures to other countries.

The United Nations Development Programme (UNDP) has produced a set of per capita GDP measures based on relative prices as these offer a better idea of local purchasing power (what can be bought with the local currency in any given place rather than what can be bought with a US dollar). This is known as purchasing power parity (PPP). The UNDP has also drawn up a human development index (HDI), based on three main elements: resources, knowledge and longevity (expected life span).

Human development statistics, 1994

	Real GDP per capita (PPP$)	GNP per capita (US$)	Life expectancy at birth (years)	Adult literacy rate (%)	Combined gross school enrolment (%)	Human development index	Military expenditure as % of health and education	% of population with access to safe water	Population with <$1 per day in PPP$ (%)
Rwanda	352	80	22.6	59.2	37	0.187	25	–	45.7
Ethiopia	427	100	48.2	34.5	18	0.244	190	25	33.8
Uganda	1 370	190	40.2	61.1	34	0.328	18	38	50.0
Tanzania	656	140	50.3	66.8	34	0.357	77	38	16.4
Nigeria	1 351	280	51.0	55.6	50	0.393	33	51	28.9
Pakistan	2 154	430	62.3	37.1	38	0.445	125	74	11.6
India	1 348	320	61.3	51.2	56	0.446	65	81	52.5
Moldova	1 576	870	67.7	98.9	67	0.612	–	–	6.8
China	2 604	530	68.9	80.9	58	0.626	114	67	29.4
Indonesia	3 740	880	63.5	83.2	62	0.668	49	62	14.5
Brazil	5 362	2 970	66.4	82.7	72	0.783	23	73	28.7
Malaysia	8 865	3 480	71.2	83.0	62	0.832	38	78	5.6
Thailand	7 104	2 410	69.5	93.5	53	0.833	71	89	0.1
Czech Republic	9 201	3 200	72.2	99.0	70	0.882	–	–	3.1
Singapore	20 987	25 500	77.1	91.0	72	0.900	129	100	–
Greece	11 265	7 700	77.8	96.7	82	0.923	71	–	–
UK	18 620	18 340	76.7	99.0	86	0.931	40	100	–
Canada	21 459	19 510	79.0	99.0	100	0.960	15	100	–

(Source: Economic Review, September 1998.)

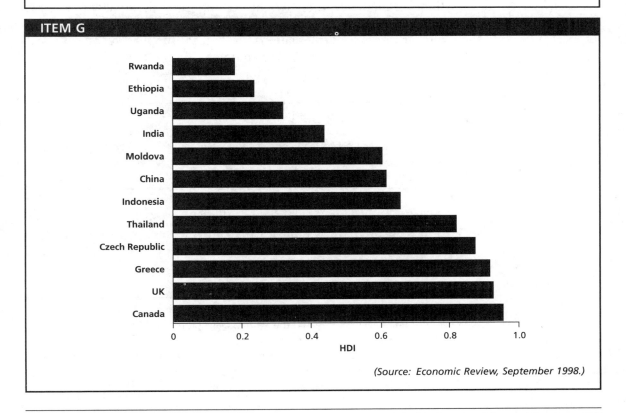

(Source: Economic Review, September 1998.)

ITEM F AND G

Exercise 7.14

Study Items F and G carefully and answer the following questions:

i
1. The last column of the table in Item F shows the percentage of people who lived on less than $1 per day in 1994. Which country had the highest number of such people?

i *a*
2. Which country had the lowest literacy rate? How would you explain this?

i *a*
3. Which country had the highest military expenditure? How would you explain this?

i
4. Which country has the highest human development index in 1994?

i
5. Which country had the lowest?

i *a*
6. Using the information in Item F, summarise the trends that occurred.

Aid

The other side of the debt-reduction coin is to give aid to countries, on top of that provided in response to natural and man-made disasters. Aid can be short, medium or long term and the nature of it varies from situation to situation. Aid can be multilateral, whereby countries channel their donations through international organisations, or bilateral, where by one country gives aid directly to another. Aid can take numerous forms, such as military arms, equipment and/or forces in war situations, or medical supplies, technical expertise and aerial water bombing equipment in the case of forest fires.

Exercise 7.15

Since 1998, which countries have been given military aid?

For what reasons was it given? (Hint: you do not know, go to your library or learning resource centre and consult the December 1998 to February 1999 issues of the *Guardian*, *The Times* or the *Telegraph*. If you have access to a CD Rom, information can be obtained by typing in UN Forces.)

There is also project aid for specific purposes, such as the building of a dam or roads. Countries that provide such aid expect to have control over the project and how it is developed.

Exercise 7.16

Go to your library or learning resource centre and using CD Roms or the Internet (if available) research the Pergau Dam project in Malaysia. Internet site www.oneworld.org/news/reportswdm-nov97.html is useful. The Pergau dam affair happened in 1994 and reports from that time are available. The geography department of your institution may be able to help with articles. On the basis of your research, answer the following questions:

1. Why did the project cause a storm of protest?

2. Who funded the project?

3. For what purpose was the dam built?

4. Who would benefit most from the dam?

5. How would the indigenous population be affected by the dam?

Because of the strong correlation between lack of education and the growth of poverty, aid is also given to build schools or improve educational facilities. This is meant to offer hope of future employment and generally benefit the nation by improving the education of the populace. However some forms of education do not lead to employment and may even be counter productive because the skills taught are not those needed to improve the life chances and day-to-day circumstances of the poor.

According to a Unicef report published in 1998 (Bellpmy, 1998), 50 per cent of 15–18 year old Sri Lankan children drop out of school each year, and 12 per cent of 5–14 year olds in low-income areas never attend school. The overall rate of non-attendance can be as high as 30 per cent. Despite government claims of a 90 per cent literacy rate in Sri Lanka, the UN (1998) estimates that the rate of functional literacy is only 50 per cent.

Exercise 7.17

1. What is meant by functional literacy?

2. How would education help to improve the lot of the Sri Lankan people?

3. Who would benefit most if Sri Lankan people were better educated? Explain your answer.

Theoretical arguments on globalisation

It is possible to identify three broad theoretical positions on globalisation.

Firstly, there are those who consider that globalisation really is taking place and that it will have a huge effect on our lives. This view is associated with a number of writers from the new right who believe that benefits will flow from the globalisation of the free market. This view is also held by many supporters of New Labour, notably Anthony Giddens (1999b), David Held (1995) and Geoff Mulgan (1998). The reluctance of the New Labour government to raise taxes can be partly explained by the effect this would have on UK competitiveness in the global economy.

Secondly, there are those who believe that the issue is being over-hyped and that the old economic roles still apply. Further more Paul Hirst and Graham Thompson (1999) argue that the world economy was more internationalised before the First World War than it is today.

Finally, commentators such as Wiseman (1998) argue that while there has been a significant shift in the way that things are organised in the world, notably in relation to work with the emergence of transnational corporations and almost instantaneous communication, this does not mean that the full-blown globalisation thesis can be accepted. Rather globalisation is uneven, sporadic and uncertain.

Hence we can see that there is no consensus on the issue of globalisation. But one thing is clear: wherever people happen to live, the actions of people living on the other side of the world will affect their lives in one way or another.

8 Welfare and the welfare state

By the end of this chapter you should be able to:

- define the term the welfare state;
- explain what the welfare state does;
- Outline the different perspectives on the welfare state.

Introduction

> This is the greatest advance in our history. There can be no turning back. From now on Beveridge is not the name of a man; it is the name of a way of life, and not only for Britain, but for the whole civilised world (Beveridge, 1942).

This chapter examines the rationale behind the concept and development of the UK welfare state. It explores different theoretical perspectives on the role of the state in welfare provision as these perspectives have had a profound effect on social policy and the way in which it has been operationalised. The historical evolution of the welfare state is examined so as present day welfare provision can be more easily understood if the principles that produced it are taken into consideration.

What is the welfare state?

Exercise 8.1

You live in a welfare state. What does that mean to you?

a 1. Write down what you think a welfare state is and what it does.

i e 2. Compare what you have written with the definition set out below.

There appears to be a general consensus that a welfare state is one in which the government intervenes in the workings of the economy to ensure a minimum income for all, and commits itself to providing essential services such as health care according to need. All of us use the welfare state and are recipients of the benefits provided by it.

Exercise 8.2

a Which of the provisions of the welfare state have you or your family received? Write your answers in a table copied from the one below. We have provided two examples to start you off.

Welfare service	How I benefit
Social security	Child benefit
Education	Free schooling
Health care	

According to government figures, about 14 per cent of the population are totally dependent on the state for their income, and it can be argued that the welfare state is actually causing them to live in poverty because benefit payments are so low. There are a number of reasons for this. At the time of the implementation of the Beveridge Report (which will be discussed in a later section) benefits were set some 40–45 per cent lower than the level deemed necessary to avoid poverty. In more recent times the benefits received by single unemployed people as a percentage of average earnings were effectively reduced from 20.8 per cent in 1986 to 19.1 per cent in 1988 (*Guardian*, 12 May 1989). Hence we cannot consider the welfare state as unproblematic, and in fact it may reinforce the very problems it set out to solve because it is not generous enough with its money.

However an alternative view is that providing people with money for doing nothing will cause them to become helpless and dependent. For example as long ago as 1846 *The Economist* warned of 'The general helplessness of the masses that is sure to be induced by the state undertaking to pay for their welfare. They come to rely on it and take no care for themselves. They trust in it and become its dependants.' This view continues to prevail amongst the new right and to guide their thinking on the welfare state.

To summarise, on the one hand there those who view the welfare state as a vital part of a civilised and humane society and sometimes criticise it for being insufficiently generous to achieve this aim; on the other hand there are those who view it as creating a culture of dependency. It is important to bear in mind that arguments about the function and structure of the welfare state have been going on since the earliest days of welfare provision in this country.

The origins of the welfare state

In order to understand how the present system developed it is necessary to study the changes that have taken place in the last 400 years in respect of state intervention in the welfare of its citizens. Figure 8.1 traces the history of welfare provision and gives a breakdown of how the system has evolved.

Exercise 8.3

Update the diagram by providing a summary of developments since 1988.

Trowler (1989) suggests that there have been four ages of provision, as follows.

The first age

In the sixteenth century, help for the poor and sick was largely provided by family and friends, although the church gave some help by dispensing alms. This kind of help is now referred to as voluntary or informal welfare provision, and it still exists today.

The Poor Law of 1601 and associated legislation made parishes (local areas) responsible for poor relief, paid for by local rates. These laws established several key principles:

- The state had a responsibility to prevent destitution, to raise taxes in order to do so and to ensure that an administrative framework existed to provide the necessary services.
- Any assistance offered to those who were able to work should be made conditional.
- A distinction should be made between those who were unable to work and those who were capable of working but were jobless.

Link Exercise 8.1

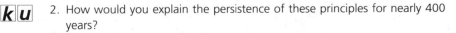

i *a* 1. Drawing on information in Chapter 9 and this chapter, list the similarities and differences between the principles of the Poor Law of 1601 and those of today.

k *u* 2. How would you explain the persistence of these principles for nearly 400 years?

The Poor Law made a distinction between the deserving and the undeserving poor, and this still exists to day.

The second age

In 1832 a commission was set up to examine the Poor Law and as a result of its findings the Poor Law Amendment Act was passed in 1834. The commission was opposed to giving cash assistance to the working poor and recommended that dependency on the state should be discouraged by harsh measures. This led to the establishment of workhouses, where the able-bodied poor were housed and fed in exchange for work. Conditions in the workhouses were so harsh that only the desperate would go there as a last resort. (Charles Dickens' *Oliver Twist* contains graphic descriptions of workhouse conditions.)

The opposite approach to workers was taken by the social reformer Robert Owen in the early part of the nineteenth century. Owen, a mill owner, was convinced of the importance of a good social environment and beneficial working conditions, so he provided good-quality housing for his workers, schools for their children and good working conditions in his factories, and attempted to prove to the world the benefits of such measures.

The third age

The Victorian age epitomised the idea that state intervention was not the best policy, but increasingly the state did have to intervene due to industrialisation and the growth of towns. Pressure for change and reform grew because by the late 1880s some sections of the working class had been given voting rights and there was need for an educated and healthy workforce. Furthermore the studies on poverty by Charles Booth (1901) and Seebohm Rowntree (1901) drew attention to the extent of the poverty that prevailed.

These factors prompted policy reviews, and in 1905 labour exchanges were set up (the equivalent of today's Job Centres). In 1906 the Liberal Party, which was in government at the time, introduced the policies that formed the bedrock of the welfare state. Among the measures introduced were school meals and school medical inspections, and (in 1908) an old age pension for those aged 70 and over. In 1909 the Trades Board Act laid the foundation for minimum wages in vulnerable industries. The 1911 National Insurance Act brought into existence a compulsory health insurance scheme, into which workers and employers paid flat-rate contributions.

After the First World War (1914–18) there was a huge economic depression and mass unemployment. A Ministry of War Pensions was set up in 1917 to deal with claims from those who had served in the war. In 1920 unemployment insurance was extended to almost all workers below a certain income level, and in 1925 pensions for widows and orphans were introduced. By the late 1920s economic recession and rising unemployment meant that large numbers of people were exhausting their time-limited access to benefit and were forced to turn to local poor relief. The 1934 Unemployment Assistance Act created a two-tier benefit system, with contribution-based benefits being paid for the first six months of unemployment followed by centrally administered, means-tested benefits for as long as necessary.

The fourth age

In 1942 the *Report on Social Insurance and Allied Services* (or as it came to be known, the Beveridge Report) was published. Within a month 100 000 copies had been sold, which was unprecedented, as was its impact on the general public at the time and on future governments once its recommendations were implemented.

The main goal of the recommendations was to eradicate what Beveridge termed the 'five giant evils': disease, want, idleness, ignorance and squalor. Disease meant illnesses such as measles in children, tuberculosis in the general population, diphtheria and general illnesses that affected large numbers of people. Want is another term for poverty and Beveridge used it in that context. Idleness referred to people who had no livelihood, and was therefore another term for unemployment. Ignorance meant lack of education – illiteracy and innumeracy were preventing many people from achieving their full potential. Squalor meant dirty, unhygienic conditions and was linked to poor housing (see Chapter 10).

Exercise 8.4

1. List the ways in which you would tackle the five giant evils.

2. Working in a group of four, copy the following table onto a large sheet of paper and write down your solutions to the five evils. Would the eradication of any one of these lead to the eradication of one or more of the others?

Beveridge's giant evils	How it could be tackled?	Would this lead to the eradication of any of the other evils?
Disease	Free national health service	
Want		
Idleness		
Ignorance		
Squalor		

Having worked out your solutions, read on and see what Beveridge suggested.

- To eradicate disease the new National Health Service would provide free health care for the entire population. All health care would be funded by the state.
- To eradicate want there would be a universal National Insurance system for all adults, funded by compulsory, contribution by all those in work. This system would provide sickness benefit, old age pensions and a family allowance for second and subsequent children.
- To eradicate idleness there would be a return to full employment by means of state intervention in the economy. Only those unable to work because of sickness or disability would be excused from work and awarded benefits.
- To eradicate ignorance there would be free education for all in state-funded schools, colleges of further education and universities.
- To eradicate squalor there would be a nationwide programme to build low-rent public housing of a good standard for those who needed it. These homes would be 'fit for heroes to live in' (see Chapter 4).

Link Exercise 8.2

[i] [a] Drawing on information in Chapter 10 and this chapter, describe (1) how the welfare state brought about changes in housing policy and (2) the effects these changes had.'

Since the inception of the welfare state the revenue needed to finance it has been raised in two ways: through general taxation and through National Insurance payments. The welfare state operates at both the central government and the local government level and provides a variety of services, based on the recommendations of the Beveridge Report.

The various aspects of the welfare state are handled by a range of designated departments, the names of which change from time to time. For instance in 1988 the Department for Health and Social Security (DHSS) was split into two separate departments, namely the Department of Health (DoH) and the Department of Social Security (DSS), and in the early 1990s the Department for Education and Science (DES) was changed to the Department for Education and Employment (DfEE). In 2001 the government created the Department of Work and Pensions, which took over many of the tasks of the DSS and the employment section of the DfEE. In 2001 the name of the latter was changed again, this time to the Department for Education and Skills (DfES).

Exercise 8.5

a **i**
u

Draw up a list of the government departments that are currently responsible for the administration of the welfare state and summarise the main areas each one deals with.

Exercise 8.6

k u a

1. Make a list of the services provided by your local authorities. (Hint: do they provide a library, home help, meals on wheels?)

k u e

2. Which services do you use? Does this depend on your age, gender or class?

The golden age of welfare

The Labour government of 1945–51 implemented Beveridge's proposals through various Acts of Parliament. In the main the Conservative governments of 1951–64 maintained Labour's welfare policies and it was during this time (1957), in an election rally in Bedford, that Prime Minister Harold Macmillan made his famous 'You've never had it so good' speech. The British public apparently agreed with this statement and voted the Conservative Party into office for another term (1959–64). By 'never had it so good' Macmillan meant that employment was at an all-time high, free education had improved people's employment prospects, there was better housing and an efficient health service, and the benefit system provided a safety net for those in need.

Since 1948 more than 120 Acts of Parliament and thousands of pieces of lesser legislation have altered the welfare system in both minor and major ways. For example there have been nine separate Acts on pensions since the first one was passed in 1906. Within five years of the introduction of pensions they were costing the government twice as much as had been expected, and because people are now living to a more advanced age a quarter of a million of today's pensioners began their working lives before the first contributory pensions were introduced in 1925. The contributions made today by a 16 year old may affect their income in 50 years' time. The amounts spent on the disability and care benefits introduced in the 1970s have also massively exceeded the original estimates. (Some of these changes and challenges, along with the other two ages of welfare, are discussed in Chapter 8.) The welfare state was set up with the notion of universal provision as its guiding principle. This principle has since been criticised by successive governments for its economic unviability.

Theoretical perspectives on the welfare state

There are a number of differing perspectives on the welfare state in terms of its inception, development, in whose interests it is run and who the main beneficiaries are.

New Right theories

A state which does for its citizens what they can do for themselves is an evil state . . . in such an irresponsible society no one cares, no one saves, no one bothers – why should they when the state spends all its energies taking money from the energetic, successful and thrifty to give to the idle, the failures and the feckless?, said Charles Murray (quoted in Trowler, 1989).

This line of thought originated in the nineteenth century with Adam Smith and John Stuart Mill and was later taken up by the economist Milton Friedman and new right thinkers such as Friedrich Hayek. At its heart is the idea that for a capitalist economy to operate efficiently there has to be a free market in labour and goods, with minimum of state intervention. People should not have to contribute to the welfare of others unless they choose to do so through charitable donations. There is an emphasis on individual endeavour and free choice. In order to nurture this, state intervention has to be kept to the minimum.

Proponents of this view are not totally opposed to state welfare provision, but believe that help should only be offered to those who truly need it because they cannot help themselves. Welfare should not be provided as a right, nor viewed as such. According to some on the new right it would have been better if the welfare state had never been established. For example, in Friedman's view, 'Most of the present welfare programmes should never have been enacted. If they had not been, many of the people now dependent on them would have become self-reliant individuals instead of wards of state' (Friedman, 1980, p. 22).

Exercise 8.7

To what extent do you agree with Friedman? Write a reasoned argument in 500 words.

According to Saunders (1995), a sociologist with new right sympathies, the welfare state has added to the growth of human unhappiness rather than alleviated it. For example 'Single parenthood . . . was not a viable option for most women before various welfare reforms from the 1960s onwards provided financial support for it' (ibid., p. 96). Until the 1960s there was no single-parent allowance and bringing up children alone could cause severe economic hardship. However changes to the benefit system made lone-parenting financially easier and many women chose to follow that course. Hence the welfare state came to be seen as encouraging women to become single parents.

In one respect the New Right position is rather contradictory. According to the New Right, married women should be encouraged to stay at home to look after their children and provide a stable home and loving maternal care so that their children will become upright, responsible citizens. However, single mothers are expected to leave their children to go to work and cease being a benefitclaimant. Is money at the heart of the matter here, rather than maternal care?

The New Right is concerned that, in order to ensure votes at election time, the government may be forced to give in to pressure groups and provide more and more benefits. This will put a financial strain on other areas where the money and resources would be better utilised. Universal benefits such as Family Allowance are paid to many people who do not need them, and therefore all benefits should be made selective and subject to need.

These ideas formed the basis of the ideology of Margaret Thatcher and her government. The emphasis was placed on individuals taking responsibility for themselves and their families rather than depending on the state. The Conservative minister Sir Keith Joseph (now deceased) believed that 'The only lasting help we can give to the poor is to help them to help themselves; to do the opposite, to create more dependency, is to destroy them morally, whilst throwing an unfair burden on society' Government policy was aimed at creating a more dynamic economy in which the extra wealth generated would 'trickle down' (see Chapter 2) to those on lower incomes.

More recently David Marsland (1996) has contended that welfare provision should be made subject to contract – that is, benefit claimants should be made to sign contracts listing their obligations as claimants, rather than being given benefits with no responsibilities attached to them. Like Saunders (1995) he focuses on the negative aspects of welfare: 'The welfare state inflicts damaging levels of moral and psychological harm on its supposed beneficiaries. It has seduced the British public away from their natural independence of spirit and their traditional commitment to hard work, honesty and high standards' (Marsland, 1996, p. 102). If people had to sign a contract that bound them to certain obligations they would be less keen to remain dependent on the state and would be encouraged to provide for themselves through hard work and endeavour.

In 1994 the right-wing Adam Smith Institute said the welfare state should be scrapped because the benefit system was costing the country up to £79 billion a year, which was one third of the government's total expenditure. Not only was the welfare state expensive, it was also eroding people's will to work. The president of the institute, Madsen Pirie, suggested that automatic benefits should be scaled down, and that people should be encouraged to make private provision for health care and pensions.

In summary, those on the new right consider that benefits are handed out far too readily and the state is encouraging people to become welfare-dependent by being overly generous. It must allow market forces to dominate, and it should introduce policies to make the poor less dependent and more self-reliant.

Marxist theories

For Marxists, as long as capitalism remains at the heart of society it is impossible to envisage great changes taking place in the provision of welfare. It is because inequality is deliberately created that the welfare state fails those who need it most. The welfare state is seen as an instrument to manipulate the working class. A healthy workforce is needed to keep industry running and that workforce needs to be educated to a certain standard to be able to operate efficiently; the health service and education system answer these needs. Welfare reforms can also be seen as manipulating the working class in that they tend to make the working class feel that something is being done and therefore they complain less. The welfare state is used to pacify the working class, to make them believe they hold a stake in society and will receive fair treatment and consideration.

O'Connor (1984) believes that the state has to legitimate itself by appearing to be just to all its citizens, but this causes conflict as capitalism has to generate profits at little cost – and the welfare state does cost. Taxpayers many want more services but they are not really prepared to pay for them, and high state expenditure on welfare makes the system dysfunctional for the purposes of capitalism. As the problems the welfare state was set up to overcome were created by capitalist society in the first place, it is unlikely that the system will operate to the benefit of the less well off in society. O'Connor (1973) contends that the modern capitalist state has two functions: to aid the accumulation of capital and to legitimate its social relations. Hence state expenditure can be divided into investment in social capital, and social expenses. Welfare benefits are a social expense, and the production processes factories that produce profits are part of social capital. Due to the increasingly social nature of production under modern capitaism, state investment becomes ever more necessary to ensure profitability and the private accumulation of wealth, so cuts have to be made elsewhere, usually in social expenses.

As Kincaid (1973) points out, the benefits paid to the poor are pitifully low – deliberately so as the poor have to be kept poor so that capitalism can thrive. The state cannot afford to eliminate poverty if it is done at the expense of capitalism and the making of profits. The welfare state is profit-depleting rather than is profit-making if it is run in a truly altruistic way.

According to Offe (1984), 'While capitalism cannot coexist with the welfare state neither can it exist without the welfare state.' The welfare state both sustains and threatens the existence of capitalism. He believes that capitalism can survive with a minimal welfare state for the very poor, with others relying on private provision. He refers to an era of 'disorganised capitalism' in which the precarious balance between the market economy, political democracy and the welfare state has become destabilised.

In Offe's view there needs to be a strategy for equality that involves higher taxation for the better off and the provision of more benefits for the worse off. In this regard Offe envisages a pivotal role being played by new social movements such as feminism, environmentalism and pacifism, which offer the possibility of socially oriented policies being brought to play. At the moment state provision of education, health services and housing, for example, is promoted to remedy the weaknesses of capitalism. It is provided in the form of policy, subject to the rules of the political subsystem. The problems that social policy appears to address are issues within the political and administrative system rather than strategies designed to benefit those in need.

Regardless of whether social policy is designed to prevent or relieve hardship, to institutionalise (keep in hospitals) or help the needy (care in the community) it confronts a 'compatibility' problem – who is providing the services, and why? The services must be funded and this is the heart of the problem. The provision of welfare absorbs taxes and labour power at the expense of the market economy. The development of welfare services involves the expansion of forms of production that are not governed by the rules of market exchange, and certain interest groups have tried to increase the size of the welfare state in order to generate expectations that the state cannot meet.

Underpinning the policies on and strategies for the welfare state have been the fundamental economic changes associated with global capital investment (see Chapter 3). These have undermined the prospect of full employment, upon which the Keynesian welfare state was built, and divided the workforce into a secure core and a vulnerable periphery with different welfare interests.

Marxists have been criticised for insisting that the economic base of society is the determining factor in all spheres of life and for disregarding other factors. The welfare state can be seen as being autonomous from the economy while still having some relationship with it, in that it is not entirely economically driven but has an ideological basis as well.

In recent years, thinkers who straddle the Social Democratic and Marxist lines have outlined an alternative approach to the problem of welfare that seeks to avoid the problems of bureaucracy and central control inherent in the standard social democratic model. For example the Basic Income European Network (BIEN) utilises the notion of citizenship to argue that all adults should be provided with a basic income. This would give people greater choice over their working lives by removing their dependence on unsatisfactory employment as the main source of income. This proposal also accords with environmentalists' desire to remove work from the central place it holds in our lives as they consider we can get by with less.

Andre Gorz (1999), a key advocate of this strategy, argues that giving all citizens a basic social income would free them from the constraints of the labour market and enable them to reject jobs with inhuman working conditions. One key problem here is, why would anyone work if the basic income was sufficient to live on? But if no-one worked there would be no production and no money to fund this basic income. Gorz argues that this problem could be solved by redistributing society's wealth. While it might be argued that this would provide sufficient money, the questions of political resistance to it and what to do once the wealth runs out have not been satisfactorily answered.

Michael Burawoy and Erik Olin Wright (2000, pp. 39–40) also argue in favour of an unconditional and universal basic grant:

> while the details may vary, the basic idea is quite simple: Every citizen receives a monthly living stipend sufficient to live at a culturally-defined respectable standard of living, say 125% of the 'poverty line'. The grant is unconditional on the performance of any labour or other form of contribution, and it is universal – everyone receives the grant as a matter of citizenship right. Grants go to individuals, not families. Parents are the custodians of minority children's grants.

Since this grant would replace all other welfare benefits, they argue that the extra cost would not be excessive. They recognise that questions have to be addressed about the practical feasibility of such a scheme, notably whether anyone would bother to work and whether wealthy people would move their money elsewhere to avoid having it confiscated to pay for the grant. With this in mind they argue that in many countries it may only be possible to institute such a system if socialism is achieved, although in some rich countries it might be possible to implement such a policy within capitalism.

Another question to be addressed is the level of basic income to be provided. Burawoy and Olin Wright talk about the level being set with reference to a 'culturally-defined respectable standard of living', which by its nature will vary from place to place and is therefore akin to the notion of relative poverty.

In her book *Low Cost but Acceptable: a Minimum Income Standard for the UK*, Hermione Parker *et al.* (2000) insists that any discussion of the level of income necessary to avoid poverty needs to be grounded in facts and figures generated from objective study rather than involving subjective issues such as participation and citizenship. Parker's approach to a minimum income standard, which is based on what the terms low cost but acceptable budgets for families, is not as radical as Burawoy and Olin Wright's proposal, and it is important to be aware that there are differing versions of the notion of a basic income that in some ways mirror the distinction between absolute and relative notions of poverty. (You can find out more about these ideas at www.citizensincome.org.uk/ and Erik Olin Wright's website: www.ssc.wisc.edu/~wright/)

Feminist theories

Like Marxists, feminists see the welfare state as perpetuating inequality. However they see it in terms of the inequality that results from male dominance and patriarchy. Patriarchy is a power structure in which dominant men have control and power over women, who are viewed as weak and subordinate. This is part of the fabric of the welfare state in that the latter contains the notion of female dependency. As Land (1978) points out, cited in Oppenheim (1990) when the National Insurance Act came into being in 1911 it was mainly concerned with insuring male workers against unemployment and sickness. Later, in accordance with the recommendations of the Beveridge Report (1942), married women were allowed to opt out of paying full national insurance contributions as it was presumed that their husbands would provide for them and that they would not work outside the home. Even today, if a woman cohabits with a man it is presumed he will take financial responsibility for her, their rendering her ineligible for Income Support. Until recently married women's tax affairs had to be handled by their husbands, which meant that men knew all about their wives' financial business but the wives knew nothing about their husbands' if the latter did not want them to.

Bryson (1992) argues that while women are the main recipient of welfare provision the welfare state takes better care of the interests of men. Because of the employment situation and the fact that women live longer than men, more women than men receive Family Allowance, Attendance Allowance, Single Parent Allowance, housing benefit and the state pension, and are therefore seen as more of a drain on the welfare state.

According to Doyal (1995), the main factor to consider when looking at women's experience of health is the impact of poverty and deprivation. It is necessary to investigate how women in poverty live their lives so that measures can be taken to improve their chances and allow them greater independence. Improved child care would enable more women to take part in the labour market, and this would also benefit the state in terms of reduced benefit payments.

Feminist Marxists such as Michele Barrett (1980) argue that the welfare state perpetuates female inequality by idealising the nuclear family, with a wage-earning father and a stay-at-home, caring mother. As women are expected to care for children and the elderly, this in effect means that women are unpaid workers for the state. Obviously women also work as paid employees of the state, often working part-time for low wages. It is here that dual systems theory comes into play (see Walby, 1990, and Bradley, 1989, amongst others). Capitalism and patriarchy combine to oppress women and keep them in subordinate roles in society. The two strands are structural elements of both the public sphere (the workplace and society in general) and the private sphere (the home). Policies such as care in the community place a particular burden on women, a burden they are expected to bear without complaint. The way in which women's labour is exploited in the home (being expected to care for elderly relatives, sick children and male partners) is part of the patriarchal mode of production.

In 1977 Patrick Jenkin, who was later to become a cabinet minister in the Conservative government, said: 'Quite frankly I don't think that mothers have the same right to work as fathers do. . . . We hear a lot about social work – perhaps the most important social work is motherhood' (Walby (1990) p. 62). This attitude still prevailed when the Conservative government took power in 1979 and it formed the backbone of many of its policies, as will be discussed in Chapter 9.

Hence feminists see the welfare state as exercising social control over women by making them responsible for the wellbeing of both themselves and others. Women also lack autonomy in other areas. For example in childbirth, which usually takes place in NHS maternity units, the terms are mainly dictated by doctors and midwives, who are often not willing to allow pregnant women to do as they would like during labour and delivery. Many women report feeling dehumanised by their treatment. Radical feminists call for the provision of women-only hospitals and clinics, and for the setting up of women's cooperatives so that women can opt out of the patriarchal system and have a voice in their own welfare and welfare rights. As long as the welfare state remains a patriarchal institution it will continue to fail women.

Social democratic views

For social democrats, social and economic objectives are linked. For example the promotion of full employment was at the heart of the Beveridge Report and is now an objective of the New Labour government. In the UK social democracy is associated with the Fabian tradition on the left of the Labour Party. The Fabian Society was founded in 1884 to pursue social reform through gradual but persistent democratic means. Fabianism was based on practical politics and moral principles. The practical politics later involved the exercise of working-class power through the trade union movement to persuade the holders of wealth to agree to the redistribution of the privileges they possessed. The moral principles were those of fraternity and solidarity (see also the following section). It could be argued that this ideology only exerted a real political influence between 1945 and 1951 when the Labour Party was in office, and even then not all members of the party were in tune with social democrat thinking.

A well-known exposition of social democratic thought is *Equality* by R.H. Tawney (1964, first published in 1931). The discussion centres on the introduction of state welfare services and redistributive tax policies to bring about social justice. While the subsequent welfare state embodied the principles of social democracy it seems to have failed to produce social justice and equality. In a truly civilised, just and egalitarian society everyone would be guaranteed economic security and welfare provision, regardless of race, class, gender or age and without stigmatisation. As things stand the welfare state is failing because fiscal policies by successive governments have been aimed at cutting costs rather than improving conditions, and even the cost-cutting has proved to be a false economy in the long run.

Postmodern views

Postmodernists believe that the era of modernity has come to an end and that society has entered a new era of thought and ideology. Modernity has its origins in the Enlightenment, a philosophical movement that emerged towards the end of the eighteenth century and was founded on a belief in the power of reason over ignorance, order over disorder and science over superstition. The application of reason would enable the emancipation of humanity to take place – emancipation from ignorance, poverty and insecurity (the same ideas upon which the modern welfare state was founded).

The fundamental assumption of modernity is that knowledge is based on primary processes in the real world that are beyond and independent of discourses about them. Modernity brought about changes that were historically unprecedented and revolutionary in nature. For example the Industrial Revolution brought about a total shift in the way people lived, propelling them from an agrarian premodern world into an industrialised modern one. The era of modernity was also an era of more bloody revolutions: the English Revolution of the seventeenth century, the American and French Revolutions of the eighteenth century and the Russian Revolution of the twentieth century. All these revolutions sought to change the structure of politics and consequently the structure of society. The French Revolution in particular was based on three ideals that can still be seen as the guiding principles of democratic reform today: liberty, equality and fraternity.

As an idea postmodernity has become disparate and ragged because it has been contested and stretched thin by its multiple applications in the fields of social science, the arts and the humanities. However in general it can be regarded as a critique of modernity and a challenge to social scientific orthodoxy that is rooted in rejection of modernism's self-validating claims to knowledge. Postmodernists see the world as ambiguous, are not convinced by the natural and social sciences' claims to knowledge and are prepared to question every claim to truth. They call for a more sensitive approach to social identities, diversity and social divisions. A common characteristic of all postmodernists is their deep scepticism about the idea of the 'good society'.

Postmodernity has marked the end of the isms: Marxism, socialism, capitalism and feminism, which are viewed as being in disarray or dying. Instead postmodernists point to the existence of fragmentation and the consequent need for diversity in welfare provision. In this regard Carter (1998) considers that some of the points made by postmodernists cannot be argued with, particular by their assertion that the Fabian notion of a benefical state operating in the interest of the people is simplistic and outdated and that today's welfare provision should be attuned to the diversity and fragmentation of society. However Carter also acknowledges the dangers of this approach, for example the concept of universal provision is very difficult to square with the idea of fragmentation, and that most postmodern analysis consists of long outlines of Foucault's thoughts followed up by a rather vague notion that this might have some relevance to social policy.

From a postmodern point of view, then, modernist explanations are seen as conceptually too narrow and therefore stultifying, leaving large swathes of society unexplained. Furthermore they are monolithic dogmas that have little relevance to present society. Even the idea that we can promote social policies to try to engineer the future are in conflict with the postmodernist approach. As Williams (1996) points out, welfare states and social policy are essentially modern in origin and are therefore diametrically opposed to all postmodernity. The founders of the modern welfare state are portrayed as naive and shortsighted because in the postmodernist view there can be no unitary cause and no single truth about the way the world should be. As Baudrillard notes: 'For all practical purposes, the social has disappeared, since there is no longer any social referent of the classical kind (a people, a class, a proletariat, objective conditions)' (quoted in Bertens, 1995, p. 34).

Developing knowledge about individual and social problems requires us to go beyond the boundaries of scientific and professional disciplines and to encompass everyday practices in social institutions such as the family, the workplace and state agencies. As such, a discourse on a welfare issue such as dependency on state benefits is not simply a set of statements or questions, but a discourse about the real world. It should focus on the question of who needs the welfare state and for what reasons so that decisions can be made about the provision of welfare. It is not the policies of the welfare state *per se* that have to be addressed but the ideas underlying the reasons for provision.

Postmodern analyses of social policy have variously been described as 'a small step forwards' (O'Brien & Penna, 1998), a 'great leap backwards (Taylor-Gooby, 1998) and a 'contradiction in terms' (Hillyard and Watson, 1996). Ferge (1996) argues that postmodernism is part of the neoliberal paradigm that undermines the commitment to welfare. The message from postmodernists is that welfare needs to utilise fundamentally different tools and to reconceptualise itself. Hillyard and Watson (1996, p. 62) point to the 'general reluctance of the social policy community to acquaint themselves with the tidal wave of postmodern thinking'. However postmodernists themselves fail to define what they mean by social policy and pay scant attention to the fact that different traditions (for example Marxism and feminism) have provided different interpretations of welfare and social policy.

Exercise 8.8

a i e

Reread all the theories on the welfare state. According to each of these theories, why has the welfare state failed to achieve its aims? Compare and contrast the reasons in 500 words.

While some of these perspectives have been around for a long time they are still relevant to the debates on the contemporary welfare state. These debates are the topic of the next chapter.

9 Contemporary debates on welfare provision

By the end of this chapter you should be able to:

- describe the recent changes in the welfare state and its provisions;
- outline the ideologies behind the debate on the future of the welfare state;
- describe the way in which government policies on welfare can affect the whole of society;
- explain the key arguments behind the selectivism versus universalism debate on the development of the welfare state.

Introduction

> This is the end of an era for the British welfare state. The post war settlement has not stood the test of time and both Conservatives and Labour are intent on re-emphasising the market. (Bryson, 1992).

This chapter focuses on the current welfare state and the changes introduced since the 1970s. All three political parties have talked about reorganising welfare provision. All of them see the welfare state as problematic and are searching for solutions in a variety of ways. It is considered that the welfare state is in crisis and that new approaches to the welfare of citizens are needed. Where the welfare state is heading and why, and whether the economy can actually afford a welfare state are questions that will be addressed in this chapter.

Exercise 9.1

[i] [a]

Go to your local reference library and look up the election manifestos of the main political parties from the last two elections. Summarise in table form their policies on the welfare state.

Use these to create posters for each party to put on the classroom wall.

The welfare state in crisis?

There has been considerable debate on whether the welfare state is in crisis. After 1974 the British economy went into decline, a decline that was exacerbated by worldwide economic events. A result tax revenues began to fall, causing concern about the government's ability to finance the welfare state. By 1976 the Labour government was having to borrow money to keep the economy afloat and one of the key borrowing conditions was that cuts should be made to public expenditure. At the 1976 Labour Party conference, Prime Minister James Callaghan revealed a clear change in Labour's approach:

> We used to think that you could just spend your way out of a recession and increase employment by cutting taxes and boosting government spending. I tell you in all candour, that option no longer exists, and that in so far as it ever did exist, it worked by injecting inflation into the economy. And each time that happened the average level of unemployment has risen. Higher inflation was followed by higher unemployment. That is the history of the last twenty years (Callaghan, quoted in Walsh *et al.*, 2000, p. 50).

The result of this was cuts in public expenditure and, perhaps more importantly, rejection of the Keynesian ideal of full employment.

Such policies were maintained under the Conservative Thatcher government after 1979. This influential period of UK politics, which was dominated by the new right, saw even greater cuts in welfare expenditure and it became clear that the welfare state would be pushed even further into crisis.

Mike O'Donnell (1987) argues that this situation led to a dilemma for social democratic thinkers. Should the private sector be helped to recover from the economic downturn since a flourishing economy would enable more money to be raised from taxes and spent on welfare, or should public sector services be preserved by squeezing out the private sector? Versions of both positions were promoted and continue to this day.

Exercise 9.2

Find a copy of Mike O'Donnell's (1987) article and write down the implications of the two alternatives discussed above. Divide the class into two groups. The first group should take one of the two options and consider its implications in detail; the second groups should do the same with the other option. After careful preparation, hold a debate on the two options.

As Harloe Pickvance and Urry (1990) point out, the state continued its role as the principal provider of social services. For example in 1987 only 8 per cent of children were privately educated and only 10 per cent of people had private health insurance. This more or less remains the case, although in the boom years of the late 1980s private education expanded somewhat as the state system was seen to be failing many children and more parents were able to afford private education. Of course the key constraint on private welfare provision is cost. Burchardt and Hills (1997) estimated that the cost of private insurance for a married man on average pay (about £400 per week in April 1996) would be £900 per year to cover just three things: mortgage protection, unemployment risk and health insurance. This was equivalent to adding 6p on the basic rate of income tax. Thus, private welfare insurance was likely to be beyond the means of people on average earnings.

Exercise 9.3

a i Phone up an insurance company and dry to find out the cost of mortgage protection, unemployment risk and health insurance today.

At the heart of the current debate on state welfare provision is what should be provided and at what cost. Various surveys show that the majority of people believe that the welfare state should be maintained, and if that means paying extra then so be it. Exactly how much extra and how frequently are issues that have yet to be addressed.

Who needs a welfare state?

Bryson (1992) points out that the UK is not alone in questioning the need for a comprehensive state welfare system as the same debate has been going on in most Western industrialised countries. She believes that it is less a question of welfare *per se* than of the distribution of power and resources in capitalist countries. There is not an unlimited supply of resources so those which are available should be targeted at certain needy groups, but those with power demand the right to utilise those resources for their own benefit. However Hutton (1996) argues that it is not economic need or necessity that spurs governments to reduce welfare spending, rather it is political ideology.

The question of who should receive state benefits and who should be made to fend for themselves has been central to the debate on the future of the welfare state, as exemplified by the universalism versus selectivism argument. Proponents of universalism argue that state benefits should be made available to everybody, regardless of how much they earn, while those who favour selectivism insist that benefits should be means tested and given only to those who are unable to provide for themselves. For those on the left of the political spectrum the welfare state is what civilised society is all about; the needy should not be left to fend for themselves but enabled to lead satisfying lives.

Several independent studies have been conducted on the questions of whether the welfare state is in crisis and which groups of people need welfare services. Various studies have all found that there is a continuing need for welfare provision because the five giant evils are still in existence (see Chapter 8, page 145), although they recognise that welfare will need to be administered in a different way, with selectivity rather than universality taking precedence. The state must provide help to those in genuine need but this should be determined by more stringent means testing than is the case at present.

Exercise 9.4

Hold a class debate on the proposition that all welfare provision should be selective.

Contemporary approaches to welfare provision

We shall now look at two broad approaches to the provision of welfare that have emerged from and been shaped by the debates on the crisis of the welfare state, namely the new right views associated with the Conservative governments of 1979–97 and the New Labour views associated with the Labour governments elected since 1997.

New Right views on the welfare state

The changes introduced during the 1980s were strongly influenced by New Right thinking and the running of the economy was based on new right economic theories. According to Willets (1992), because modern life was so complex (as postmodernists would agree) there was no logic in centralised planning, rather the terms should be dictated by the free market and the role of the state should be marginalised. The welfare state was undesirable because it interfered with the workings of the free market.

The Thatcher government elected in 1979 was heavily influenced by the New Right argument that wages were too high, causing a natural level of unemployment, and because employer could not afford to employ people to counteract this phenomenon there should be at these rates downward pressure on both wages and benefit levels. Beveridge had worked on the assumption that the successful administration of a welfare state depended on full employment, and that the use of unemployment as an instrument of government policy would turn the welfare state into a burden. However the Thatcher administration took the view that unemployment was a necessary component of a low inflation policy and therefore was an acceptable consequence of its economic strategy. Due to the rise in unemployment the financing of the welfare state became increasingly difficult, as predicted by Beveridge. In 1979 the proportion of households where all adults of employable age were out of work was 9 per cent, but by the mid 1990s this proportion had risen to 21 per cent.

In the opinion of the New Right, because public expenditure was being pushed up by welfare payments there was a need for welfare pluralism, meaning that agencies other than state ones should play a part, and that community and family care should be encouraged. The New Right did not envisage a state without some welfare provision, but this should be a residual system that would act as a safety net to be used only when all other avenues of help had been explored. This reflected the idea of selectivism rather than the universalism upon which the welfare state was based. As Alcock (1996, p. 6) has said, 'the new right perspective thus remain[ed] within the bounds of a mixed economy of welfare . . . New Right ideology might shift the boundary between the state and the market sectors of welfare but it would retain both'.

Hayek believed in welfare pluralism, that the part played by the state should be kept to a minimum so that individual freedom would be maintained. Each individual should be free to pay into a private scheme, and to opt out of the NHS if they so wished, and thus have control over how their own money was used. Likewise Saunders (1990) argued that individual choice was all important and that people often preferred private services. The middle class should be able to provide for themselves with little or no state cash. But what about individuals who could not afford that choice? State care would become limited for them and worsen their circumstances. The welfare state would end up as a poor system for poor people.

The 1986 and 1988 new Social Security Acts introduced a number of changes that had obvious implications for individuals and for the future of welfare in general. These included:

- Social security grants for household necessities such as beds and bedding were replaced by loans. These loans were discretionary and many people were turned down because it was felt that they would be unable to repay the loan from their benefit payments. This naturally saved the state money but led certain individuals into greater poverty.
- A lower rate of Income Support was given to under 25 year olds.
- People aged 16–18 became ineligible for benefit and were required to take part in training schemes.
- The provision of free eye tests was withdrawn, and the ever-increasing paperwork required from NHS dentists resulted in many taking on only private, fee-paying patients, leading to a decrease in the availability of dentists for those who had no choice but to rely on the NHS.

- Child benefit and housing benefits were not increased in line with inflation, which meant that their actual value decreased.
- Prescription charges were increased (and have been increased a number of times since) by more than the rate of inflation.
- Right to buy legislation enabled council tenants to buy the property they occupied (see Chapter 10).
- The link between current earnings and pensions was abolished, meaning that the value of the state pension fell.

Exercise 9.5

a i Draw up a list of arguments for and against the changes introduced by the new right, as outlined above.

These changes can be seen as part of the general move from universal to selective benefit provision. Although universal benefits survived (for example the state pension and Family Allowance) others were made subject to a means test, for example Family Credit.

Universal benefits were very costly and the Family Allowance and pensions in particular were placing a great strain on the Department of Social Security's budget. It was the overall cost that was causing concern, not the plight of those in need of benefits. Means testing would result in the social security bill being drastically cut, allowing the government to channel the funds thus released into other areas. New Right theorists argued that if the state could persuade other sections of society to take some responsibility the state's economic position would improve even further. For example Marsland (1996) argued that as recipients of state benefits families should be made to accept their responsibility to the provider of those benefits. Families could and should provide informal care for each other and rely less on formal state provision.

There was also a move to promote care in the community, which cost half as much as keeping individuals in long-term residential institutions. The responsibility of the state was also reduced by the introduction into the NHS and the education sector of market principles such as trust funded hospitals and the local management of schools by governing bodies.

From the New Right to New Labour

The 1997 general election brought the defeat of the Conservative Party and the retreat of New Right thinking in government. The conservatives were replaced by the Labour Party under the leadership of Tony

Blair, who had made substantial and somewhat controversial reforms to the approach and policies of the party and adopted the name 'New Labour' to underline this change. While rejecting many elements of new right thinking it is clear that Blair and New Labour shared the New Right's belief in the efficiency of private sector service provision. When the Labour government was reelected in 2001 this belief caused conflict between the government and the traditional supporters of the Labour movement. This section starts by looking at the changes made by New Labour and then goes on to consider the debate on private–public partnerships (PPPs).

New Labour's views on welfare

In May 1997 the New Labour government came to power after 18 years of Conservative rule. New Labour claimed to espouse ethical socialism and pledged that Beveridge's principles would be maintained, believing that:

- Society had a responsibility to help people in genuine need who were unable to look after themselves.
- Employment was the best route out of poverty for people who were able to work.
- Individuals had a responsibility to provide for themselves when they could do so.

Exercise 9.6

1. What problems might arise from these principles?

2. To what extent do you agree that work is the best route out of poverty? Is this true for all people?

3. What responsibilities do you believe people should have?

Hence the government envisaged a welfare state that would provide for those in genuine need while encouraging others to take responsibility for their own lives. According to Skidelsky, Jacob and Nye (1998, p. 16), 'In order to build a stakeholder welfare state, and make it politically acceptable, the government believes it has to increase benefits for all. Then, it realises that the poorest are falling behind, so it increases benefits again. The whole process is one which rachets spending higher.' In Nye's view benefits had to be made more selective and spending should be curbed to provide a better service to those in most need. More was being spent on welfare than on health, education and law and order combined, but the poorest 20 per cent were receiving a lower share of social security benefits than they had in 1979. If welfare was to be redesigned it had to direct more money and services to the poor while keeping the main beneficiaries (the middle classes) happy (see Chapter 8). Priorities had to be decided upon as resources were not infinite. Should all benefits be means tested or should some remain universal, and if so, which and why? Any decision had to take political, social and economic factors into consideration if progress was to be made.

In October 1996 Tony Blair (then leader of the Opposition) had said that a new Labour government would have failed if it had not at least laid the foundation stones of a modernised welfare state by the end of its first five years in office. The next year he had outlined the three main principles upon which this modernised welfare state would be built:

- Greater emphasis on the responsibilities and obligations of claimants.
- A less dogmatic approach to the balance between public and private provision.
- A move towards provision that was active rather than passive.

The first point echoed the new right idea that the recipients of benefits should take more responsibility for their own actions and not rely on the state for handouts. The second point referred to the private sector being a necessary part of overall welfare provision. The third point was akin to the New Right's belief that active participation was vital it progress was to be made and changes implemented.

In *New Ambitions for our Country* (DSS, 1998) the government stated that

> Reform will not come overnight. It will be a long term process which we will have already begun with the £3.5 billion New Deal for young people, the long term unemployed, lone parents and people who are sick and disabled. Pilot projects are underway and the programme will start to go nation-wide in April 1998. We want the debate to be based on facts, without scaremongering. Our aim is to fight poverty, not increase it; narrow social division, not widen it; and extend opportunities, not deny them (p. 28).

The thrust of Labour's thinking was that if people were helped to establish themselves in employment and society in their youth they would not need state help in the future and this would lower welfare spending, reduce poverty and allow people to make a positive contribution to society.

In February 1998 Blair spoke of his intention to create an international consensus of the centre-left for the twenty-first century, a modernising 'third way' that would differ from the old left and the new right. Whilst maintaining the central social democratic ideals of social justice, the third way would reject class politics and seek cross-class support. The values upon which the third way would be based were specified as democracy, liberty, justice, mutual obligation and internationalism. The welfare state was in need of radical reform to make it responsive to the altered circumstances of contemporary life.

Giddens (1999a) argued that the third way would give the welfare state a new direction. In Giddens' view there should be a change to a social investment state in which there would be a balance between state management of risk and security on the one hand and individual and collective responsibility on the other. Giddens distinguished between external risks (risks emanating from outside) and the natural or manufactured risks that resulted from conscious human activity. The main aim the social investment state should be to invest in human capital rather than concentrate on provision benefit. New ways should be found for citizens to share in the making of decisions that affected them and their everyday lives. As Giddens (1994, p. 10) said: 'We should be prepared to rethink the welfare state in a fundamental way.' At the present time welfare policy was responding *post hoc* to mishaps rather than taking the proactive role he advocated, in which welfare 'mobilises life political measures, aimed once more at connecting autonomy with personal and collective responsibility' (ibid., p. 4).

Giddens pointed out that the original welfare state was set up to address social conditions that had markedly changed, and therefore the welfare state had to be reformed to take account of those changes. There was a need to take account of the experiences, needs and views of those for whom the benefits of the welfare state were intended. The welfare state had generally come to be equated with improving the lot of the underprivileged, but the affluent also had welfare needs: 'Security, self-respect, self-actualisation – these are scarce goods for the affluent as well as for the poor, and they are compromised by the ethos of productivism, not just distributive inequalities' (ibid., p. 14). Instead of perpetuating universal welfare measures that could result in welfare dependency there was a need for 'Schemes of positive welfare, oriented to manufactured rather than external risk, ... directed to fostering the autotelic self. The autotelic self is one with an inner confidence which comes from self respect, and one where a sense of ontological security, originating in basic trust, allows for the positive appreciation of difference' (ibid., p. 16). Giddens was of the opinion that the state should foster individual responsibility, which would give people a sense of self-worth, self-belief and self-reliance.

In Giddens' view the welfare state had not proved effective in reducing economic inequality because of the considerable involvement of the middle classes in social programmes. Poverty could not be alleviated by redistribution of wealth from the affluent to the poor but could be reduced by the sharing of risk. The affluent benefited most from the present system and in order for this to change a risk assessment should take place and risk should be shared by all.

Exercise 9.7

Refer to your sociology textbook and answer the following questions:

1. What do you understand by the term work ethic?

2. What kind of work ethic do you possess, and why?

A new contract for welfare

Before the general election of May 1997, in its party manifesto the Labour Party set out its policy for reform of the welfare state. Once the party was elected to power it appointed a minister for welfare reform to produce measures appropriate. Amongst the measures announced the following year were the New Deal scheme, to be handled by the Department of Education and Employment, and the contract for welfare, to be administered by the Department of Social Security. Both schemes were part of the 'third way' discussed above. By 2020 welfare would be based on a contract between the government on the one hand and individuals and families on the other. This contract would essentially be about duty – the duties of the government would be matched by the duties of the individual:

- The government's duty would be to provide a proactive, work-focused service to ensure the speedy return to work of the unemployed; individuals' duty would be to seek work or training wherever practicable.
- The government's duty would be to help parents meet the cost of raising their children; individual's duty would be to support their children and other family members both financially and emotionally.
- The government's duty would be to prevent poverty in old age and regulate pension provision; individuals' duty would be to save for their old age.

The reforms would be based on the twin pillars of work and security: work for those that could and security for those that could not. There was also a belief that the current system was encouraging fraud and deception rather than honesty and hard work, and dependence rather than independence, so reform was vital to combat these phenomena. There were eight prime objectives:

- To alleviate social exclusion and help those in poverty.
- To help and encourage people to work if they were capable of doing so (the New Deal scheme).
- To enable disabled people to lead dignified, fulfilling lives.
- To form a partnership between the public and private sectors to ensure that people were insured against foreseeable risks and made provision for their retirement.
- To provide high-quality public services as well as cash benefits.
- To support families and children while tackling the scourge of child poverty.
- To encourage openness and honesty, with the gateways to benefit being clear and enforceable.
- To deliver a modern welfare system that was flexible, efficient and easy for people to use.

Exercise 9.8

In groups, discuss each of the objectives outlined above.

1. Decide whether you agree or disagree.
2. What are the policy implications of your decisions?

Social exclusion

The government acknowledged that low earnings were at the heart of the poverty and welfare issue and that growing inequality had to be tackled. Accordingly the Centre for the Analysis of Social Exclusion was established on 13 November 1997, situated at the London School of Economics, and a new Social Exclusion Unit was set up in the Cabinet Office to embark on a new programme of welfare reform. These two units would enable the academic world and the government to come together to discuss the problems inherent in the administration of the welfare state and to develop strategies to tackle these problems.

The Social Exclusion Unit reports to the prime minister and works closely with the Policy Unit at 10 Downing Street. It is staffed by civil servants from other Whitehall departments and representatives of local authorities, voluntary bodies and other key agencies. The prime minister steers the work of the unit and chairs meetings with ministers from the Departments of Education and Employment, Social Security, and the Environment to review the ongoing work.

Social exclusion is a complex issue, for many people, social exclusion means feeling isolated from the rest of society because they live in substandard housing with few comforts, their diet is of a poor quality, they cannot afford to do the things that other people do (for example have family days out at theme parks) and they feel they are merely existing rather than living a full and satisfying life.

The two Social Exclusion units set out to develop policies to deal with individual problems in order to bring about wholesale change. The problems identified included low educational achievement, drug abuse, worklessness, poor health and poor housing. The first problems to be tackled were truancy and school exclusion as children who truanted or were excluded tended to leave school with few qualifications and were unlikely to obtain employment. Homelessness was also given priority as those living rough were treated as outcasts from the rest of society. Those who were housed but lived on problem estates where crime, drugs, unemployment, community breakdown and substandard schools were most likely to be found needed help to better their living conditions and their lives in general. (Although problem estates, living rough and substandard schools are found mainly in inner city areas it must be borne in mind that social exclusion is not just an inner city problem that is confined to certain areas, it is a nation-wide problem that occurs in both urban and rural areas.)

The first phase of the reforms focused on drawing up key indicators of social exclusion and recommending how these could be located and monitored, and on improving mechanisms for integrating the work of the relevant government departments, local authorities and other agencies at the national and local levels so that the allocated funds would be used effectively to bring about the declared objectives.

Exercise 9.9

1. How would you define social exclusion?

2. Using information in this chapter and your sociology textbook(s), together with your sociological imagination, in 500 words answer the following question: Which groups of people are most likely to be socially excluded, and for what reasons?

In September 1998 the Social Exclusion Unit announced a concerted attack on area deprivation. Seventeen areas were chosen for pilot schemes; 18 action teams were to be set up, with the team members being drawn from business and community organisations, the world of academia and government departments; and a three-year budget of £800 million was allocated to the project. (This amounted to between £50 and £200 per household, which would not have covered the cost of rebuilding rundown housing let alone tackling all the other elements of exclusion.)

Labour: have things got better?

The 1997 Labour manifesto contained a total of 177 commitments. Although most of these and the famous five pledges have been met, the records show that some things have remained the same or even worsened during the period 1997–2001. In relation to welfare spending the government:

- Cut the Lone Parent Benefit.
- Made Incapacity Benefit subject to a means test.
- Increased pensions by a mere 75p per week (in 2000).
- In 1999/2000, reduced the proportion of the economy taken in taxes by the state from the 41.2 per cent that prevailed in John Major's last year as Prime Minister (1996/7) to 37.7 per cent.

Despite all this, through stealth taxes Chancellor Gordon Brown has brought about a degree of redistribution. In 2000 the Institute for Fiscal Studies (IFS) estimated that the poorest 10 per cent of the population had become 8.8 per cent better off while the richest 10 per cent had become 0.5 per cent worse off (Ichimura and Taber, 2000). Nonetheless there are clear signs that the government is trying to force people off welfare and into work.

In relation to education the government:

- Sanctioned the use of private contractors.
- Failed to spend the promised 5 per cent of GDP on education.
- Allowed pupil–teacher ratios in secondary schools to rise to a 15-year high, from 16.4 : 1 in 1997 to 17.2 : 1 in 2000.
- Declared that Labour was the 'friend' of private schools.
- Abolished grants for higher education and introduced means-tested loans, leading to a fall in university enrolment in 1998, the first in many years.

In relation to health the government:

- Increased spending on health to a lesser degree than had been the case under its conservative predecessor.
- Used the Private Finance Initiative (PFI, see below) to finance the hospital building programme, leading to a reduction of beds in some hospitals and the closure of others.
- Formally introduced drug rationing through the National Institute for Clinical Effectiveness (which decides whether the cost of drugs exceeds their effectiveness).

- Recruited 4000 extra nurses rather than the 20000 it had promised.

In relation to investment the government:

- Increased the amount raised through PFI-totalling 150 projects worth £12 billion.
- Cut government debt from 39.4 per cent of GDP to 33 per cent (in comparison Germany's stands at 59.5 per cent and France's at 57.1 per cent).
- Continued its plan to set up a public–private partnership for the London Underground despite the objection of the elected mayor of London.

PPPs and PFIs

One of the most controversial aspects of New Labour's approach to public provision is its promotion of public–private partnerships (PPPs) in various sectors of the welfare state, notably education and health. Traditionalists in the party are committed to Labour's founding principle of people over profits, and therefore they and the unions are against the idea of profit-making private-sector involvement in the provision of public services.

A crucial aspect of this approach is the continuation of the Private Finance Initiative (PFI), which was introduced by the Conservative chancellor, Norman Lamont, in 1992. The aim of PFI was to raise money for capital investment without having to raise taxes or increase government borrowing. As Gordon Brown has also pledged not to raise income tax he too has turned to PFI to finance the large-scale investment in public services that New Labour has promised.

The justification given for PFI is that the private sector will bear all the financial risk of large-scale building projects, thus freeing the government from the well-known phenomenon of cost overrun, whereby more has to be paid out than anticipated, leaving less money for other areas of government spending. Hence PFI is a means of shifting the risk of overspending onto the private sector. However in Hobson's (1999, p. 337) view:

> Contrary to political rhetoric, investment is a cost, not a benefit. By asking the private sector to raise the capital, the government forfeited its chief advantage: that it can always borrow more cheaply than anybody else. The purpose of the PFI is to transfer the risk of projects from the taxpayer to private financiers, but the greater the risk investors are asked to bear, the higher the premium they will demand for advancing funds. The cost of finance for PFI projects will always be higher than conventional government borrowing.

Most of the risks associated with big public-sector building projects occur during the construction stage, but once this is over the firms concerned are guaranteed payments by the government for up to 30 years and some have the added possibility of reaping very large profits. For instance the new Fazackerly prison will start to generate profits after two years and government payments will continue for about 30 years. Even known supporters of the government are lukewarm about PFI:

> PFI had been invented by the Tories as a way to get private money on the table now, leaving the state to pay instalments later. Under Treasury pressure, health trusts were instructed to sign deals, bringing in private consortia to build and maintain new buildings. The trusts were then committed to a stream of repayments stretching far into the future, mortgaging future generations' health spending for as long as sixty years, by which time these hospitals would be long redundant, still paying money which might have to come out of savings on health care. Critics claimed that new hospitals in Worcester, Durham, Edinburgh and elsewhere cut rather than expanded bed numbers; funds had to be diverted from clinical needs to pay for the schemes (Toynbee and Walker, 2001, p. 78).

PFI has sparked real controversy in respect of the NHS and the London Underground. Pollock *et al.* (2001) highlights the problems relating to PFI and the NHS. One of the supposed benefits of PFI is reduced cost escalation. However Pollock *et al.* have found that public sector projects have a cost escalation of 8 per cent while that of PFI projects is more than 16 per cent. Secondly, PFI hospitals tend to have 31 per cent fewer beds than the hospitals they replace, with a consequent reduction in medical and in nursing staff. Key examples of these points are provided by the Worcester Royal Infirmary, whose building costs of escalated by 188 per cent. This meant that the planned savings (by reducing the number of beds by 28 per cent) were no longer enough and this led to the decision to close Kidderminster Hospital to the north of Worcester. On top of this the new hospital would have 32 per cent fever ancillary workers and 17 per cent fewer nurses. This issue hit the political headlines during the 2001 general election, when Dr Richard Taylor unseated the Labour MP for Wyre Forest as a result of the closure of part of Kidderminster Hospital.

With regard to the London Underground, the government has refused to abandon its planned PPP despite opposition by the mayor of London, Ken Livingstone, and his transport commissioner, Bob Kiley – the issue is to go to court for judicial review. At the heart of the debate is the fact that greater risk is attached to private sector lending because borrowing companies may go bankrupt. This means that public sector organisations can borrow more cheaply than private companies and therefore the costs of PPPs are higher.

Goodin *et al.* (2000) provide a clear analysis of how governmental ideology can impact on inequality and therefore social inclusion. They compared life in the US, Germany and the Netherlands between approximately 1989 and 1999. The US bases its welfare provision on the liberal free-market model, the conservative model is utilised in Germany and the social democratic model in the Netherlands. Goodin *et al.* found that the different political approaches produced very different outcomes. The percentage of people who remained poor after the implementation of government antipoverty action varied from 0.75 per cent in the Netherlands to 13 per cent in the US. In the US poverty was only reduced by 20 per cent, whereas in the Netherlands it was reduced by over 90 per cent. Goodin *et al.* conclude that:

> Whatever it is we want from welfare regimes – whether it is income stability, income equality, low poverty or high economic prosperity – the social democratic welfare regime seems the best on offer. It is at least as good as the other two on all of those dimensions, and far better on some of them. Conversely, the liberal regime is unambiguously the worst on offer, no matter which of those values are prioritised (ibid., p. 184).

This shows that (1) governments can make a difference and (2) the trickle-down approach is not an effective means of imposing welfare.

New Labour and inequality

One other pressing problem for New Labour is growing inequality in British society. For traditional Labour thinkers such as Roy Hattersley, the reduction of inequality was a founding aim of the Labour Party and the seeming abandonment of that aim by those involved in the New Labour projects has angered him and many others (for a summary of these views visit www.catalyst-trust.co.uk).

It has been estimated that in 2001 British chief executives' remuneration package averaged £509 000 compared with the £298 200 received by German executives (*Guardian*, 26 July 2001). At the same time the average wage of workers in the manufacturing industry was £20 475 in the UK and £26 124 in Germany. Chief executives in Germany therefore earned 11.5 times the average wage of workers compared with 25 times in the UK. This suggests that New Labour is not really concerned with reducing inequality and is moving away from the continental model of social organisation towards that of the US. Along with PFI and PPPs, this is likely to cause dissention within the labour movement that may affect the future development of welfare policies.

Exercise 9.10

1. Using information in the section above and elsewhere, draw up a list of arguments for and against private sector involvement in the provision of welfare services.

2. If there are any examples of this in your area, produce a poster outlining what has happened and how local people feel about it.

10 Aspects of contemporary welfare provision

By the end of this chapter you should be able to:

- describe the services provided by social security, housing and personal social services;
- describe the conflicting arguments on welfare provision in these areas;
- outline the similarities and differences between the new right and New Labour in terms of contemporary welfare provision;
- describe the various agencies involved in contemporary welfare provision.

This chapter looks at some of the contemporary debates on the provision of welfare in three distinct areas: social security, housing, and personal social services.

Social security

Welfare to work

Work is central to the government's attack on social exclusion. The government sees work as more than just earning a living, it is a way of life and the key to independence, self-respect and advancement. It enables us to support ourselves during our working lives and to save for our retirement.

The welfare to work scheme is crucial to welfare reform. It was originally introduced in the US, and in Wisconsin it took little more than a year to reduce the number on welfare by 75 per cent. A House of Commons select committee on social security visited Wisconsin in December 1998 to see how the system operated. A mixture of tough work requirements and help with childcare and training called 'Winconsin Works' seemed to be the main ingredients of the scheme's success.

The UK welfare to work package is essentially based on two economic theories on long-term unemployment: the replacement ratio theory and the withering flowers theory. According to the latter, being unemployed makes people less employable, whilst the former states that people remain unemployed because the benefit system is arranged in such a way that it allows them to. The government believes it has a duty to invest in helping those who can work to do so, thus enabling them to enjoy a decent standard of living rather than suffering benefit dependency. Policy is based ensuring that:

- people receive the right education and training to maximise their employability;
- obstacles to work are cleared away, for example by making sure that affordable child care is available (especially to single parents, mainly mothers);
- expert advice is provided to those trying to get back into work and suitable housing policies are developed;
- a national minimum wage is implemented and the tax and benefit systems are reformed.

Exercise 10.1

Based on what you have just read about welfare to work, in a copy of the table below list the strengths and weaknesses of this scheme. Two examples are provided to start you off.

Strengths	Weaknesses
Incentives such as child care are provided for single parents	The minimum wage is still set at a low level

The minimum wage

Exercise 10.2

a

If you were setting a minimum wage, how much would it be, and why?

In June 1998 the first national minimum wage was set at £3.60 per hour for people aged 21 and over and £3.20 per hour for those aged 18–21. No minimum was placed on the pay of workers below the age of 18. The minimum wage included service charges, tips and incentive payments such as commissions. Employers were also allowed to take the provision of accommodation into account (for example rooms for hotel and care workers) up to a limit of £20 per week.

At £3.60 per hour the minimum wage was less than 50 per cent of the median full-time hourly rate. It was also lower than the *de facto* poverty level of £210 per week for a family of four. It was set below those of the UK's main economic rivals (for example Belgium, France, the US and the Netherlands) in order to boost the UK's competitive position. Nonetheless it allowed many workers to come off housing benefit and Family Credit and some families actually crossed the income tax threshold for the first time (see Chapter 2). It is estimated that this cut the social security bill by £300 million a year and increased tax revenues and National Insurance contributions by £700 million.

It is difficult to enforce the minimum wage in places such as sweatshops (see Chapter 6), which are largely unregulated, and many people work for less than the minimum wage because they have no alternative. The latter include illegal immigrants, those under the legal age for full-time work, and those who are registered as unemployed and claiming benefit. Others may be unaware of the minimum wage.

Sachdev (2001) draws attention to inconsistencies in the uprating of the minimum wage over time. As can be seen in Table 10.1, the rise in the adult rate in October 2001 was more than five times that in October 2000 and more than four times the rise promised for October 2002. Sachdev points out that two of the three rises shown in the table are below the actual or likely rise in the average wage. Hence although the minimum wage was introduced to eliminate poverty it has not reduced the gap between those on the average wage and those on the legal minimum. Indeed if the minimum wage continues to be based on what seems to be political whim, this may lead 'to avoidable and intense political lobbying; to greater instability and uncertainty for low paying firms; and [it] is unfair to those on or near the minimum wages who are held captive to the vagaries of the political process to main-

Table 10.1   Changes to the UK minimum wage

	Adult rate (£)	Average annual increase (%)	Development rate (18–21 year olds) (£)	Average annual increase (%)
April 1999	3.60		3.00	
June 2000			3.20	5.7
October 2000	3.70	1.85		
October 2001	4.10	10.8	3.50	7.0
October 2002	4.20	2.4	3.60	2.9

(*Source*: Sachdev (2001), p. 8.)

tain the value of their incomes' (ibid., p. 4). In this respect the UK is more like the US than Europe. In France, for instance, the minimum wage is increased in line with inflation and with at least half the increase in the average wage.

Exercise 10.3

How does the national minimum wage compare with the wage you set in the previous exercise? By how much and why does it differ?

Private and public sector pensions

The fact that the average age of the population is rising has to be faced and addressed. In 1991 only 16 per cent of the population was aged over 64, but it is estimated that by 2041 this figure will have risen to 24 per cent. Older people receive more welfare resources than any other age group, so naturally the more of them there are, the higher the welfare bill will be. At present the state provides a pension to all retired people, funded by the National Insurance contributions paid by those in work. In 1998 there were 3.4 working people for every pensioner, but this ratio is contracting and in time the system will reach the point where it will become unsustainable. Therefore the government is urging people in work to provide for their retirement by taking out a private pension.

Exercise 10.4

Do you have any form of life assurance? If so, why? If not, why not?

For many people, joining a private pension scheme is problematic if not nigh on impossible due to the conditions laid down for the present schemes. In 2000 three quarters of workers had a private pension and eleven million employees belonged to a company scheme, 4.5 million more than in 1953. However, many catagories of workers are not eligible for such schemes and the unemployed will find it impossible to pay into a private pension if their unemployment runs into the long term.

At present pension provision consists of three tiers. The first tier is the universal state retirement pension, funded by National Insurance contributions on a pay as you earn basis. The second tier consists mostly of company schemes. Nearly everyone in full-time work is compelled to pay into a second-tier pension. The third tier consists of private pension plans and at the moment some 14 million people, including the self-employed, have such plans.

Exercise 10.1

[i]

1. How much financial disparity is there likely to be between a care worker and a finance director when they retire?

k u a i

2. Using information in this chapter and Chapters 5, 6, 7 and 8, explain the likely reasons for this and other possible disparities between them. (Hint: class, race, education.)

Some illustrations of pension provision:

- A care assistant earning £8000 a year pays National Insurance contributions and upon retirement will be entitled to a state pension, both basic and also State Second Pension (SP2). The State Second Pension replaced SERPS in April 2002. If her earnings remain the same in real terms for the rest of her working life and she is unable to pay for a private pension she will receive a pension of £4550 for each year of retirement (at today's rates).
- A finance director earning £50000 a year is a member of a contracted-out, salary-related occupational pension scheme and pays National Insurance contributions towards the state pension. Additional employee/employer contributions (equal to 5 per cent of her earnings) are paid into an occupational fund. She receives £1670 a year in tax relief and a National Insurance rebate of £960 a year, giving a total £2630 a year in relief and rebates. Assuming she stays in her job until the official retirement age she will receive a tax-free lump sum of £75000 and a total pension of £28250 a year (at today's rates).

As can be seen, the present pension structure fails to deliver a decent standard of living for all pensioners. Furthermore retirement is lasting longer as life expectancy has risen and looks set to rise even further. This 'greying of society' has important implications for policy decisions on the welfare state and future provision for the elderly.

The government introduced low-cost stakeholder pension schemes in 2001 to give low-paid workers the chance to save for a decent second pension. To keep costs low these schemes are collectively operated and can be delivered by trade unions or mutual societies. The state pension will continue to be provided.

In his March 1999 budget speech Chancellor Gordon Brown announced that single pensioners would be aworded a minimum income guarantee of £78 per week and couples £120 per week (suggesting that two can live more cheaply than one). The winter fuel allowance, which was paid to all eight million elderly households would be raised from £20 to £100. The personal tax allowance was also to be raised, so single pensioners would not have to pay any tax if their income was less than £5720 per year. The equivalent threshold for married couples was set at £15000. In total, two thirds of pensioners would not have to pay income tax.

Exercise 10.5

1. How much were single pensioners allowed to earn each week before tax had to be paid?

2. Would this have been enough to live on comfortably?

Another controversial political issue is that of pensions adjustment. In 1980 the Conservative government decided to index the state pension to inflation rather than the annual rise in average earnings. As a result its value fell from 20 per cent of the average male earnings in 1978 to 15 per cent in the early 1990s, and by 2020 its value would have fallen to 9 per cent of the average male earnings. In 2000 the Labour government did agree to raise pensioners' minimum income guarantee in line with earnings, but since this is unlikely to cover all of a pensioner's needs it does not entirely address the problem of poverty in old age.

Childcare provision

The majority of single parents are women and for those who wish to work childcare provision is vital. Once at work they can begin to become self-reliant and less dependent on the state.

Likewise Colette Kelleher (1998), director of the Childcare Trust, stresses that 'Children are missing out on quality childcare because they live in an area where it does not exist or their families can't afford to pay for it. Parents are missing out on chances to work or study because they can't find childcare they can afford' (www.guardian.com).

In the government announced in 1998 a £300 million package to provide out-of-school childcare throughout the UK. Childcare was to be made available before and after school and during the school holidays. Out-of-school clubs with trained playcore workers would offer care for 4–12 year olds, but this still left the under four year olds to be catered for. In a New Deal in Oct 1997 programme was introduced in eight areas (North Surrey, Clyde Valley, Cambridgeshire, North Cheshire, Sheffield East, Warwickshire, North Worcestershire and Cardiff and Vale) to help 40 000 single parent households to enter or re-enter the job market. From April 1998 was extended to all single parents on Income Support, and from October 1998 it was applied nationally. In tandem with the national childcare strategy this encouraged single parents to enter or re-enter the job market. Money was also set aside for single parents with children below school age who wished to join the programme.

The New Deal

The New Deal which is funded by the Windfall Levy, caters for the young unemployed, the sick and disabled, and the long-term unemployed as well as single parents.

From April 1998 the New Deal for the young unemployed gave 18–24 year olds throughout the UK a choice between:

- Working in a subsidised job in the private sector for up to 26 weeks, with at least one day a week being spent on education or training to acquire accredited qualifications. Young entrepreneurs who wished to start their own business were offered training and support plus a weekly allowance.
- Taking part in full-time education or training to improve their employment prospects.
- Working in the voluntary sector, with day releases to study for accredited qualifications.
- Working in official environmental task forces, with day release education or training for accredited qualifications.

Failure to accept any one of these choices resulted in loss of benefit.

In March 1998 there were 118 000 18–24 year olds who had been unemployed for six months or more, and each month up to 15 000 more passed the six-month threshold. By April 1998 over 16 000 young people had joined the New Deal programme in pilot areas and over 250 000 companies had been asked to provide jobs.

Exercise 10.6

a i

1. Try to find someone who has taken part in the New Deal. Ask him or her about the experience, perhaps using a semistructured interview. You could tape the interview and allow other students in your group to hear it (obviously with the permission of the interviewee). Your questions could include the following:

- How did you find out about the New Deal?
- What options were you offered?
- What advice were you given?
- Who gave you that advice?
- Has the new deal proved beneficial to you? If so, how? If not, why?

Welfare to work for the disabled

The disabled are particularly disadvantaged in terms of employment as their individual needs have to be addressed. However, simple provisions such as large-print documents and magnetic loop telephones (developed for people with hearing difficulties) cost very little and make certain disabled people employable. In fact the additional costs of employing disabled people are generally low whilst their value to employers is high. Disabled employees tend to be more punctual than other workers, have better attendance records, work harder and show greater enthusiasm. The provision of access ramps and so on is seen as sound business practice if it allows firms to obtain the best people for the job.

Later that month it was duly announced that a new personal adviser service for disabled people would be piloted in 12 areas, covering over a quarter of a million people on incapacity benefit. The first six, to be run by the Employment Service, were launched in October with a budget of £5 million. The remainder were put out to open tender and started early in 1999 with a £12 million budget.

Other New Deal measures for the disabled included benefit changes to remove the disincentive to work. For example people on incapacity benefit were encouraged to work for a trial period and could earn up to £15 a week whilst remaining on benefit. In October 1999 a Disabled Person's Tax Credit replaced the Disability Working Allowance.

In March 1998 over 120 bids were made to run innovative schemes to help people with disabilities find work. The client group for these scheme consisted of 2.2 million people of working age with a disability or long-term illness who were receiving either Incapacity Benefit, Income Support or Severe Disablement Allowance. It was hoped that employers could be made to realise that the disabled were capable of contributing fully and purposefully as employees.

Besides the welfare to work measures the government pledged that these benefits paid to cover the additional costs incurred by disabled people (the Disability Living Allowance and Attendance Allowance) would not be made subject to a means test. There would be a focus on what people could do rather than what they could not do. In this way savings would be made and these could be targeted at the severely disabled in greatest need.

Criticisms of the New Deal

It is rather early to say how successful the New Deal has been, but conflicting opinions have already been expressed. The government continues to depict the associated programmes as offering hope and opportunity, and it views them as a success. However potential problems have been pointed out:

- The options available in unemployment blackspots are likely to be limited.
- Changing economic circumstances may adversely affect the programmes.
- The income offered to some New Deal claimants might be too low.

- Administration problems might arise.
- The most appropriate groups might not have been targeted.
- The training provided might not bring the desired results.

It has also been argued that the type of companies that have agreed to take part in the New Deal are those which would have employed young people anyway. Furthermore there are hundreds of thousands of unemployed people aged 40–55, but to date the government has done little to improve their situation. Pamela Meadows (1999) argues that the emphasis on youth unemployment is misplaced and that older people who could and should be economically active are being ignored. The New Deal programme has been extended to cover these people but the budget allocated is less than 10 per cent of that for the young unemployed.

Housing

'While the housing of the working class has always been a question of the greatest social importance, never has it been so important as now. It is not too much to say that an adequate solution of the housing question is the foundation of all social progress (speech by King Geerge V to local authority representatives at Buckingham Palace, April 1919).

Housing tenure

Housing tenure takes two basic forms: rented and owner-occupied. Traditionally the type of tenure held has tended to be related to social class and economic status. In 1996–97, for example, nearly nine out of ten households headed by people with professional or managerial occupations were owner-occupied, compared with four out of ten of those headed by unskilled manual workers.

Rented accommodation

There are four main categories of rented accommodation:

- Local authority housing, where the property is owned by the local authority and the tenant pays rent. Some people in this sector qualify for help with housing costs (housing benefit), depending on the household income.
- Housing association accommodation, where the property is owned by a housing association and rented to the tenant. As with local authority housing, tenants may receive housing benefit if their

income is below a certain level. (This and local authority accommodation are also known as social housing.)

- Private furnished, where privately owned furnished property is rented out by a landlord/lady to make a profit. Furnished accommodation can be very expensive, and although some benefits may be available to tenants they may not cover all the extras involved in renting in this sector.
- Private unfurnished – as above but tenants provide their own furniture.

Along with the Irish Republic and the Netherlands, the UK has one of the smallest privately rented sectors in the European Union, amounting to 10 per cent of dwellings.

Owner-occupied accommodation

There are two categories of owner-occupied housing:

- Owner-occupied with mortgage – properties being bought by the occupant(s) via a mortgage. The number of such dwellings more than doubled between 1961 and 1996 whilst the number of rented dwellings fell by one sixth.
- Owner-occupied, fully paid. While outright ownership might seem desirable at first glance, no subsidies are availlable from the government and the full cost of repairs and so on falls on the owners. Many people in this category are retired and have paid off their mortgages.

Exercise 10.7

k u

1. Which kind of tenure do you, your family or the people you live with have? Does this have anything to do with age, gender, race social class? Give reasons for your answer.

a

2. Construct a short closed questionnaire on housing tenure that could be distributed around your school/college. This might be a sensitive topic for some people, so bear this in mind. Your questions should include the following:

    1. Does the person being questioned live in a city, town or village?

    2. What types of housing are these in the area?

    3. If there are council estates in the area, where are they situated?

    4. Are new housing estates being built? Are these council or private houses?

    5. Where are the oldest houses in the area?

    6. What type of tenure does the household have? (You will need to explain what tenure means in the questionnaire and give examples.)

Social housing

The Conservative Manifesto of 1979 referred to housing under the heading 'Helping the family' and emphasised 'Homes of Our Own', 'The Sale of Council Houses' and 'Reviving the Private Rented Sector'.

The private rented sector has been in decline for a number of years and now accounts for only around 8 per cent of housing tenure compared with more than 50 per cent in the 1950s (Hill, 1993). Why did this sector suddenly go into such a steep decline? One of the main arguments put forward is that the purchase of houses was no longer considered a good investment and much better returns could be obtained elsewhere.

The Conservatives wished to revitalise the private sector by attracting new investment, and after the election of the Thatcher government in 1979 there was a shift away from the provision of social housing and encouragement of owner-occupation. Fewer local authority dwellings were built, and the government's right to buy scheme (see below) reduced the number of existing dwellings available to rent, resulting in long waiting lists and contributing to an increase in homelessness. Furthermore, many of the remaining dwellings were in poor condition and unsuited to needs of, for example, the sick and disabled.

The role of local authorities as providers of housing reduced even further when the market became more diverse, with housing associations, private sector providers and changes in tenure all playing a part. The introduction of market force, in the construction of social housing, with private builders competing, for contracts, led to rent increases throughout the sector, thus placing financial pressure on the lower paid members of society.

These changes in housing policy and provision had a profound effect on society in general and specific groups in particular. The following subsections describe the changes, the ideology behind them and the implications for the future.

Exercise 10.8

i Go to the library or a learning resource centre and find out whether the Conservative government actually cut expenditure between 1979 and 1989. Using government papers, national statistics (available at www.open.gov.uk.) and *Social Trends* volumes 26, 27 and 28, compile a list of data on housing expenditure and council house building. Compare it over time and note down any changes. Write a summary of these changes in 150 words.

The sale of council houses

As noted throughout this book, the Conservative government was strongly influenced by new right thinking (see Chapters 2, 7 and 9). It believed in individual enterprise, that market forces should direct policy, and that those who wished to better themselves should be enabled to so do. The sale of council housing to sitting tenants at favourable prices was seen as one way of promoting these ideals. Furthermore it would boost the government's revenues and reduce the cost of housing maintenance by making it the responsibility of the new private owners, thus freeing up money for use in other areas of expenditure. Pride of ownership, it was hoped, would also help to solve the social problems found on council estates.

The proposal to sell off council housing appealed to free-market purists, to those who already owned their homes and saw this as socially important, and to those tenants who stood to benefit, particularly those occupying the more desirable terraced and semidetached council houses with gardens.

The proposal duly materialised as the Right to Buy Scheme (RTB), which formed part of the 1980 Housing Act. Although the Act did not come into force until October, over 81 000 council dwellings were sold that year (the majority under previous schemes). In 1981 more than 100 000 dwellings were sold, with sales peaking at 201 880 in 1982. RTB accounted for 90 per cent of these sales (Hughes and Lowe,1995). Overall, between 1979 and 1990 over 1.5 million council dwellings were sold, or around 20 per cent of all council dwellings. This had obvious implications for future housing policies as far fewer council houses were available to rent.

However popular the RTB scheme may have been it was not without problems:

- The sales were very uneven, both geographically and socially.
- A large number of sales were in areas where there was already a high proportion of owner-occupied properties.
- A large number of RTB purchasers were middle-aged, non-manual workers.
- A large proportion of the houses sold were in the more desirable suburban estates. This meant that new council tenants from the poorer social groups – such as single parents, the unemployed and the elderly – were offen confined to less desirable accommodation in high-rise blocks or rundown inner city areas.

With regard to the latter point, it has been suggested that RTB served to polarise the housing market along class lines, in that the middle classes seemed to benefit at the expense of the working-class. As Loney (1986, p. 62) puts it: 'The new owner-occupiers might largely have joined the comfortable majority but they left behind an increasingly impoverished public sector.'

Right to buy applications[1] for and sales[2] of dwellings owned by council sector,[3] 1980–96 (thousands)

Notes:
1. Applications data for 1980 and 1981 are not available.
2. Includes shared ownership sales.
3. Includes local authorities, new towns and Scottish Homes.

(Source: Social Trends, vol. 28, London: HMSO, 1998.)

ITEM A *Exercise 10.9*

Study Item A carefully and answer the following questions:

1. In which year did applications peak?

2. How might this be explained?

3. In which year did sales peak?

4. Why would the proposal to sell off council housing have appealed to free-market purists?

5. The social problems that occurred in public sector housing areas could, it was thought, be solved by home ownership. In what ways could pride of ownership help to solve social problems?

Finally, it is clear that the sales brought political benefits to the government: 59 per cent of those council tenants who had voted Labour in 1979 and subsequently bought their houses deserted Labour and switched to the Conservatives or the SDP – Liberal Alliance (now the Liberal Democrats).

Housing associations

Housing associations are non-profit-making organisations governed by their own constitutions and registered with the Housing Corporation. They provide homes to people on low incomes, the homeless and those living in very poor conditions. Housing associations were important providers of social housing in the nineteenth century, but their position declined with the growth of council housing (Hill, 1993). However in recent years they have experienced something of a revival and according to Hill they now account for a large proportion of new investment in rented housing. In 1993 they owned over half a million homes, or around 3 per cent of the total housing stock.

In the conservative government envisaged that housing associations would become the main providers of social housing, operating within a market (or quasimarket) environment that would promote greater efficiency, economy and output. Indeed the movement's tradition of small-scale provision for people with particular housing needs has in many areas been superseded by an altogether different kind of organisation, 'a larger scale, more homogeneous style of development mounted mainly by a few large national associations' (Hughes and Lowe, 1995). Hughes and Lowe argue that a 'commercial ethos' has undermined the voluntary tradition in that the risks and liabilities of the market environment have influenced the kind of accommodation on offer.

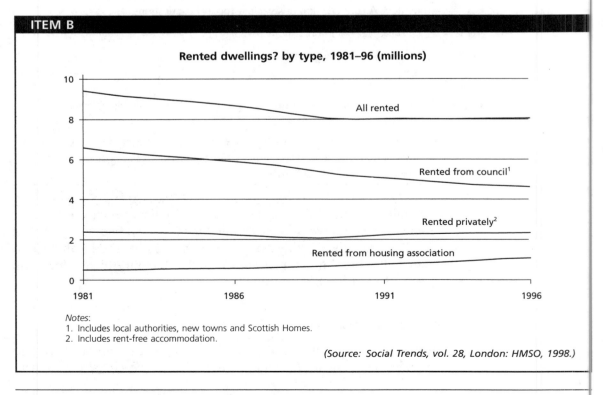

ITEM B

Rented dwellings? by type, 1981–96 (millions)

All rented

Rented from council[1]

Rented privately[2]

Rented from housing association

Notes:
1. Includes local authorities, new towns and Scottish Homes.
2. Includes rent-free accommodation.

(Source: Social Trends, vol. 28, London: HMSO, 1998.)

ITEM B

Exercise 10.10

Study Item B carefully and answer the following questions:

1. What was the rise in the number of dwellings rented from housing associations between 1981 and 1996?

2. Which housing sector rented out the most?

3. Which housing sector experienced a decrease?

Gender and housing

Watson and Cooper (1992) argue that the emergence of owner-occupation as the dominant form of housing tenure, aided by the conservative government's privatisation programme, has had serious consequences for some household groups in terms of access to tenure. Approximately one in three marriages ends in divorce, and finding accommodation after the breakdown of a relationship is crucial for women and men alike. There is a tendency to assume that the female partner will remain in the marital home (and changes to the law have to some extent helped make this so), but Sullivan (1986) claims that nearly half of women leave the marital home, or four out of ten when children are involved. Although the sale of the marital home may provide some cash, acquiring a mortgage for a new property is not a realistic option for many women. There are now more women than ever in the labour market, but the majority tend to be in low-paid, low-status occupations, making it difficult for them to take out mortgages. Another factor affecting women's borrowing power is that many experience quite long periods of economic inactivity, usually as a result of having to care for children or other family members, so overall there is no guarantee that the sale of the marital home will do anything to help the housing situation of the female partner. There is also evidence to suggest that when women do manage to gather the funds to buy a dwelling they are forced to go further downmarket than their former partners and buy an older and cheaper property.

ITEM C

**Tenure of male and female heads of household, 1991
(as percentage of each tenure category)**

	Women	Men
Owner occupation	23.81	76.19
Private rented	30.37	69.63
Housing association	53.78	46.22
Local authority	47.467	52.54
All tenures	30.54	69.46

(Source: 1991 Census.)

ITEM C   *Exercise 10.11*

i   1. According to Item C, who had the highest rate of owner occupation in 1991?

*k**u*   2. How would you explain this?

i   3. Who had the highest rate of tenancy for housing associations?

*k**u*   4. How would you explain this?

ITEM D

**Economic position of men and women heads of household,
all tenures, 1991 (per cent)**

	Men	Women
Economically active	66.32	34.73
Unemployed	6.24	3.54
Economically inactive	27.42	61.72

(Source: 1991 Census.)

ITEM D   *Exercise 10.12*

i   1. According to Item D, what percentage of women were economically active in 1991?

    2. What explanations can you give for the lower percentage of economically active women?

Many women who divorce or separate and do not remarry move into public sector housing, the tenure of which is based on need rather than ability to pay (Ginsburg and Watson, 1992).

ITEM E

Home ownership is the most rewarding form of housing tenure. It satisfies a deep and natural desire on the part of the householder to have independent control of the home that shelters him and his family. It gives him the greatest possible security against the loss of his home; and particularly against the price changes that may threaten his ability to keep it. If the householder buys his house on a mortgage he builds by steady saving a capital asset for himself and his dependents.

(Source: Gilroy and Woods, 1994: 123.)

Exercise 10.13

Read Item E and answer the following questions:

i **a** 1. What assumption is made about home ownership?

i **a** 2. What changes have taken place since 1971 that make this view of home ownership inappropriate today?

In many ways the extract in Item E underlines, much of what is wrong with current housing policy. Watson and Cooper (1992, p. 82) argue that 'The nuclear family household, which has dominated the thinking of policy makers and politicians, is becoming less and less the norm.' It could be argued that certain assumptions about the nature of the family have been instrumental in reproducing and maintaining the patriarchal relations that exist in society. Housing provision in both the public and the private sector often revolves around the needs of the conventional family, to the detriment of single people and lone parents. In the private sector the preference is for two-wage households, and single women and lone parents are viewed as a risk in terms of mortgage lending. The acquisition of public sector accommodation can also be difficult when notions about the deserving and undeserving poor drive allocation policy. Single parents (especially women) are often viewed as undeserving – they may be stereotyped as unreliable, as having had a series of relationships and bearing children for whom the state will have to provide (see to Chapter, 7 pp. 83–9).

Housing and class

The original purpose of public sector housing was to provide homes for the working class, who had long endured the squalor and associated ills of poor and inadequate housing. However it came to be occupied by all social classes, so this type of tenure was not always a useful indicator of status. Many people rented accommodation out of choice rather than necessity, as home ownership was not an issue of any note. Individuals with capital to invest were unlikely to tie up large sums of money in domestic property when far better returns could be obtained by investing it elsewhere. When owner-occupation did expand the purchasers tended to be non-manual workers, managers, business owners and skilled manual workers. The unskilled and the economically inactive remained in the public sector. This led to sociological debate on the likely effects of increased owner-occupation on the UK class structure. The idea that consumption (or the ability to consume) is the driving force in the postmodern world one focus of this debate.

Saunders [1986] argues that just as class relations are determined by the (non)ownership of the means of production, so the main cleavage within the sphere of consumption is determined by the (non)ownership of the means to fulfill consumption requirements. Thus the major consumption sector cleavage is that between those people who can meet their consumption needs through personal ownership of the means of consumption – the middle class – and those who can not, and are thus reliant on the state to provide it for them – the residualised underclass. . . . Saunders . . . claims that three different modes of consumption can be identified within a British context over the past 150 years: a market mode, a socialised mode and a newly emerging privatised mode. In the nineteenth century the primary form of consumption was provided through the market and the main contradiction was between low wages and high costs of consumption. This contradiction provided the context within which a more socialised system of collective consumption developed. This socialised mode of cash benefits and payments in kind attempted to deal with the contradiction by supplementing wages and lowering consumption costs. However, this socialised mode has given rise to a new set of contradictions – expressed in terms of the 'fiscal crisis of the state' on the left and theories of 'overload' on the right – and this has ushered in the latest mode of consumption – privatised . . .

In the long run Saunders suggests that the socialised mode will be seen as a 'holding operation' between the market and the privatised modes of consumption. This developing privatised mode will, he argues, have deep implications for the British social structure. His central conclusion is that we are moving towards a position in which the majority of the population will be able to satisfy most of their consumption requirements through some form of market – subsidised where appropriate by the state – whilst the minority will be 'cast adrift on the waterlogged raft of what remains of the welfare state.'

He goes further by arguing that this consumption cleavage is at least as fundamental as the traditional class cleavage in the determination of many spheres of people's existence and especially with respect to housing 'may actually come to outweigh class location.'

(Source: Burrows and Butler, 1989, pp. 340.)

Income of households in council housing, UK, 1968–86 (per cent)

Proportion of council tenants who were among the:	1968	1978	1983	1986
Poorest 30% of all households	31	42	52	60
Middle 20% of all households	23	23	23	22
Richest 50% of all households	46	35	25	18

(Source: Social Trends, vol. 23, London: HMSO, 1993, p. 62.)

Exercise 10.14

Study Items F and G and answer the following questions:

i 1. What is meant by 'a residualised underclass' (Item F)?

i 2. According to Saunders (Item F), what are class relations are determined by?

i 3. What are the three modes of consumption that Saunders claims can be identified?

i 4. Summarise Saunders' central conclusion.

i 5. According to Item G, in 1968–86 which household group experienced (a) the greatest increase in council house tenure, (b) the greatest decrease in council house tenure?

In June 1998 Serplan (the committee of local authorities that works out how many houses need to be built in the South-East) announced a reduction of 200 000 from its previous estimate. It decided that fewer new homes would be needed in the South-East because the rents and mortgages in the area would be too high for poor people to afford. It appears that there was no plan to build houses that the poor could afford. Homes would continue to be built for the affluent middle classes while an increasing number of the poor would become homeless. Those that were housed would be 'ghettoised' in the worst estates or privately rented, run-down accommodation whilst the middle classes and the rich enjoyed the comforts of private developments away from the poor.

Housing and race

The Nationality Act of 1948 gave citizenship to the peoples of Britain's former colonies. In theory this should have given them access to all that citizenship entailed (equal entitlement, employment and residential rights, protection under the law, access to the welfare state and so on), but in practice things turned out rather differently. Labour shortages during the late 1940s had increased the demand for cheap labour, and pressure to address these shortages led to the encouragement of immigration from the Commonwealth countries. However little effort was made to accommodate the influx of new residents, with housing policies being at best uncoordinated and at worst negligible.

According to Smith, Robinson and Peach (1981) the use of migrant labour was viewed as a short-term measure and it was thought that the migrants would leave the UK once the labour shortages were over. To provide them with accommodation would in all likelihood encourage them to stay, so the government remade relatively little effort in this particular area of housing policy.

Exercise 10.15

Henderson and Karn (1987) used a range of methods to study racism in the allocation of council housing in Birmingham, including an ethnographic study of how the allocation process operated. They found evidence of institutional racism, particularly in the case of six explicit policies that in their view discriminated against Afro-Caribbean and Asian applicants:

- Applicants were required to have resided in the city for at least five years (reduced to two years in 1977).
- Applications from owner-occupiers were disqualified.
- Applications from single people of all ages were disqualified.
- Applications from unmarried couples were disqualified unless they had cohabitated for five years in the case of childless couples and two years in the case of couples with children.
- Applications from joint or re-constituted families were disqualified.
- Black families were dispersed to different areas of Birmingham (dropped in 1975).

1. How did these policies discriminate against ethnic groups?

2. Do you consider the policies to be racist? Give reasons for your answer.

ITEM H

Tenure patterns by ethnic origin of household, 1983 (per cent)

	White	West Indian	Asian	Indian	Pakistani
Owner-occupied	59	41	72	77	80
Council rented	30	46	19	16	13
Private rented	9	6	6	5	5
Housing association	2	8	2	2	1
	Bangladeshi	**African Asian**	**Muslim**	**Hindu**	**Sikh**
Owner occupied	30	73	67	73	91
Council rented	53	19	24	16	6
Private rented	11	5	6	8	3
Housing association	4	2	2	3	–

(Source: Brown, 1984.)

ITEM H

Exercise 10.16

Examine Item H and answer the following questions:

1. Which ethnic group had the highest percentage of its members in council accommodation?

2. Which group had the lowest?

3. Which group had the highest number in private accommodation?

4. Which group had the lowest?

Personal social services

Informal care

Before the modern welfare state existed families were the main providers of care. This type of care is referred to as informal care. As you have read in Chapters 6 and 8, assumptions were made in the Beveridge Report about the role of women as primary carers and the dependants of males. Other social services were seen as secondary to those provided by the family, or rather the woman of the family.

According to Finch (1989) there was a mythological 'golden age' of the family in which the family provided care for the sick and elderly, but in the nineteenth century few people lived long enough to become dependent on the family, either economically or physically. Therefore to say that families provide less case these days is misguided – as far as elderly people are concerned, many families may well provide more.

Government policy on informal care relies heavily on women carers, care in the community being a prime example. However since the early 1980s women's participation in the labour force has grown significantly and may continue to grow, which has implications for the provision of informal care. In addition the rising divorce rate has resulted in an increase in single parent families, and given the additional tasks involved in lone parenting, single mothers are unlikely to the time to care for sick or elderly relatives.

Exercise 10.17

'Normalising lives for dependent people may in effect de-normalise the lives of the carers' (Acker and Abbot, 1996, p. 12).

1. List the kind of work you think might be involved in informal care.

2. What do you think the quote by Acker and Abbot means?

The Thatcher government and New Right thinkers believed that the wider community should play a part in welfare provision, and in 1990 the National Health Service and Community Care Act came into being. Amongst its aims was greater participation by the voluntary sector, charities and the private sector. There should be more choices available to the consumer and the needs of each individual should be assessed. Individuals would be able to choose, with the support and help of medical staff, to leave the isolation of mental health institutions and live in the community.

The Mental Health Foundation (Thompson, 1994 p. 62) provided the following explanation of community care: 'Community care is intended to provide help and support for people who could not otherwise manage on their own. The sort of people who may be eligible for community care, include frail older people, those with physical disabilities, drug or alcohol problems learning disabilities, or mental health problems.' Most of the concerns expressed about community care related to the care of the mentally ill and the provisions that would be made for them. It was thought that some mentally ill people could prove a danger to the community. Conversely, rather than benefiting from life in the community they could suffer from the consequences of being labelled as mentally ill – as labelling theory points out in the case of criminals, those in society generally react negatively to such labels.

The rights and wrongs of community care have been much debated and many negative arguments have been raised. Nonetheless we as a society have to take responsibility for the vulnerable and decide how to provide the necessary care, be it formal, informal or voluntary.

Voluntary care

Voluntary care has its roots in the late eighteenth and nineteenth centuries. The Industrial Revolution led to the mass migration of rural people to the new industrial towns to find work in the factories. With this came overcrowding, poverty, squalor, drunkenness and disease. There was widespread concern about this state of affairs and voluntary organisations were set up to try to alleviate some of the problems. The voluntary sector now comprises an estimated 400 000 charitable organisations that provide services for or represent the interests of particular social groups. These vary considerably in size and structure, ranging from large national or international organisations with local branches to small local groups. Some of the larger organisations employ full-time staff at a central office and rely on unpaid volunteers to perform various functions at the local level. Oxfam and Help the Aged are two such organisations.

Exercise 10.18

1. Consult a register of voluntary organisations at your library or resource centre. How many organisations are listed? What areas of care do they participate in (for example helping the elderly, children, the poor, the disabled)? Draw up a table showing the main national/international organisations and the groups of people they help.

2. More women than men are involved in voluntary work. Suggest possible reasons for this.

Organisations in the voluntary sector can obtain charitable status if they are able to meet set criteria. Charitable donations can then be solicited from individuals or businesses. Other sources of funds are charity shops, which have become commonplace in most high streets and are run by volunteers, and mail order sales from charity catalogues. Voluntary organisations may also receive funds from central or local government, and without this many organisations would find it difficult to continue.

Studies indicate that the distribution of voluntary services is far from uniform. Affluent areas and those with a high proportion of middle-class people tend to have a high degree of voluntary provision but a low degree of need. This conforms with with the inverse care law (discussed in Chapter 8), which states that areas with the greatest need receive less help than areas with less need. As Johnson (1981 p. 67) points out, 'the voluntary sector is characterised by fragmentation and poor co-ordination, leading to overlapping and gaps, with ample facilities in some areas and shortages in others'. Hence those in most need do not receive as much help as they should because voluntary care is not logically organised.

In a sense the increased use of voluntary sector care represents a return to the 'Victorian values' that were close to the heart of Conservative social policy. As we have seen, the voluntary sector has a long history and for a considerable time it filled in the gaps left by statutory welfare provison. Today, however, it has returned to its central position.

Exercise 10.19

a i k u e

Arrange to visit the local branch of a voluntary organisation to conduct a short interview with some of the volunteers. Your interview should be structured and the questions preprepared. This will allow you to concentrate on the answers. Amongst other things, try to find out:

- What a volunteer does.
- The nature of the 'client' group.
- The background of the volunteers.
- The reasons why the volunteers do this work.

After your visit write up your findings in a short report and comment on your chosen methodology – how well did it work, how could it have been improved?

Bibliography

Abel-Smith, B. and P. Townsend (1965) *The Poor and the Poorest* (London: G. Bell and Sons).

Acker, S. and D. Abbot (1996) *Social Policy for Nurses and the Caring Professions* (Oxford: Oxford University Press).

Alcock, P. (1996) *Social policy in Britain: themes and issues* (Basingstoke: Macmillan).

Atkinson, J. (1985) 'The Changing Corporation' in D. Clutterbuck (ed.) *New Patterns of Work* (Aldershot: Gowe).

Bagguley, P. and K. Mann (1992) 'Idle Thieving Bastards: Scholarly Representations of the Underclass', *Work, Employment and Society*, vol. 6, no. 1.

Balchin (1990) *Housing Policy* (London: Routledge).

Baldwin, P. (1999) 'Postcodes chart growing income divide', *Guardian*, 25 October.

Banfield, E. C. (1970) *The unheavenly city: the nature and future of our urban crisis* (Boston: Little Brown).

Barrett, M. (1988) *Women's Oppression Today: Problems in Marxist Feminist Analysis* (London: Verso).

Bell, D. (1973) *The Coming of Post-Industrial Society* (New York: Basic Books).

Bellamy, C. (1998) *The state of the world's children, 1998* (Oxford; New York: Published for UNICEF by Oxford University Press).

Benn, Melissa (2002) 'The hour of reckoning', *The Guardian*, 30 January.

Bertens, H. (1995) *The idea of the postmodern: a history* (London: Routledge).

Beveridge, W. (1942) *Report on Social Insurance and Allied Services* (London: HMSO).

Booth, C. (1891–1903) *The Life and Labour of the People in London*, 17 vols (London: Williams & Norgate).

Bradley, H. (1989) *Men's Work, Women's Work* (Cambridge: Polity).

Bradshaw, J. and H. Holmes (1989) *Living on the edge: a study of the living standards of families on benefit in Tyne & Wear* (London: Tyneside Child Poverty Action Group).

Bradshaw, J., National Children's Bureau and Unicef (1990) *Child poverty and deprivation in the UK* (London: National Children's Bureau).

Braun, J. (1997) *Industrialisation and Everyday Life* (Cambridge: Cambridge University Press).

Brown, C. (1984) *Black and White in Britain: The Third PSI Survey* (Oxford: Heinemann).

Brown, C, and J. Lawton (1993) *Training for Equality* (London: PSI).

Brundtland, G. H. (1988) *Our common future: a perspective by the United Kingdom on the report of the World Commission on Environment and Development* (London: Department of the Environment).

Brundtland, G. H. (1996) *Our Common Future* (Oxford: Oxford University Press).

Bryson, L. (1992) *Welfare and the State: Who Benefits?* (London: Macmillan).

Burchart, T. and J. Hills (1997) *Private Welfare Insurance and Social Security* (York: Joseph Rowntree Foundation).

Buroway, M. and E. O. Wright (2000) Sociological Marxism, unpublished manuscript available at: *www.ssc.wisc.edu/~wright/SocMarx.pdf*

Burrows, R. and T. Butler (1989) 'Middle Mass and the Pit: A critical review of Peter Saunder's *Sociology of Consumption*', *Sociological Review*, vol. 37, no. 2.

Byrne, D. (1997) 'Chaotic places or complex places: cities in a post-industrial era', in S. Westwwod and J. Williams (eds), *Imagining Cities* (London: Routledge).

Byrne, D. (1999) *Social Exclusion* (Buckingham: Open University Press).

Callinicos, A. (1989) *Against Postmodernism: A Marxist Critique* (Cambridge: Polity).

Carter, J. (ed.) (1998) *Postmodernity and the Fragmentation of the Welfare State* (London: Routledge).

Central Statistical Office (1994) *Urban Trends 33* (London: HMSO).

Central Statistical Office (1996) *Regional Trends 1996* (London: HMSO).

Coates, K. and R. Silburn (1970) *Poverty: The Forgotten Englishmen* (Harmondsworth: Penguin).

Cooper, A., R. Nye and Social Market Foundation (1995) *The Rowntree inquiry and 'trickle down'* (London: Social Market Foundation).

Crosland, A. (1956) *The future of socialism* (London: Jonathan Cape).

Davis, K. and W. E. Moore (1945) 'Some principles of stratification', *American Sociological Review*, vol. 10.

Dean, H. and P. Taylor-Gooby (1990) *Dependency Culture: The Explosion of a Myth* (Hemel Hempstead: Harvester Wheatsheaf).

Devine, F. (1992) *Affluent Workers Revisited* (Edinburgh: Edinburgh University Press).

Dobson, B. (1994) *Diet, choice and poverty: social, cultural and nutritional aspects of food consumption among low-income families* (London: Family Policy Studies Centre / Joseph Rowntree Foundation).

DoE (1971) 'Home Ownership', White Paper (London: HMSO).

Doyal, L. (1995) *What Makes Women Sick? Gender and the Political Economy of Health* (London: Macmillan).

DSS (1998) *New Ambitions for our Country: A New Contract for Welfare* (London: HMSO).

Economic Review – Data Supplement, September 1998.

Elliott, L., P. Wintour and R. Kelly (1994) 'Tory taxes favour rich says study', *Guardian*, 9 February.

Ermisch, J. (1986) *The economics of the family: applications to divorce and remarriage* (London: Centre for Economic Policy Research).

Esping-Anderson, G. (1990) *The Three Worlds of Welfare Capitalism* (Cambridge: Polity).

Falkingham, J. and J. Hills (1995) *The Dynamic of Welfare: the Welfare State and the Life Cycle* (New York: Prentice Hall).

Ferge, J. (1996) *Dynamics of Deprivation* (London: Avebury Press).

Field, F. (1997) *Are Low Wages Inevitable?* (Nottingham: Spokesman).

Finch, J. (1989) *Family Obligations and Social Change* (Cambridge: Polity Press).

Finch, J. (2001) 'A boss is worth 45 workers', *Guardian*, 30 August.

Finch, J. and J. Mason (1993) *Negotiating Family Responsibilities* (London: Routledge).

Friedman, M. (1980) *Free to Choose* (Harmondsworth: Penguin).

Gaffney, D., A. Pollack, D. Price and J. Shaoul (1999) 'The Politics of the Private Finance Initiative and the New NHS', *British Medical Journal*, 319.

Gardner, H. (1995) 'Cracking Open the IQ Box' in Fraser, S. (ed.) *The Bell Curve Wars* (New York: Basic Books).

Giddens, A. (1994) *Beyond Left and Right* (Cambridge: Polity).

Giddens, A. (1999a) *The Third Way* (Cambridge: Polity).

Giddens, A. (1999b) *Runaway World*, The BBC Reith Lectures (London: BBC).

Gilroy, R. and R. Woods (1996) *Housing Women* (London: Routledge).

Glass, D. V. (ed.) (1954) *Social Mobility in Modern Britain* (London: Routledge).

Glendenning, C. and J. Millar (1987) *Women and Poverty in Britain* (Hemel Hempstead: Harvester Wheatsheaf).

Glendenning, C. and J. Millar (1994) *Women and Poverty in Britain: The 1990s* (Hemel Hempstead: Harvester Wheatsheaf).

Glyn, A. and D. Miliband (eds) (1994) *Paying for Inequality* (London: IPPR).

Goldthorpe, J. (1980) *Social Mobility and Class Structure in Modern Britain* (Oxford: Clarendon Press).

Goodhart, D. (1999) 'Don't Mind the Gap', *Prospect*, August/September.

Goodin, R. E., B. Hepples, R. Muffeus and H. Dirven (2000) 'The Real Worlds of Welfare Capitalism', in C. Pierson and F. Castles (eds), *The Welfare State Reader* (Cambridge: Polity).

Goodman, A., P. Johnson and S. Webb (1997) *Inequality in the UK* (Oxford: Oxford University Press).

Gordon, D., P. Townsend, R. Levitas, C. Pantazis, S. Payne, D. Patsios, S. Middleton, K. Ashworth, L. Adelman, J. Bradshaw and J. Williams (2000) *Poverty and Social Exclusion in Britain* (York: York Publishing Services for Joseph Rowntree Foundation).

Gordon, D. M. (1996) *Fat and mean: the corporate squeeze of working Americans and the myth of managerial 'downsizing'* (New York: Martin Kessler Books).

Gordon, P. and A. Newnham (1985) *Passports to Benefits: Racism in Social Security* (London: CPAG).

Gorz, A. (1982) *Farewell to the Working Class* (London: Pluto).

Gorz, A. (1999) *Reclaiming work: beyond the wage-based society* (Cambridge: Polity Press).

Gove Philip, B. (1993) *Webster's third new international dictionary of the English language* (Chicago: Encyclopaedia Britannica).

Gramsci, A. (1971) *Selections from the Prison Notebooks* (London: Lawrence & Wishart).

Halsey, A. H. (1985) *British Social Trends since 1900* (London: Macmillan).

Hamilton, M. and M. Hirszowicz (1993) *Class and Inequality* (London: Harvester Wheatsheaf).

Haralambos, M. and M. Holborn (2000) *Sociology: Themes and Perspectives*, 5th edn (London: Collins).

Harrington, M. (1962) *The Other America: Poverty in the US* (Harmondsworth: Penguin).

Harloe, M., C. Pickvance and J. Urry (1990) *Place, policy and politics: do localities matter?* (London: Unwin Hyman).

Hawkins, J., A. Delahunty and F. McDonald (1997) *The Concise Oxford School Dictionary* (Oxford: Oxford University Press).

Hayter, T. (1989) *Creation of World Poverty* (London: Pluto).

Heath, A. (1992) 'The attitudes of the underclass', in D. J. Smith (ed.), *Understanding the Underclass* (London: PSI).

Held, D. (1995) *Democracy and the Global Order* (Cambridge: Polity).

Henderson, J. W. and V. A. Karn (1987) *Race, class and state housing: inequality and the allocation of public housing in Britain* (Aldershot: Gower).

Herrnstein, R. and C. Murray (1994) *The Bell Curve* (New York: Free Press).

Hill, M. (1993) *The Welfare State in Britain* (Aldershot: Edward Elgar).

Hills, J. (1995) *Inquiry into Income and Wealth* (York: Joseph Rowntree Foundation).

Hills, J. (1998) *Income and Wealth: the latest evidence* (York: Joseph Rowntree Foundation).

Hillyard, P. and S. Watson (1996) 'Postmodernism and Social Policy: A contradiction in terms?' *Journal of Social Policy* vol. 25, no. 3.

Hirst, P. and G. Thompson (1999) *Globalization in Question*, 2nd edn (Cambridge: Polity Press).

Hobson, D. (1999) *The National Wealth* (London: HarperCollins).

Hoogvelt, A. (1982) *Globalisation and the Post-Colonial World* (London: Palgrave Macmillan).

Howarth, C., P. Kenway, G. Palmer and R. Miorelli (1999) *Monitoring Poverty and Social Exclusion 1999* (York: Joseph Rowntree Foundation).

Howarth, C., P. Kenway, G. Palmer and C. Street (1998) *Monitoring Poverty and Social Exclusion: Labour's Inheritance* (York: Joseph Rowntree Foundation).

Hughes, D. and S. Lowe (1995) *Social housing law and policy* (London: Butterworths).

Hurl, B. (1988) *Privatization and the public sector* (London: Heinemann Educational).

Hurst, C. (2001) 'Pay – and display', *Guardian*, 30 August.

Hutton, W. (1996) *The State We're In* (London: Vintage).

Hutton, W. (2001) 'Accountants' words that shame a whole strategy', *Observer*, 26 August.

Ichimura, H. and C. Taber (2000) *Direct estimation of policy impacts* (London: Institute for Fiscal Studies).

Institute for Fiscal, Studies and Goldman Sachs International (1997) *The IFS green budget: summer 1997* (London: Institute for Fiscal Studies in collaboration with Goldman Sachs).

Johnson, N. (1981) *Voluntary social services* (Oxford: Basil Blackwell).

Johnson, P. and H. Reed. (1996) *Two Nations: The Inheritance of Poverty and Affluence* (London: IFS).

Jones, T. (1993) *Britain's Ethnic Minorities: an analysis of the Labour Force Survey* (London: PSI).

Joseph, K. and J. Sumption (1979) *Equality* (London: J. Murray).

Judge, A. (1982) 'The growth and decline of public expenditure', in A. Walker (ed.), *Public Expenditure and Social Policy* (London: Heinemann).

Kempson, E. (1996) *Life on a low income* (York: York Publishing Services for the Joseph Rowntree Foundation).

Keynes, J. M. (1936) *General Theory of Employment, Interest and Money* (London: Papermac).

Kilty, Keith M., Virginia E. Richardson and Elizabeth A. Segal (1997) *Income security and public assistance for women and children* (New York: Haworth Press).

Kincaid, J. (1973) *Poverty and Equality in Britain* (Harmondsworth: Penguin).

Kirby, M. (1999) *Stratification and Differentiation* (Basingstoke: Macmillan).

Kirby, M., W. Kidd, F. Koubel, J. Barter, T. Hope, A. Kirton, N. Madry, P. Manning and K. Triggs (1997) *Sociology in Perspective* (Oxford: Heinemann).

Kirby, M., W. Kidd, F. Koubel, J. Barter, T. Hope, A. Kirton, N. Madry, P. Manning and K. Triggs (2000) *Sociology in Perspective: AQA Edition* (Oxford: Heinemann).

Kirby, M., W. Kidd, F. Koubel, J. Barter, T. Hope, A. Kirton, N. Madry, P. Manning and K. Triggs (2000) *Sociology in Perspective for OCR* (Oxford: Heinemann).

Kodias, J. E. and J. P. Jones (1991) 'A contextual examination of the feminization of poverty' *Geoforum*, vol. 22, no. 2.

Labour Research Survey (1995) *Survey of Directors*, Labour Research, August.

Land, H. and H. Rose (1995) *Compulsory Altruism for Some or Altruistic Society for All? In Defence of Welfare* (London: Tavistock).

Lassman, P. and J. Speirs (1994) *Weber* (Cambridge: Cambridge University Press).

Lawson, T. and J. Garrod (1996) *The Complete A-Z Sociology Handbook* (London: Hodder & Stoughton).

Lawson, T. and T. Heaton (1996) *Education and Training* (Basingstoke: Macmillan).

Lazear, E. P. and R. T. Michael (1988) *Allocation of Income within the Household* (Chicago, Ill.: University of Chicago Press).

Le Grand, J. (1990a) 'The State of Welfare', in J. Hills (ed.) *The State of Welfare: The Welfare State in Britain since 1974* (Oxford: Oxford University Press).

Le Grand, J. (1990b) *Privatisation and the Welfare State* (London: Allen & Unwin).

Lewis, O. (1965) *La Vida* (Harmondsworth: Penguin).

Liebow, E. (1964) *Tally's Corner* (Boston, Mass.: Little, Brown).

Lister, R. (1991) 'Concepts of Poverty', *Social Studies Review*, vol. 6, no. 5.

Loney, M. (1986) *The politics of greed: the New Right and the welfare state* (London: Pluto Press).

Mack, J. and S. Lansley (1985) *Poor Britain* (London: George Allen & Unwin).

Mack, J. and S. Lansley (1992) *Breadline Britain 1990s* (London: London Weekend Television).

Madry, N. and M. Kirby (1996) *Investigating Work, Unemployment and Leisure* (London: Collins).

Mann, N. (1995) 'Britain "second among equals"', *New Statesman and Society*, 10 February.

Marshall, G., H. Newby, D. Rose and C. Vogler (1988) *Social Class in Modern Britain* (London: Hutchinson).

Marshall, T. H. (1963) 'Citizenship and Social Class', in Marshall, T. H. (ed) *Sociology at the Crossroads* (London: Heinemann).

Marsland, D. (1996) *Welfare or Welfare State* (London: Macmillan).

Mayer, Susan E. (1997) *What money can't buy: family income and children's life chances* (Cambridge, Mass.: London: Harvard University Press).

Mead, L. (1992) *The New Politics of Poverty – The Non-Working Poor in America* (New York: Basic Books).

Meadows, P. (1999) *The flexible labour market: implications for pensions provision* (London: National Association of Pension Funds).

Meager, N., J. Moralee and J. Court (1996) *Winners and Losers* (London: Institute for Employment Studies).

Miliband, R. (1969) *The State in Capitalist Society* (London: Weidenfeld & Nicolson).

Miller, W. B. (1962) 'Lower class culture as a generating milieu of gang delinquency' in M. E. Wolfgang and N. Johnson (eds), *The Sociology of Crime and Deviance* (New York: John Wiley & Sons).

Modood, T., S. Beishon and S. Virdee (1997) *Ethnic Minorities in Britain: Diversity and Disadvantage* (London: PSI).

Morgan, P. (1995) *Farewell to the Family?* (London: IEA).

Mulgan, G. (1998) *Connexity* (London: Vintage).

Murray, C. (1990) *The Emerging British Underclass* (London: IEA).

Myrdal, G. (1962) *Challenge to Affluence* (London: Victor Gollancz).

Nisbett, R. (1995) 'Race, IQ and Scientism' in Fraser, S. (ed.) *The Bell Curve Wars* (Harmondsworth: Penguin).

O'Brien, M. and S. Penna (1998) *Theorising Welfare* (London: Sage).

O'Connor, J. (1973) *The Fiscal Crisis of the State* (New York: St Martin's Press).

O'Connor, J. (1984) *Accumulation Crisis* (Oxford: Blackwell).

O'Donnell, M. (1987) 'Ideology, social policy and the welfare state', *Social Studies Review*, vol. 2, no. 4.

Offe, C. (1984) *The contradictions of the welfare state* (London: Hutchinson).

Offe, C. (1977) *Industry and inequality: the achievement principle in work and social status* (New York: St Martin's Press).

ONS (1993) *Social Trends*, vol. 23 (London: HMSO).

ONS (1998) *Social Trends*, vol. 28 (London: HMSO).

ONS (1999) *New Earnings Survey 1999* (London: HMSO).

Oppenheim, C. (1990) *Poverty: The Facts* (London: CPAG).

Oppenheim, C. (1993) *Poverty: The Facts*, 2nd edn (London: CPAG).

Oppenheim, C. and L. Harker (1996) *Poverty: The Facts*, 3rd edn (London: CPAG).

OUP (1997) *The Concise Oxford Dictionary* (Oxford: Oxford University Press).

Orshansky, M. (1977) *Documentation of background information and rationale for current poverty matrix* (Washington: US Department of Health Education and Welfare).

Parker, H. and M. Nelson (2000) *Low cost but acceptable incomes for older people: a minimum income standard for households aged 65–74 years in the UK: January 1999 prices* (Bristol: Policy Press: Family Budget Unit).

Parsons, T. (1977) *The Evolution of Societies* (Englewood Cliffs, NJ: Prentice-Hall).

Pen, J. (1971) *Income distribution* (London: Allen Lane).

Phillips, M. (1992) 'The truth gap over the poverty gap', *The Guardian*, 3 April.

Philo, G. and D. Miller (2001) *Market killing: what the free market does and what social scientists can do about it* (Harlow: Longman).

Piachaud, D. (1981) 'Peter Townsend and the Holy Grail', *New Society*, 10 September.

Piachaud, D. (1987) 'Problems in the definition and measurement of poverty', *Journal of Social Policy*, vol. 16, no. 2, pp. 147–64.

Piore, M. and C. Sabel (1984) *The Second Industrial Divide* (New York: Basic Books).

Pollock, A., J. Shaoul, D. Rowland and S. Player (2001) *A Response to the IPPR Commission on Public–Private Partnerships* (London: Catalyst).

Rein, M. (1970) *Social policy: issues of choice and change* (New York: Random House).

Rentoul, J. (1987) *The Rich Get Richer* (London: Unwin Hyman).

Rex, J. (1986) *Race and Ethnicity* (Buckingham: Open University Press).

Robertson, R. (1992) *Globalization: Social Theory and Global Culture* (London: Sage).

Rosen, J. and C. Lane (1995) 'The Sources of the Bell Curve' in Fraser, S. (ed.) *The Bell Curve Wars* (Harmondsworth: Penguin).

Rowntree, S. (1901) *Poverty: A Study of Town Life* (London: Macmillan).

Rowntree, B. S. (1941) *Poverty and Progress: a second social survey of York* (London: Longmans Green).

Rowntree, B. S. and G. R. Lavers (1951) *Poverty and the Welfare State: a third social survey of York dealing only with economic questions* (London: Longmans Green).

Rubinow, I. M. (1969) *Social Insurance* (New York: Arno).

Rutter, M. and N. Madge (1976) *Cycles of Deprivation* (London: Heinemann).

Ryan, A. (1999) 'Britain: Recycling the Third Way', *Dissent*, Spring.

Sabel, C. (1982) *Work and Politics: The Division of Labour in Industry* (Cambridge: Cambridge University Press).

Saunders, P. (1986) *Social Theory of the Urban Question* (London: Routledge).

Saunders, P. (1990) *Social Class and Stratification* (London: Routledge).

Saunders, P. (1995) *Capitalism: A Social Audit* (Buckingham: Open University Press).

Saunders, P. and C. Harris (1994) *Privatization and popular capitalism* (Buckingham: Open University Press).

Scott, J. (1994) *Poverty and Wealth* (London: Longman).

Sefton, T. (1997) *The changing distribution of the social wage* (London: Suntory Toyota International Centre for Economics and Related Disciplines, London School of Economics and Political Science).

Shaoul, J. (2001) 'Privatisation: Claims, outcomes and explanations' in Philo, G. and Miller, D. (eds) *Market Killing* (London: Longman).

Skidelsky, Robert, A. Jacob and R. Nye (1998) *The future of welfare* (London: Social Market Foundation).

Smith, Susan, V. Robinson and C. Peach (1991) *Ethnic segregation in cities* (London: Croom Helm).

Tawney, R. H. (1961) *Equality* (London: Unwin).

Taylor-Gooby, P. (1998) *The future of giving: evidence from the British Social Attitudes Survey* (Tonbridge: Charities Aid Foundation).

Thomas, G. M. (1997) *The Extent of the Atonement: a dilemma for Reformed theology from Calvin to the Consensus (1536–1675)* (Carlisle: Paternoster).

Thompson, D. (1994) *Mental illness: the fundamental facts* (London: Mental Health Foundation).

Townsend, P. (1979) *Poverty in the UK* (Harmondsworth: Penguin).

Townsend Alan, R. and J. Lewis (1989) *The North–South divide: regional change in Britain in the 1980s* (London: Paul Chapman).

Townsend, P. (1997) 'Poverty and Policy: what can we do about the poor?' *Sociology Review*.

Toynbee, P. and D. Walker (2001) *Did Things Get Better?* (Harmondsworth: Penguin).

Treanor, J. (2001) 'Executive pay shoots up by 28%', *Guardian*, 29 August.

Trowler, P. (1989) *Investigating Health, Welfare and Poverty* (London: Collins).

Tudor-Hart , J. (1971) 'The inverse care law', *The Lancet*, 27 February.

United Nations Development, Programme (1996) *Human development report* (New York; Oxford: Oxford University Press).

United Nations Development, Programme (1998) *Human development report* (New York; Oxford: Oxford University Press).

United Nations (1999) *Platform for Action: Women and Poverty* (New York: UN).

Valentine, C. (1968) *Culture and Poverty* (Chicago, Ill.: University of Chicago Press).

Van der Werff, M. and C. Donellan (1996) *Poverty Trap* (Cambridge: Independence Publishers).

Veit-Wilson, John (1994) *Dignity not poverty: a minimum income standard for the UK* (London: Institute for Public Policy Research).

Walby, S. (1990) *Theorizing Patriarchy* (Oxford: Blackwell).

Walker, A (1997) *Britain Divided: The Growth of Social Exclusion in the 1980s and 1990s* (London: CPAG).

Walker, C. (1993) *Managing Poverty* (London: Routledge).

Walker, L. (1994) *Managing Poverty* (London: Routledge).

Walker, Robert L., K. Ashworth and S. Middleton (1994) *Family fortunes: pressures on parents and children in the 1990s* (London: Child Poverty Action Group).

Walker, Robert L. and L. Leisering (1998) *The dynamics of modern society: poverty, policy and welfare* (Bristol: Policy Press).

Walsh, M., P. Stephens and S. Moore (2000) *Social Policy and Welfare* (Cheltenham: Stanley Thornes).

Waters, M. (1997) 'Inequality After Class', in D. Owen (ed.), *Sociology After Postmodernism* (London: Sage).

Watson, L. and R. Cooper (1992) *Housing with care: supported housing and housing associations* (York: Joseph Rowntree Foundation).

Webb, S. (1993) 'Women's incomes, past, present and prospects', *Fiscal Studies*, vol. 14, no. 4.

Webb, S. and A. Goodman (1996) *For Richer, for Poorer* (London: IFS).

Westergaard, J. (1995) *Who Gets What? The Hardening of Class Inequality in the Late Twentieth Century* (Cambridge: Polity).

Westergaard, J. and H. Resler (1976) *Class in a Capitalist Society* (Harmondsworth: Penguin).

White, P. (1995) 'Where income support falls short', *Young People Now*.

Willetts, D. (1992) *Modern Conservatism* (Harmondsworth: Penguin).

Williams, F. (1989) *Social Policy: A Critical Introduction* (Cambridge: Polity).

Wilson, W. J. (1987) *The Truly Disadvantaged* (Chicago, Ill.: University of Chicago Press).

Wiseman, J. (1998) *Global Nation?* (Cambridge: Cambridge University Press).

Answers to examination questions

Chapter 5, p. 94
The logical order is: **(g), (d), (c), (b), (h), (e), (a), (f)**.

Chapter 6, p. 117
The logical order is: **(c), (a), (b), (f), (e), (d), (g)**.

Author index

Subject index

absolute definitions   43, 44, 45, 47, 48, 51, 60
absolute poverty   43, 44, 45, 48

bourgeoisie   39

capability poverty   61
capitalism   34, 36, 39, 111, 112, 115, 118, 128, 150, 151, 152, 154, 156
capitalist   30, 70, 97, 115, 116, 119, 128, 150, 151, 152, 154, 156
Care in the Community   154, 195
Child Poverty Action Group   60, 65, 76
Child Support Agency   84
citizenship   34, 54, 62, 117, 153, 193
claiming class   101
coercion   31
consumption property   16
contribution principle   39, 40
cost of living   13
culture of dependency   104, 143
culture of poverty   98, 99, 100, 138, 143

debt   133, 134, 135
deindustrialisation   123
dependency culture   103, 108, 117
deprivation index   55, 56
disability   45, 80, 82, 83
Disability Discrimination Act   81
discourse   157
disposable income   6, 7
dual systems   36

employment   5, 22, 48, 78, 85, 108, 121
equal opportunities   26, 28
Equal Pay Act   86
equality   3, 32, 33
ethnicity   8, 9, 10, 11, 13, 38, 72

Fabian Society   155
Fabianism   155
feminisation   84, 89
feminism   40, 151, 156, 157
feminist   32, 33, 36, 97, 115, 153, 154

Fordism   99
  post-Fordism   97
Fordist   125
  post-Fordist   127
functionalism   27, 119
functionalist   27, 29, 30
functionalists   28, 29, 43

gender   10, 11, 13, 38, 45, 72, 79, 80, 83, 86, 87, 97, 189
globalisation   40, 88, 97, 120, 126, 128, 131, 139
gross domestic product   7, 136

housing associations   187, 188, 189
housing   3, 183, 184, 185, 186, 188, 189, 191, 192, 193, 194
human rights   33

ideological   67
ideologies   2, 3
ideology   149, 155, 160, 173, 185
indirect taxes   6
income   3, 4, 5, 6, 7, 8, 9, 10, 11, 12, 13, 20, 21, 22, 26, 27, 29, 30, 32, 34, 37, 38, 40, 48, 50, 61, 85, 90, 109, 115, 116, 117, 184
income support   75, 76, 77
inequality   1, 3, 4, 6, 8, 9, 10, 11, 18, 19, 20, 25, 26, 28, 30, 31, 32, 33, 36, 37, 38, 54, 62, 69, 78, 94, 100, 101, 111, 112, 114, 115, 120, 129, 150, 153, 154, 167, 168, 173
infant mortality   75, 133
inflation   79, 116
informal care   195

lone parenting   149
lone parents   73, 85, 165, 170, 191
low pay   48

marketable wealth   17, 18
Marx   37, 38, 40, 70, 111
Marxism   40, 72, 119, 156, 157
Marxist   32, 36, 38, 39, 40, 67, 72, 95, 96, 97, 111, 113, 114, 115, 116, 118, 125, 150, 151, 152, 153, 154